Also by Linda Bird Francke

Growing Up Divorced
The Ambivalence of Abortion

As Collaborator
Daughter of Destiny (by Benazir Bhutto)
A Woman of Egypt (by Jehan Sadat)
Ferraro: My Story (by Geraldine Ferraro)
First Lady from Plains (by Rosalynn Carter)

LINDA BIRD FRANCKE

GROUND ZERO

The Gender Wars in the Military

SIMON & SCHUSTER

SIMON & SCHUSTER
Rockefeller Center
1230 Avenue of the Americas
New York, NY 10020

Copyright © 1997 by Linda Bird Francke
All rights reserved,
including the right of reproduction
in whole or in part in any form.
SIMON & SCHUSTER and colophon are
registered trademarks of Simon & Schuster Inc.
Designed by Edith Fowler
Manufactured in the United States of America

10   9   8   7   6   5   4   3   2   1

Library of Congress Cataloging-in-Publication Data
Francke, Linda Bird.
   Ground zero : the gender wars in the military / Linda Bird
Francke.
      p.   cm.
   Includes bibliographical references and index.
   1. United States—Armed Forces—Women.
   2. Sex discrimination against women—United States.
   I. Title.
   UB418.W65F73   1997
   355'.0082—dc21   *97-10748*
                                                          CIP

ISBN 0-684-80974-5

Acknowledgments

SO MANY people contributed to this book that I have limited my thanks to those who went out of their way to either fax, mail or personally deliver information. That list includes Richard Casabianca, Maryann Calendrille, Tanya Domi, Linda Bray, Kathleen White, Eleanor and Ray Lewis, Jane Howard, the Southampton College and Bridgehampton libraries, Arnot Walker, Isabelle Katz Pinzler, James Brady, Judith Daniels, Lisa Moreno, Nancy Duff Campbell, Leo Rathbun, Rena Coughlin, Carolyn Dreyer, Kayce Freed, Peter Copeland, the Center of Military History (Army), Dr. Linda Grant De Pauw, Alice Booher, Betty Friedan, Julie Mackenzie, Peter Jennings, Caitlin Francke, Carolyn Becraft, Elaine Donnelly, Trish Beckman, Jeanne Kelser, Deborah Gill, Ted Paynther, Gertrude Rossi, Rhonda Cornum, Jane Nissen, Andrew Mackenzie, Joe Fox, Joan Vallance Whitacre, Bob Loomis, Ngaere Macray, Scott and Jodi Tekell, Dr. Dorothy Zinberg, Patrick Cummings, Anne Isaak, Linda Ritchie, Tapp Francke, Polly Kraft, Lloyd Cutler, and Marty Humphreys. Thanks to the faculty and students at DEOMI, the staff and cadets at West Point, the U.S. Army Military History Institute, Carlisle Barracks, Pennsylvania, and to Harvey Loomis, Lynn Nesbit, Elizabeth Stein and my editor and friend Alice Mayhew, for their unswerving support.

FOR CURTIS AND KELSEY

"Make war on the men—the ladies have too-long memories."
—Stephen Vincent Benet,
John Brown's Body, Book 4, 1928

Contents

PROLOGUE

The Life and Death of Major Marie Rossi

MAJOR MARIE ROSSI's funeral on March 9, 1991, in her hometown of Oradell, New Jersey, was an international news event. A phalanx of journalists, including a Japanese television crew, covered the ceremony. Her matter-of-fact sentiments to ABC's Mike von Fremd as she prepared to fly into Iraq in the first wave of the Allied ground offensive had saturated television networks just two weeks before.

"We thought it was pretty neat that three women were going to be across the border before the rest of the battalion," the helicopter company commander had said. Rossi's death five days later, when her Chinook helicopter crashed into an unlit microwave tower, made her an international celebrity.

I went to Marie Rossi's funeral. Like many other civilian women, I had been both awed and puzzled by Rossi. What was a woman like her doing in the Army? She hardly fit the stereotype of the butch, tough-talking women traditionally associated with military service. She was, as one of my friends said, someone you'd like to have lunch with. Yet the eulogies at her funeral bore little resemblance to civilian experience. "I prayed that guidance be given to her so that she could command the company, so she could lead her troops into battle," her Army husband, John Anderson Cayton, told the packed church. "And I prayed to the Lord to take care of my sweet little wife."

I wanted to know more about Marie Rossi, to write about her and the servicewomen like her who had dominated the nightly news during Operation Desert Shield in the Gulf. There were crowds of them gathered at Arlington National Cemetery for her military burial on March 11, including Captain Jodi Tekell, an Army intelligence officer who had become close to Rossi during an earlier tour of duty in Korea. Tekell's husband, Scott Tekell, had been Rossi's commanding officer.

Women seemed to have reached a new plateau in equal opportunity and acceptance. The Tekells described the high-risk missions Rossi had flown in Korea dodging through the antennae and wires the Koreans had strung haphazardly between mountaintops, the tent she'd shared on monthlong field exercises with Scott as his executive officer and the company's first sergeant. The men had left early each morning for the mess tent to afford Rossi the Army version of privacy. "It gave Marie time to do whatever women have to do to get ready for work, take a little sponge bath if the water wasn't frozen, comb the dirt out of her hair."

Rossi had earned pilot in command status during her first six months in Korea, an unusual accomplishment for commissioned officers who had so many additional duties on the ground. Tekell had asked the most experienced instructor in the company, a Vietnam veteran with five years in Korea, to check her out. "This was a tough guy from the old school, just the one you'd think would be against a female flying around Korea."

The only potential black mark against Rossi had been her growing relationship with Andy Cayton, a warrant officer in her company. The Army's "fraternization" policy forbade "unduly familiar" relationships between officers and enlisted, and officers of different ranks, especially if they were in the same line of command.[1] And Rossi was senior to Cayton.

Tekell had run interference for Rossi and Cayton, protecting them from reprimand by the base commander, ignoring the whisper campaign among the troops. Bending fraternization regulations, or any regulation, turned out to be commonplace in the Army. On the monthlong field exercises, Tekell encouraged Cayton to sneak out of his tent at night to join him and Marie in their tent for a game of cards.

The complexities of Rossi's military service began to come clear with her career success. While Rossi's friends and her brigade commander attributed the three hotly contested company command assignments she'd won after Korea to merit, the angry white men she had beaten out laid her success to reverse discrimination.

The negative beat continued in the Gulf, where a superior male officer raised questions behind Rossi's back about her skills as a pilot and her ability to lead the company. The only female company commander in her battalion, Rossi was not extended the tenet of command loyalty. "He broke the Army code," says an intelligence officer who heard the daily undermining of Rossi.

The gender discrimination institutionalized by the Army's combat exclusion policies almost cost Rossi her command. When rumors of impending war with Iraq swept the forces in November 1990, Army commanders worried that sending women into harm's way might violate the Army's complicated Direct Combat Probability Coding, which supposedly kept the highest-risk positions closed to women. If women were injured or killed in jobs which could be construed as male-only combat slots, their commanders might have to take the political heat.

Rossi had to fight for her command when her aviation company was identified as one of the units moving to the front line, and senior officers in the 101st Airborne Division to which she was attached moved defensively to replace her with a man. "You're telling me now that my command is supposed to be a male slot?" she had confronted her male superiors. "Then you tell me why in hell I was ever here in the first place?" The male officers had backed down, but the no-confidence vote remained.

When a sergeant reported Rossi for crying in her tent on the tense eve of the ground war, Rossi almost lost her command again. Only after explaining to her supportive brigade commander that crying was no different as a stress reliever than the male propensity to swear or throw things was she allowed to keep her job. "Do you have any problem continuing on?" he had asked her. "None," she'd replied.

The more I learned about Marie Rossi, the clearer it became that the book I intended to write about women in the military had less to do with women than with men in the military. Almost twenty years had passed since President Richard Nixon ended the draft and women started being integrated into the new All-Volunteer Force, and women were still not fully assimilated.

Servicewomen's critics blamed the political pressures of "special interest groups" and the women's rights movement in the 70s for forcing women on the All-Volunteer Force. While it was true that congressional passage of the Equal Rights Amendment in 1972 and its expected ratification had promised equal opportunities for women both inside and outside the military, the answer to women's presence in the All-Volunteer Force lay more in the shortage of men. The declining fertility rate among the post–World War II baby-boom generation forecast a 25 percent drop between 1976 and 1992 in the pool of young men from which the services traditionally drew their members.[2]

The Defense Department had turned to women to save the All-Volunteer Force. The women drawn to military service were smarter and better educated than the men, it was pointed out in an influential 1977 study, *Women and the Military.* Over 90 percent of women recruited between 1971 and 1976 had high school diplomas, compared to 63 percent of the men, and scored ten points higher on the service entrance exams.[3] The women stayed longer, proving the accepted correlation between retention and high school degrees: 70 percent of the women who had joined the services in 1973 were still on active duty in 1976, compared to only 64 percent of the men.[4]

Women were seen as a counterbalance to the high rate of absenteeism, or "lost time," among men for disciplinary problems and substance abuse, and were projected to be cheaper to maintain and recruit. Because of the reluctance of male high school graduates to voluntarily settle for lower military pay than potential civilian pay, the Army had to spend $3,700 in recruiting and advertising costs for each quality male recruit. Conversely, the services had to spend only $150 to recruit a woman because even the low military pay was a step up for women, who could hope to earn only 59 cents for every dollar earned by men in the civilian world.

Weighing the good with the not so good, the balance had come down in favor of women. "The trade-off in today's recruiting market is between a high quality female and a low quality male," read a 1978 Defense Department report. "The average woman available to be recruited is smaller, weighs less, and is physically weaker than the vast majority of male recruits. She is also much brighter, better educated, scores much higher on the aptitude tests and is much less likely to become a disciplinary problem."[5]

Marie Rossi had joined the Army through the Reserve Officer Training Command (ROTC) two years later, though no one is quite sure why. Her brother, Paul, attributed it to "adventurousness." "It was something unusual for a woman to be doing, and she wanted to see what it was like," he says. Andy Cayton remembers his wife saying that joining the Army "seemed like a neat thing to do for a couple of years" until she found out what she "really wanted to do. Marie never thought she'd stay in the Army," he says. "But she seemed to do so well in it, she never could justify getting out. She was a natural."

At the Port Mortuary in Dover, Delaware, where all fatalities from the Gulf were processed for identification, the young male "body handlers" had fallen apart when Rossi's body and other female remains came through. Servicemen were supposed to die in war, not servicewomen. "The guys were grief-stricken," says Lieutenant Colonel "Happy" Maguire, a twenty-year veteran of the Mortuary Affairs unit. "They didn't feel women should die that way."

While Rossi and, by extension, all servicewomen were being lauded by civilians as heroes (*Glamour* magazine named Rossi one of 1991's Women of the Year, along with Anita Hill, and *People* proclaimed her one of the "15 most intriguing people" in its special "heroes of the war" issue [Summer 1991], she was being disparaged by some in the Army.

Male aviators expressed bitterness at Rossi's posthumous election to the Army Aviation Hall of Fame while her male co-pilot had been ignored. Male colleagues and families of the three men who had died along with Rossi were upset at the attention focused on her death. No television cameras had recorded the funerals of Staff Sergeant Garret, Specialist Bill Brace or Warrant Officer Bob Hughes. "There was a backlash against Rossi because of the families of the other dead crew," a female officer told me at the U.S. military academy. "There was no mention of her at West Point."

The women pilots from all the services eulogized Rossi and prayed for her at the convention of Women Military Aviators in 1991, and set up a memorial flight scholarship in her name. An honor contingent of women pilots attended her funeral, her burial and the dedication of her headstone at Arlington in September. Rossi joined the WMA roster of fifteen women military aviators killed "in service" since 1980 and the thirty-eight World War II women aviators killed "in service" between 1942 and 1944. Until her high-profile death in the Gulf, little or no recognition had been afforded the other women aviators. Women had had to record the military service of their own. Rossi's military death put women pilots in the spotlight. Rossi's military life illuminated the cultural problems and ambiguities faced by all women in uniform.

■

Ground Zero has two, opposing themes. One is a story of women in the military. The other is a story of men in the military. It is not a history, though I have attempted to portray significant events in a historical context. Rather, it is a narrative of the cultural and biological forces at work within the military culture that divide the sexes, dictate women's harassment and demean their achievements.

What started out as a straightforward exploration of women in uniform turned into a labyrinth of social, cultural and political contradictions. Wherever I went, whether to West Point, the bi-annual conventions of Women Military Aviators, the twice yearly meetings of the Defense Advisory Committee on Women in the Services or Marie Rossi's funeral, there were always two different interpretations of the same realities.

The All-Volunteer Force depends on women to fill its ranks. Men and women are trained together, advance together. Women have moved into senior positions in the two decades since the inception of the AVF. But though the civilian and service leaders in the Pentagon know the military cannot perform without women, they have not been able to break down the resistance to women.

Women's presence in the military is enormously complex. For centuries, the warrior class has been male. The women who voluntarily joined every military campaign since the American Revolution have never been admitted to that class; they have been accepted as helpful but temporary military appendages. The All-Volunteer Force started to upset the male status quo in the 70s. The post-Gulf war move in the 90s to open combat positions to women threatened the last intact all-male domain, save for the priesthood. And the gender wars escalated sharply.

Ground Zero concentrates on the two years following the Gulf war and the issues raised in the polarized debate over women in combat. The biological differences between men and women, including menstruation, pregnancy and motherhood, would be cast as threats to national security by servicewomen's opponents, while servicewomen's advocates would use those same issues to press for expanded child care, parental leave and gynecological services. The exposure of women's harassment at the military academies and in the services would signal a call for women's retreat by their opponents but serve as a mandate to overhaul the male culture by their advocates. In the combat debate, the average woman's lesser physical strength would mask the core divide. The cultural issue was not whether women could perform combat roles, but whether women should.

The dynamics are as timeless within the military culture as they are predictable. The seeds for Tailhook and the sexual misconduct exposed in the Army in 1997 were sown the first day women were accepted into the military but categorically excluded from men's jobs. Women's token presence in the overwhelmingly male military dictated the reduction of Marie Rossi's career successes to affirmative action. And her highly publicized death in the Gulf paved the way for women's challenge to the combat exclusion laws and the inevitable battle at ground zero.

1

THE SILK AND
CHIFFON GENERALS

The Opening Shot in the Gender Wars

THE MOOD was euphoric at the dinner for three hundred hosted by the Defense Department on April 22, 1991, at the Radisson Mark Plaza Hotel in Alexandria, Virginia, six weeks after American and Allied forces liberated Kuwait and declared victory in the Gulf war. Members of the military in full dress uniform, their chests ablaze with service ribbons and awards, mingled with members of Congress, Defense Department officials and a Supreme Court justice. There hadn't been a headier moment for the U.S. military and their civilian watchdogs in Congress since V-E Day in 1945.

When an honor guard posted the colors, hands snapped the salute like karate black belts cleaving bricks. During the "President's Own" Marine Corps Band's full-bore brass rendering of "The Star-Spangled Banner," the American flag seemed brighter, more robust. In this room full of armed forces fresh from defeating Iraq, you could almost feel the heightened levels of testosterone. It was a startling reminder of the new gender order in the military that almost one-third of those uniformed personnel were women.

The dinner was held on the second night of a four-day semiannual conference of a little-known but powerful Defense Department civilian committee, the Defense Advisory Committee on Women in the Services, known by its acronym, DACOWITS. Defense Secretary George C. Marshall had formed the committee in 1951 to advise the Defense Department on the ways to enlist and retain women during the manpower crisis of the Korean War.

The military's attitude toward women at the time was a familiar one. In times of national crisis, women are suddenly indispensable to the services. In times of peace, they are just as quickly disposable. "I want all the women off this base by noon," a Navy nurse recalls the orders of her base commander at the conclusion of World War II.

Marshall's advisory committee had recognized that attitude, and by the time of the Gulf war it had become an uncompromising advocate for servicewomen. On this occasion, dressed for dinner in silk and chiffon, the white, affluent Republican loyalists (their three-year appointments to DACOWITS were rewards from the Bush administration for their financial and political support) hardly fit the image of gender revolutionaries. But they were lawyers, business-women, academics and public officials, and they were appalled by the treatment of women in the services and the gender discrimination institutionalized by law and policy in the military.

It did not matter that few of the thirty-five women and two men on DACOWITS in 1991 had any firsthand experience in the armed services. They did not speak the insider language of acronyms like MLRS, SAC and CONUS. They frequently instructed uniformed briefers at the spring conference to speak to them "in civilian." They had not studied military history, shot an automatic weapon, commanded an air wing or served on a ship. But they outranked almost everybody in the hotel dining room who had. Anticipating the resistance of military men to his predominantly female civilian appointees, Marshall had awarded members of DACOWITS the protocol rank of three-star general.

What even the farsighted Marshall could not have anticipated was that his prized creation would evolve until it was ready to mutiny in 1991. On the momentum of the Gulf war, DACOWITS was about to turn its considerable influence on the Pentagon and the commander in chief to put an end to discrimination by pushing for congressional repeal of the combat exclusion laws.

Save for a brief flurry of legislative advocacy for Army women following Panama in 1990, the last time the issue of repeal had received congressional consideration was in 1979 during Jimmy Carter's presidency. DACOWITS and Carter's assistant secretary of defense, Robert Pirie, had argued then that the laws did not offer the individual services any flexibility in setting their own policies for women. Moreover, the Defense Department pointed out, the use of the term "combat" in expanding women's assignments was artificial. Though technically women were considered noncombatants, they had received hostile-fire pay and combat awards in past conflicts, from the Revolutionary War to Vietnam.[1]

But the 1979 bid for repeal never got out of subcommittee. While the civilian secretaries and undersecretaries of the Air Force and the Navy supported repeal in their testimony, the chief of naval operations was not so sure. The Marine Corps personnel chief testified flat out against it, as did retired Army Chief of Staff General William Westmoreland: "No man with gumption wants a woman to fight his nation's battles."[2]

The Gulf war, in which so many women served, had pushed the issue of repeal to the front burner of congressional and public notice. DACOWITS wanted to move on it fast to take advantage. The DACOWITS executive committee had already mustered support for their proposal among many of the fifteen new appointees arriving for their first meeting. The chair, Becky Costantino, wanted a unanimous vote. "The words 'timing' and 'historic' kept coming up in support of the repeal," says one member. "I was absolutely lost. I'd never even met a woman in uniform before."

To the hundred or so uniformed women at the dinner and their allies on DACOWITS, the combat exclusion laws were designed to perpetuate an all-male preserve and career advantages. There could be no other rational explanation for Section 8549 of Title 10 of the U.S. Code, which held: "Female members of the Air Force . . . may not be assigned to duty in aircraft engaged in combat missions." Women instructor pilots had been flying high-performance Air Force jets for years, teaching men to fly the supersonic jets similar to those that the men, but not the women, could go on to fly in combat squadrons. Top pilots among them, like test pilot Jackie Parker, had withstood "G-forces" up to 7.3 times the gravitational pull on earth and flown the contour-hugging F-111 two hundred feet above the ground through the canyons of New Mexico at 600 knots. Flying ability could not be the issue.

There was no rationale either for Section 6015 of Title 10, which held that Navy women "may not be assigned to duty on vessels or in aircraft that are engaged in combat missions. . . ." Female sailors were already serving on the Navy oilers and ammunition and supply ships that followed the forbidden aircraft carriers around the seas of the world, while Navy pilots were catapulting off the flight deck of the USS *Lexington,* the one aircraft carrier open to women for training.

Only the Coast Guard, a peacetime service under the Department of Transportation but a wartime service under the Navy, had unequivocally supported repeal at the 1979 congressional hearings. Unconstrained by any laws, men and women had been serving together on all Coast Guard ships since 1977. If the Navy took over the Coast Guard during an emergency and the laws were still in place, women would have to be removed from the positions they were already holding.

Compared to its NATO allies, the United States was well behind on the gender curve. The Canadian Air Force trained women for combat cockpits. So did the U.S. Air Force, if the woman was not American. At the same time DACOWITS was meeting in 1991, the U.S. Air Force was training Lieutenant Manja Blok of the Royal Netherlands Air Force to fly the F-16 on combat missions.[3]

The Canadian, Scandinavian and Dutch Navies had long opened all their ships to women as, more recently, had Britain's Royal Navy. "We have concluded that to attempt to categorise ships into 'combat' and 'non-combat' would be artificial and misleading . . . when all ships will be liable to service in potentially dangerous waters," Britain's Conservative armed forces minister, Archie Hamilton, had concluded in 1989.[4] The day before the air war kicked off in Iraq in January 1991, twenty female sailors were among a crew of 254 deployed from England to the Gulf aboard the British frigate HMS *Brilliant*.[5]

What came to be known as the combat exclusion laws in America were a by-product of the post–World War II congressional debate over the formation of permanent women's components in all the services. The case for establishing the first female corps in peacetime rested on the perceived military need to mobilize the entire citizenry quickly in the event of a national emergency. The military projection after Hiroshima and Nagasaki held that any future conflict would not be played by traditional rules, but would be an all-out nuclear war. "I do not believe that anyone in the city of Pittsburgh or any other industrial center is going to be in a rear area in the next war," Army General Willard S. Paul had testified in support of the Women's Armed Services Integration Act. "We must have the full use of the total personnel power of the nation."[6]

The assumption at the hearings was not that women in the WAC and the WAVES would be in combat, but would do "women's work," the administrative and clerical roles they had done so well during World War II. It seemed natural at the time that women would want to do the typing while the men would want to do the fighting. "If a soldier is in the field and you detail him to a switchboard where efficient service is most important, he gets to feeling, 'Well, this is not a very good job for a big 200 pounder,'" testified General Dwight David Eisenhower, who had become so high on women during the war that as Army chief of staff in 1946 he had directed the Army legislation formalizing women's military service to be written up and submitted to Congress.[7] "You do not have that with women. The jobs to which they are assigned are performed more efficiently than men do in the normal case."[8]

The issue at the 1947 and 1948 hearings was whether women should be admitted to the services as reservists or as members of the regular forces, or indeed at all. Of grave concern to those opposed was the potential humiliation women's authority would inflict on men. "There is not a member of the House Committee on Armed Services who has not received a telephone call or a call in person from an enlisted man objecting to the idea of having to take orders from WAVE officers," said one congressman. "Put yourself in the position of an enlisted man and I am sure you will agree with them."[9]

Legally barring women from the Navy fleet had grown out of the chauvinism of Congressman Carl Vinson from Georgia, the powerful chair of the House Naval Affairs Committee. Though the Navy had already testified that it had no intention of assigning women to ships other than the transports on which Navy wives and children sailed or hospital ships, nurses being somehow gender neutral, Vinson threatened to scuttle the legislation unless his demands were met for an amendment banning women from the heart of the Navy. "Let them serve on shore in the continental United States and outside of the United States, but keep them off the ships," Vinson told the Navy representative testifying before a House Armed Services subcommittee. ". . . Just fix it so they cannot go to sea at all."[10]

Women in planes were only slightly less offensive to the vice chief of staff of the fledgling Air Force. He testified that the Air Force had no intention of letting women fly. Though Air Force General Hoyt Vandenberg readily admitted that women in the Women's Airforce Service Pilots, or WASPs, had successfully ferried aircraft for the Army Air Forces during the war and had not only done "a fine job" but also incurred an "accident rate as low or better than that of men," when he was asked by a congressman if the Air Force planned to train women as pilots under the proposed legislation, he replied, "No, sir." There was no mention by the Air Force, however, of a legal ban against female pilots."[11]

The Air Force amendment to the Women's Armed Services Integration Act of 1948 banning women in combat cockpits didn't surface to join Vinson's Navy amendment on ships and the last-minute provision against Navy women flying combat missions until the entire bill was presented to the full House for a vote—and passed with no debate about women and combat.

Absent from the statutes was the Army, which escaped congressional control by not being able to define "combat." By the Army's testimony, the weapons and battlefields of future wars, including the entire United States, made it impossible to outline combat areas. Congress agreed to let the secretary of the Army establish his own personnel policy on the utilization of women as long as it echoed the "congressional intent" of no combat for women.[12]

The combat issue was never about women but about men. To Vinson, for whom the grateful Navy named an aircraft carrier, the legal imperative seemed to be to preserve male privilege on Navy ships. In the same vein, the issue to the Air Force was to preserve male entitlement to its most prized aircraft. It is a dynamic modern servicewomen readily understand. "The hierarchy in the Navy is all designed for the folks who are in charge of ships," said Air Force Captain Anne McGee at the 1991 DACOWITS spring conference. "In the Air Force, it's the guys who fly fighters. The Navy lets women fly fighters, but not be in charge of their boats because that is where their power base is. The Air Force power base comes from flying fighters, so women aren't allowed to fly them."

Such barriers based on gender, not ability, DACOWITS reasoned, relegated their female constituents to the separate and lesser military status that bred the host of other gender-specific problems the committee was fighting, from sexual harassment to stalled careers. With the combat exclusion laws in place, the problems facing DACOWITS in the 90s were little different from those facing their predecessors. "Without the option of equal training, equal opportunities and equal experiences, people are not always regarded as the first team," said Admiral Louise Wilmot, who served as a Navy representative to DA-

COWITS in the mid-70s and headed the women's equal opportunity branch at the Bureau of Naval Personnel.

The docket for the DACOWITS spring meeting in 1991 included variations of every "concern" the committee had been tracking for almost twenty years. Sexual harassment was high on the agenda. An officer from the Naval Academy was scheduled to brief DACO-WITS on the academy culture, which resulted in the handcuffing of a female midshipman to a urinal. An Air Force lieutenant colonel from the Pentagon would respond to a recent survey of sexual harassment in all the services by presenting yet another remedy, this one titled "Strategy for the Eradication of Sexual Harassment."

The unequal job opportunities for women legitimized by the combat exclusion laws were also familiar issues on the agenda, but increasingly urgent concerns in the post–Cold War drawdown of forces. The Air Force was threatening to close jet instructor pilot slots to women since women's exclusion from combat squadrons made such assignments impractical. The Marines were continuing to refuse to let women fly any of their aircraft at all. The Army was threatening to close field artillery to women, a branch that women had served in for ten years. Just as Marie Rossi's male superiors in the Gulf had suddenly decided her company command was combat coded for a man, the Army was trying to apply that same combat code to every position in field artillery. "The DACOWITS continues to object to the assignment of soldiers on the basis of gender," the committee report would read.

The veteran members of DACOWITS listened to their military briefers with skepticism. "They would give us what they thought we wanted to hear," says Costantino, its chair. The Air Force had assured DACOWITS in the mid-80s that it was opening the high-flying espionage planes, the TR-1 and the U-2, to women pilots, but until 1989 nothing had happened. "Suddenly I get this emergency call saying, 'Kim, we need you to come out and interview for the U-2 next week,'" says Air Force Captain Kim Corcoran, the first woman to be interviewed for the U-2. "DACOWITS had gotten on their case."

The Pentagon presentation of its sexual harassment statistics at the April 1991 conference also tried to get away with good news. Only 22 percent of the personnel who responded to a recent Defense Department survey had reported being sexually harassed, the briefer claimed. The low percentage may have been technically correct, but

it was grossly misleading: 64 percent of the women surveyed reported recurring sexual harassment. The soothing figure of 22 percent included responses from the men surveyed, whose reported rate
of sexual harassment was much lower.[13]

The civilian members of DACOWITS were not intimidated by
military rank. Unlike the original members of Marshall's committee—
officers' wives who were deferential to the male hierarchy—the current members were accomplished women in their own right. Linda
Bisson, the DACOWITS vice chair in 1991 and commissioner of New
Hampshire Public Utilities, had taken on the Marine Corps on the
subject of women and grenades. While Army women threw live
grenades in training, Marine women were not considered strong
enough to throw grenades beyond the burst radius and were issued
duds. Says Bisson, who was known among Marines as "The Grenade
Lady": "Think about it. You're in a pinch. Your support position is
being overrun and the only way out is to throw a grenade, but you've
never thrown a real one before. I see no rational reason to use
training time to have women throw inert grenades."

DACOWITS member Barbara Barrett, an Arizona lawyer and
deputy administrator of the Federal Aviation Administration, was
focusing her sights on female pilots. Barrett and Bisson had checked
out the high-flying U-2 reconnaissance planes which the Air Force
had opened to women, but qualified only one to fly. "We actually sat
in the plane," says Bisson. "And what they'd said was true. You had
to sit tall, be very strong and have a long reach." What wasn't true
was the conjecture that women would panic in the claustrophobic
constraints of a high-altitude pressure suit and that women would
pose more problems than men by not being able to urinate during
the thirteen-hour flights. "Troy Devine was the first U-2 pilot, and
she solved it by wearing a diaper," says Bisson.

Barrett also wanted to see for herself what the objections were
to women pilots on Navy aircraft carriers, so she had flown out to
one. "She had to go through a survival course and float in the water
for two hours with all her gear on," says Bisson. "She passed it the
first time, a thirty-five-year-old woman and civilian. That sort of
takes some of the mystique and macho out of it."

During their three-year tenure on DACOWITS the members
toured military bases at home and abroad, talking privately to enlisted women and female officers. Dr. Margaret Scheffelin, a research
professor and member of DACOWITS from 1982 to 1984, had made

over a hundred base visits during her term and talked individually
to over four hundred servicewomen. "Their primary concern was
being recognized for the good job they were doing as soldiers, sailors
or airmen," says Scheffelin, who was at the 1991 DACOWITS meeting. "One woman, an Army master mechanic trainer and supervisor,
was quitting after twenty-two years because she was so sick of having to prove herself over and over again. A man with the same
number of stripes on his sleeve would not have to keep proving
himself the way she did. It would just be there."

A DACOWITS executive committee tour of service bases' in
Korea, Japan, Hawaii and Alaska in 1989 had passed on the concerns
of over two thousand military women to their base commanders and
ultimately to Defense Secretary Dick Cheney, from the eight-week
wait for gynecology appointments in Hawaii to the inability of some
women to apply their skills because of the combat exclusion laws.
"As in the case of Cryptologists (and many others) one must have
hands-on experience to learn and to progress in a specialty, but
females are so often barred from the site of this necessary experience
by law," the DACOWITS trip report chided.[14]

Pressure from DACOWITS forced the Pentagon to focus on such
uncomfortable issues as sexual harassment and debasement of
women. The accounts of the prurient environment for servicewomen
that laced the 1987 DACOWITS report from the committee's first
tour of Navy and Marine installations in Hawaii, Okinawa, Japan
and the Philippines had so embarrassed the Pentagon that the report
was classified. A Freedom of Information Act filed by the *Washington
Post* had revealed the report's charges of servicewomen on liberty in
the wall-to-wall bar town of Olongapo near the huge naval base of
Subic Bay being "grabbed on the streets by military men, treating
them as though they were free game"; of the "routine public 'use' of
Philippine females" by sailors and "sexually oriented entertainment
with the alleged participation of audience members" at the enlisted
and officers' clubs on base; of the behavior of the commanding
officer of the salvage ship USS *Safeguard,* who was charged in the
DACOWITS report with "fraternizing" with the eighteen female sailors among the ninety males in his ship's crew, publicly engaging in
oral sex with a civilian woman, encouraging his male sailors to swim
nude among the female sailors and offering to "sell" his female crew
members to Korean sailors on another ship.[15]

The report's dirty details published in the media under such

headlines as the *Washington Post*'s "Salvage Ship's CO Draws Allegations of Harassment"[16] and *Time*'s "Much Too Macho,"[17] had led
Defense Secretary Caspar Weinberger to quickly announce the formation of a Defense Department Task Force on Women in the Military in 1987 and his successor, Frank Carlucci, to order the first
Defense Department survey of sexual harassment in 1988. The members of DACOWITS, including Carlucci's wife, Marcia, had been
pleased. "Our report told it like it was and it was quite an earful for
many people," says former DACOWITS member Meredith Neizer,
who had gone on the 1987 trip. "A lot of things came out of that
report that said, 'Hey, things are running amuck and a lot more
attention needs to be paid to it.' It started a lot of things."

But always, the subject at DACOWITS came back to repealing
the combat exclusion laws. The passage of the Equal Rights Amendment by the House of Representatives in 1971 had afforded DACO-
WITS the first weapon to blast through the male wall around Navy
ships. Within months of encountering the wrath of DACOWITS at
its 1971 spring meeting, Admiral Elmo R. Zumwalt Jr., the chief of
naval operations, opened the ship's company of the hospital ship
USS *Sanctuary* to women for a three-year trial period. "I foresee that
in the near future we may very well have authority to utilize officer
and enlisted women on board ships," Zumwalt's historic Z-Gram
116 had informed the stunned Navy. ". . . The ultimate goal, assignment of women to ships at sea, will be timed to coincide with full
implementation of pending legislation."[18]

The combination of DACOWITS and the ERA also caused Zumwalt to open naval flight training to women in 1973, the first service
to do so.[19] "Admiral Zumwalt saw that the ERA was just three states
short of ratification," says Navy Commander Rosemary Mariner at
the 1991 DACOWITS meeting. "Eight of us were selected for Navy
flight school. Six won their wings of gold. But we could only fly
helicopters and props, not jets."

The Navy balked at opening any other ships to Navy women. For
all the efforts of DACOWITS, the combat exclusion laws remained.
Though Z-Gram 116 also established a task force to review the "legal
or attitudinal" impediments to Navy women, the combat exclusion
laws were not among them. "We identified hundreds of discriminatory laws, put them in one package and asked Congress to overturn
them," says Admiral Louise Wilmot, who served on the 1973 task

force. "There were two of these laws that were identified that were deemed too sensitive. One was the law admitting women to service academies and the other was to change Section 6015 which prevented women from serving on ships and combat aircraft."

The Navy went to such lengths to preserve its all-male sanctuaries that in the end it would prove to be its undoing. The hypocrisy inherent in the Navy's willingness to transport Air Force and Army women, but not Navy women, on its ships, and to allow civilian women to work aboard its ships as technicians while denying the same opportunity to its own female members led one enlisted sailor to take the Navy and the Defense Department to federal court—and win a landmark lawsuit in 1978.

Yona Owens, a Navy electrician, had been looking forward to her new assignment aboard a civilian-controlled Navy survey ship in 1974. The Navy job detailers apparently had no problem with her assignment. The ship, which regularly carried female civilian scientists and already had a separate berthing area for women, needed someone with her interior communications skills and no eligible male sailor was available. When the Navy's top lawyers canceled Owens's orders two weeks after she received them, she and three other enlisted women whose careers were also stymied went to the American Civil Liberties Union and the League of Women Voters to help overturn Section 6015. A group of officers whose careers were equally stymied by this section joined the suit, among them Lieutenant JoEllen Drag, one of the Navy's three, but essentially useless, female helicopter pilots.[20]

Although the Navy allowed civilian women and female pilots from the other services to land on its ships, Navy women could not. "JoEllen couldn't deliver mail or ferry supplies to an aircraft carrier or any other ship," says retired Navy Captain Kathleen Bruyere, a fellow plaintiff in the suit and one of twelve women ironically chosen by *Time* magazine in 1976 to be its "Man of the Year." "The Navy wouldn't allow her to even *hover* over a carrier."

Such maneuvers to avoid setting a legal precedent for Navy women on ships infuriated the members of DACOWITS. "The Navy women we worked with were so intelligent and so capable," says a former member of DACOWITS. "But they weren't even allowed to *board* a Navy vessel if they were wearing their uniforms. They had to wear skirts so they would look like civilians."

It also moved Judge John J. Sirica of Watergate fame to rule that Vinson's thirty-year-old statute not only denied the Navy women their equal protection under the Fifth Amendment and was therefore unconstitutional, but also sprang from outdated values: ". . . that Section 6015's bar against assigning females to shipboard duty was premised on the notion that duty at sea is part of an essentially masculine tradition . . . more related to the traditional way of thinking about women than to military preparedness," Sirica wrote in his July 1978 decision in *Owens* v. *Brown*.[21]

Women finally went to sea three months later, but the Navy's Women in Ships program assigned women to only a few auxiliary ships, such as repair ships and tenders. The "masculine tradition" was still protected from women. "What we're trying to do is avoid having them as part of the combat team," Navy Secretary W. Graham Claytor testified before Congress in 1978.[22]

Women were further distanced in the Navy's amended combat exclusion law in 1978 by a provision that allowed them to serve temporarily on all Navy ships for up to six months, but only if the ships were sailing through peaceful waters. If the ship's noncombat mission turned into a combat mission, the women were to be evacuated. Such fairweather treatment of women would serve to reinforce women's separate and secondary status in the Navy into the 90s.

But the Navy brass was unmoved from the beginning. With men in the Navy outnumbering women at least ten to one, more weight was given to male perceptions about women than objective assessments of women's capabilities. "I had very firm reasons for not expanding women to combat ships," says retired Rear Admiral James Hogg, who developed policy for the Navy's Women in Ships program as the director of military personnel training between 1979 and 1982. "The feedback I was getting from the fleet was that women aren't strong enough for combatant ships, that cohesion will be a problem, that working conditions are too bad for women to work in. On and on. I walked away from that time frame feeling that the Women in Ships program was fine, but just for noncombatant ships."

That "time frame" was still in place when DACOWITS met in April 1991 after the Gulf war. Forty-three years after Carl Vinson decreed Navy ships off bounds to women, women were still not allowed to serve permanently on the Navy's most prized ships. Nor, in the Air Force, were women allowed to fly its most prized planes.

Nor, in the Army and Marines, were women allowed to serve in a whole host of jobs.

For all the seeming gender equality coming out of the visuals of the Gulf war, the 1948 laws and Army policy still excluded women from 48 percent of the positions in the Army, 80 percent in the Marines, 41 percent in the Navy and the prized 3 percent male-only slots in the Air Force—flying high-performance jets.[23] "The laws condone sex discrimination, pure and simple," said Becky Costantino. "They keep women from jobs they have proven they are perfectly capable of doing."

Women pilots from all the services filed into each DACOWITS subcommittee meeting room during the 1991 spring conference. They were there to educate the new members on the inequities of the laws against women in combat cockpits and to pitch the advisory committee to support repeal.

"I'm tired of fighting the same battles again and again," said Air Force Lieutenant Colonel Kelly Hamilton, who had just returned from five and a half months in the Gulf. "We train all day as if we're going to use 100 percent of our people, but then when it comes time to deploy, the leaders say, 'Wait a minute. Is this a combat zone? Can I use this woman?' I can't blame them because we've put them in that protectionist mode where they're going to get into trouble."

One by one the pilots made their case for repeal. "This is the time to do it because of the tremendous success of Operation Desert Storm," urged Navy Commander Rosemary Mariner, who had been fighting the laws since 1973. "If we hadn't had the Civil War with the resulting legislation and the Fourteenth Amendment to the Constitution, we'd be fighting slavery plantation to plantation. That is what we are doing today in the military."

The new members of DACOWITS seemed inspired by these new heroines whom they had seen only on television during the Gulf war. Many had thought Marie Rossi was unique. But there were turning out to be hundreds of Marie Rossis in the military. "We carried twenty-one human remains back from Saudi Arabia, two of whom were women," said Terry VandenDolder, a C-141 cargo transport pilot in the Air Force Reserve. "The crew felt remorse for all twenty-one, not just the two who were women."

The inequities the pilots and flight officers faced seemed absurd to the DACOWITS members. Navy Commander Trish Beckman told the committee she had spent the war in St. Louis testing $24 million F-18s just off the line at McDonnell Douglas. Though the lives of the male fighter pilots would rely on her expertise in testing the F-18's radar and weapons systems, spin recover mode and automatic "G" limiter, she wasn't allowed to fly the F-18 in the fleet. "I can test the plane but I can't fly it operationally because of my gender," said Beckman.

Similar inequities showed up during a DACOWITS field trip during the 1991 conference to the Marine Corps Combat Development ment Command at nearby Quantico, Virginia. The Marine Corps commandant found no conflict in showcasing two young women sharpshooters at Quantico's Weapons Training Battalion who had conducted crash courses for male reservists called up for the Gulf, but had not been allowed to deploy with them.

The commandant saw no discrepancy either in the Marine's newly commissioned pistol, which was too big for most women's hands. He didn't seem to notice twenty-three-year-old Corporal Barbara Evans's dejection when she demonstrated the Marine hand weapon to DACOWITS she had used to twice become the women's national pistol champion and then the Marine's new pistol, which she could barely hold. Because the redesigned butt was appreciably thicker, Evans had to stretch her hand awkwardly along the side of the pistol to reach the trigger. Under the Marines' restrictive policies, it didn't much matter if women could shoot straight.

Over at the "Tarzan" obstacle course, a drill instructor on exchange from Britain's Royal Marines watched impassively as a young female trainee struggled and failed to climb the thick rope. Though he could have taught her the technique of belaying the rope around one foot and using the slack as a "step," thereby reducing the strain on her arms, the Royal Marine used her frustration to illustrate the lack of women's upper-body strength to the members of DACOWITS. "Women always wash out on the rope," he said, shrugging his well-muscled shoulders. It fell to a female Marine major escorting DACOWITS to demonstrate the rope-climbing technique to the committee. "It's easy when you know how," she told the members as she steadily worked her way up the rope.

At the Defense Department dinner for DACOWITS in 1991, the members' momentum toward repeal built during a filmed salute to military women in general and specifically the 41,000 women who had served in the Persian Gulf. When Marie Rossi's familiar image appeared on an oversize screen in the dining room, the applause was solemn. By making "the ultimate sacrifice," the term the military uses to ennoble death, Rossi had elevated the status of all military women.

When the image played of Army Flight Surgeon Rhonda Cornum gingerly stepping out of a U.S. helicopter in Riyadh, Saudi Arabia, dressed in a yellow prisoner-of-war suit to be welcomed back to safety by General Norman Schwarzkopf, the audience erupted into applause. Shot down in a search-and-rescue mission on the day before the cease-fire and captured by Iraqi soldiers, the badly wounded Cornum had spent a harrowing and painful week as a POW with two shattered arms, a badly torn knee and a bullet lodged in her shoulder. Cornum's capture and that of an Army truck driver, Melissa Rathbun-Nealy, had staked out a place for women in what had been an exclusive, if not sought-after, male club.

When Rhonda Cornum was introduced as the film ended, her finger splinted and held together by a metal screw, the prolonged applause brought the guests to their feet. To the advocates of military change in the room, there was only one possible conclusion: women had finally, and at demonstrable cost, proved their right to serve as equals in the military.

Caught up in the spirit of the moment, neither the military women nor DACOWITS members noticed the perfunctory applause on the part of some of the military men present, the ones who looked impatiently at their watches, the ones who sat stony-faced through the speeches lauding women and the "invaluable contributions" of DACOWITS.

The very existence of the committee was enraging to many men in the military. They considered its advocacy of women as reverse discrimination and its focus on such a military minority as a waste of time and resources. "They're a pain in the you-know-what, if you'll excuse my French," muttered an Army colonel at the dinner who, like many other members of the military, would not allow the use of his name.

Equally resented was the committee's easy and envied access to the top echelons of the Department of Defense, and, to their minds, the DOD's seeming capitulation to their every demand. Women had encroached on one male preserve after another under pressure from DACOWITS, Congress and the courts. In 1967, DACOWITS won a seven-year battle to remove both the 2 percent ceiling on the number of women allowed to serve in the military and the promotion cap of lieutenant colonel on the rank women officers were allowed to achieve; in 1972, Junior ROTC programs were opened to female high school students; a year later female students were included in the required number of students to establish the programs; an eight-year battle ended victoriously in 1973 when the Supreme Court upheld the entitlement of civilian male spouses of servicewomen to the same benefits as servicemen's civilian wives in *Frontiero* v. *Ferguson;* 1973 also saw the opening of pilot training for women in the Army and Navy, followed reluctantly by the Air Force three years later; 1974 saw the overturning of yet another military tradition of involuntarily discharging women for pregnancy; in 1975 a strong campaign by DACOWITS to open West Point and the other service academies to women became law under President Ford; in 1977 male and female recruits were integrated in coeducational Army basic training; in 1978 the Navy opened berths on selected Navy ships to women. In 1979, DACOWITS joined President Carter in supporting draft registration for women, a proposal that would be rejected by the Supreme Court in 1981 in *Goldberg* v. *Rostker* because women were legally barred from combat.

Though momentum slowed under President Ronald Reagan and in some cases reversed—the Army returned to segregated basic training in 1981 and an evaluation of assignment policies for women closed some positions previously open to them—all servicewomen began to receive the same weapons training as their male counterparts, and the Marine Corps more than doubled the positions open to women. Even the most resistant military personnel knew that the silk and chiffon generals were not to be messed with.

George Marshall would have been stunned at the success of his committee in making the military a viable option for women. In 1952, a year after DACOWITS first came into being, 36,419 active duty women and 11,938 reservists served in nine all-female components within the Department of Defense, including the Army WAC, Navy WAVES, Air Force WAF, Women Marines and the Army Nurse Corps. By 1990, the number of active duty and reserve servicewomen in the integrated armed forces and the National Guard had swelled to 373,176. By the Gulf war, women accounted for one out of nine members of the modern military.

To supporters of women in the military, DACOWITS had done its job well. To its detractors, the committee had done too well. Beneath the politically correct Pentagon unctuousness that both lauded the presence of women in the military and extolled their accomplishments was the conviction of many military men that women did not belong in the military and most emphatically not in combat positions.

Their laundry list of negatives about women ranged from the physiological realities of women's lesser strength and stamina to the more nebulous disruption of "male bonding" and unit cohesion. Women alone took the brunt of "fraternization" between service members of different ranks, "Nothing has done more to cheapen rank and diminish respect for authority than cute little female lieutenants and privates," wrote Brian Mitchell in *Weak Link: The Feminization of the American Military.*[24]

Different physical standards for men and women gave an unearned advantage to women; worse, critics charged, the physical criteria had been adjusted so that men weren't challenged and women wouldn't fail. Career standards were also skewed. In the highly competitive world of the military, men charged that women were not advanced on their own merits, but on an undeclared quota system which the services called "goals."

Moreover, the rise in the number of service members married to each other to some 56,000 "dual-service" couples by 1990 overburdened the detailers who tried to find them joint-duty assignments, while the number of single mothers (but not fathers) seriously handicapped military readiness. The list went on and on. But the bottomline charge was always the same. The mission of the military was to protect and defend the U.S. Constitution, not to be an equal opportunity employment agency.

The women countered that physical strength in the age of hightech weaponry and hydraulic machinery was no longer an overriding issue, and that unit cohesion did not depend so much on male bonding as unit bonding. Any personal favoritism toward women in the chain of command was a form of paternalism and unsolicited.

Different physical standards, the women claimed, were a tired complaint: many women performed at male standards, and the alleged lowering of physical criteria was a myth created by men. As to military readiness, the women had studies to prove that men lost more time to injury or disciplinary charges than women did to pregnancy. And rather than being favored in career promotions, women were blocked from career-enhancing jobs because of the combat exclusion laws. The bottom line, the women maintained, was that they were every bit as competent and qualified as men to protect and defend the Constitution of the United States. The only barrier left was the combat exclusion laws. At the 1991 spring DACOWITS meeting, even the men thought the laws were going to fall.

Clean-shaven jaws clenched during the comments of Deputy Secretary of Defense Donald Atwood to DACOWITS at a Pentagon meeting the morning of the dinner. Citing the "outstanding performance" of servicewomen in Operation Desert Storm which "validated their importance in the U.S. military today," Atwood had gone on to say that he "wouldn't be surprised to see the role of women expand even further in the years ahead."

The military women present shuddered at the plural of the word "year." But the temporary reprieve was little solace to the men in the Pentagon meeting room when Atwood went on to cite the Defense Department's commitment "to make the best possible use of all of its people," and to "ensure that women have equal opportunities to serve their country in all branches of the armed forces." What other interpretation could there be than the Defense Department's intention to support the DACOWITS recommendation to repeal the combat exclusion laws? Breaking with military tradition in which no facial expression is the ultimate expression, the women in uniform shot stealthy thumbs-up looks at each other. The men looked as if they were at a wake.

The tide began to turn at the dinner that night, though few of the women noticed. Seated beside Assistant Secretary of Defense Christopher Jehn at the head table, Becky Costantino was relishing her good fortune at being the DACOWITS chair at the right time. The Gulf war had provided the breakthrough to accomplish the major goal of DACOWITS. "The media was supportive of women, and the American people were supportive of women, and the military and DOD had to admit the women performed well," says Costantino. "It is the chance of a lifetime, really, an opportunity that we had waited for a long, long time."

Her resolve, and that of the other members of DACOWITS, had not succumbed to seductive military pomp and privilege: fleet tours on admirals' launches and base visits in generals' helicopters, a private lunch at the Pentagon that very day with Defense Secretary Dick Cheney, a congratulatory note to DACOWITS read aloud at the dinner from Commander in Chief George Bush citing the committee's "significant contribution to our military readiness and deterrent capability."

In the optimism of the moment, no one at the dinner noticed the grim expressions on the faces of two new DACOWITS members —Eunice Van Winkle Ray, a marketing consultant to Kentucky Fried Chicken in Crestwood, Kentucky, and director of the Kentucky Quilt Project; and Claude Galbreath Swafford, a lawyer from South Pittsburg, Tennessee, who listed her membership in the Holly Avenue United Methodist Church and her "Lifetime Membership of Women in the Church" high in her DACOWITS résumé.

No one noticed either the fury on the face of former DACOWITS member and the committee's influential archenemy Elaine Donnelly. A onetime Reagan volunteer in Michigan, she had purposely sought an appointment to DACOWITS in the mid-80s to block what she considered the committee's dangerous advocacy of women in combat.

In Donnelly's view, shared by Swafford and Ray, women weakened, not strengthened, the defense of the country. Military readiness in the Gulf war had been compromised by pregnancy rates among servicewomen, field commanders having to cope with grieving, distracted service mothers separated from their children and the Pentagon's turning a blind eye under pressure from DACOWITS.

"Our priorities are getting way out of whack, as is this committee's perspective," Donnelly said in between DACOWITS subcommittee meetings at the 1991 conference. "DACOWITS deals with careerism and the advancement of women to such a distorted degree that the interests of children are secondary, the interests of field commanders are secondary, and therefore the interests of national defense are made secondary."

Donnelly's campaign against the DACOWITS agenda was not new. During her tenure on DACOWITS from 1984 to 1986 she had so fanned the flames of male resistance to women by circulating her own questionnaire on women in combat among West Point cadets and the military bases she visited that the Pentagon made her stop.

"They said it wasn't proper for a DACOWITS member," says Donnelly.

Donnelly was a protégé of Phyllis Schlafly, the far-right founder of the Eagle Forum and "Stop ERA," who had used the threat of a female draft to roll back support for the Equal Rights Amendment in the late 70s. Donnelly had picked up the Schlafly banner to wage the war against women in combat. Relentless and effective, she had lobbied Capitol Hill by foot and fax and testified against expanded opportunities for women at every congressional hearing since the 1980 hearings on registering women for the draft.

Donnelly had founded her own conservative Coalition for Military Readiness to counter the influence of DACOWITS. Funded by such organizations as the American Conservative Union, Concerned Women for America and the Eagle Forum, she had come to the 1991 spring DACOWITS meeting to drum up support among the new members to kill any DACOWITS resolution to overturn the combat exclusion laws. "The Schlafly group knows that with the media coverage of women in the Gulf, right now is probably the best time in history to get the law repealed," said an Air Force master sergeant attached to DACOWITS. "And they want to counter that. This should not be a political game, but it absolutely is."

Caught in the ideological cross fire were the servicewomen who believed, naively, that their military performance both in peacetime and at war in the Gulf would form the basis for repealing the laws. Perhaps that is why the comments of the dinner's keynote speaker, Marine Corps Commandant General Alfred M. Gray Jr., chilled the euphoria in the dining room only momentarily.

Resplendent in his dress Marine uniform, the double gold stripe on his royal blue trousers running from waist to shoe top, Gray was the personification of a Marine. A veteran of Korea, Guantánamo Bay and Vietnam, he had the deep, resonant voice, skull-baring haircut and deliberate southern accent, though he was born in Rahway, New Jersey, that spoke of military male authority. About to retire from the Marine Corps after forty-one years, Gray sounded the alarm about women in the military that would reverberate for the next eighteen months in Senate hearing rooms, congressional subcommittees, newspaper columns and on television talk shows, and end up in a damning two hundred–page report to the president at a cost to the taxpayers of $4.1 million. Instead of a call to breach the last barrier remaining for women in the military, Gray sounded a call for retreat.

"Is it really good for the military and for our women, and for our country, to have so many single parents on active duty?" he said to an ever-deepening silence. "Is the military really the place for a single parent?"

Spines stiffened under the women's dress uniforms as he went on, attacking one DACOWITS breakthrough for women after another.

"Should we have men and women who are married in the service?" Gray mused. "Is that really in the best interest over the long haul?"

There wasn't a sound in the dining room as he said what so many military traditionalists had kept to themselves, and women dreaded. To reverse the family policies that now treated men and women equally would send thousands of military women out of the forces.

"Some of the money that's flown . . . into the military to encourage families and encourage marriage could perhaps be better used in a civilian-type occupation on or near the base," he continued.

Gray made no mention of expanding opportunities for women in the military, even single, childless women, and gave no hint of support or even consideration of repealing the combat exclusion laws. His only concession was his acknowledgment that the women who had been serving in the integrated Marine Corps since 1973 resented being called Women Marines.

"Perhaps we can broaden out," said Gray to a now infuriated audience of military women. "Your Women Marines want to be known as Marines. They're getting tired of being singled out as women."

His words hung uneasily in the air as the "President's Own" Marine Corps band swung into the Marine "Hymn" and the dinner guests rose to their feet. The deafening sound and mystique of male military power seemed for the moment overwhelming and impenetrable. Standing erect and proud among their fellow comrades at arms, the women in uniform suddenly looked very small.

On the morning of April 24, the Hickory Room at the Radisson Mark Plaza Hotel was packed for the DACOWITS vote with forty-six former and current members of DACOWITS, their nineteen military representatives, eight liaison officers, two legal advisors and ten office and administrative staffers. Filling the rows behind them were DOD representatives and active, retired and reserve military women from every branch of service including the Coast Guard and the Air National Guard.

Generations of career servicewomen crowded into the back of the room: Rear Admiral Roberta Hazard, the highest-ranked woman in the Navy; retired Air Force Major General Jeanne Holm, in 1973 the first woman in U.S. military history to make that rank; Captain Kathleen Bruyere, who had joined the class-action suit against the Navy to open ships to women; Captain Carol Barkalow, a Gulf war veteran and 1976 graduate of West Point, the first class to admit women.

Into the early hours of the morning, the members of the DACOWITS executive committee had worked and reworked the wording of the recommendation's rationale for repealing the combat exclusion laws, grounding it in the enhancement of military mission rather than equal opportunity. Already printed and bound in a draft report, Recommendation #1 to repeal the combat exclusion statutes read simply:

> The events in the Persian Gulf demonstrated that the entire Theater of Operation is part of the modern battlefield, where exposure to the risks of combat extended to all members of the Armed Forces. The DACOWITS believes that with the repeal of the combat exclusion statutes:
> —Flexibility is given to the Services to fully utilize all qualified personnel
> —Ability rather than gender becomes the basis for assignment
> —Acceptance of Servicewomen as full partners is enhanced
> —Opportunities are expanded for Servicewomen to compete fairly for assignments and promotions
> Therefore, the DACOWITS support efforts to ensure total force utilization in the U.S. military through the repeal of Title 10, U.S.C. 6015 (Navy) and 8549 (Air Force).

Though the outcome of the vote was fairly well predetermined, the process was tense. Seated alone a few rows in front of Elaine Donnelly, and appropriately on the right side of the room, were Claude Swafford and Eunice Ray. In a prelude to the ideological wars to come, their objections to the recommendation were not based on women's military qualifications but on their cultural roles. "Who's going to take care of the children?" Swafford asked. "What will the cost be of providing child care?"

Correctly charging the committee with being "one-sided," and citing the lack of information she and other new members of DACOWITS had for an instructed vote, Swafford first moved to table the motion for repeal, and when that failed, introduced a motion for a secret ballot so that members could express their reservations without fear of repercussion. "That's the first time I ever remember there being a secret ballot," says an Air Force representative to DACOWITS.

The military women sat tensely in the back of the room while civilian women who had never trained as they had or lived in tents or truck cabs for weeks on end in the Saudi desert debated their future.

Seventy-four-year-old columnist Sarah McClendon, a former DACOWITS member and ERA activist who had seen the ERA fall to Phyllis Schlafly's scare tactics in the 70s, sent a written message down the row to Swafford: "Are you a member of the Eagle Forum?" Swafford did not respond.

The tension broke when the vote was finally counted and the servicewomen erupted into applause. Twenty-nine members had voted for repeal, four had voted against. Swafford's political ploy had gained a vote or two, but not enough to derail the momentum toward repeal.

"This committee is loaded," said Eunice Ray as she left the meeting room. "We've been processed like baloney. The fight is going to be on the home front now and this committee has taken a position on women in combat without doing any homework. What about the child care issue which was about to blow up in the Gulf? What about the draft? If we're called upon to testify by Congress and we don't have research, then we're going to look like a garden club."

Emotions were just as raw on the other side. At the luncheon following the secret vote, a new DACOWITS member was close to tears. "They're spreading rumors that I voted against. You know I wouldn't do that to you," she whispered to Becky Costantino, who had made the history she wanted, but without the public relations weight of a unanimous vote. If women were divided among themselves, it would be harder to sway Congress and the Defense Department to their support.

The preliminary signs, however, were positive. When the executive committee of DACOWITS arrived at the White House in a Radisson airport minivan to deliver their historic recommendation to the commander in chief, both Dick Cheney and Colin Powell made sure to join the women for the photo op with the president in the Rose Garden.

The four minutes allotted to the DACOWITS visit stretched to ten when Bush asked what major issue had come out of the convention. "You may be sorry you asked," replied Costantino, who then told him about the call for repeal. Bush laughed. "Well, I'm a little old-fashioned about this issue," said the World War II Navy pilot. "I might have a little trouble with it." Diane Ruebling, a cheek-kissing friend of the president who had campaigned on a tractor with him in Minnesota, sent him a look. "Just don't sic Diane on me," Bush quipped. "That's exactly what we intend to do," replied Costantino as hearty laughter filled the Rose Garden.

In the jolly Rose Garden moment, the humor bonding the secretary of defense, the chairman of the Joint Chiefs and the commander in chief did not seem dismissive to Costantino. The extra, unscheduled time the president was spending with the committee members was a positive sign, as was the photograph which appeared to align the top military and civilian defense officials in the country with the up-front goals of DACOWITS. "The historical timing and significance of the gathering right after DACOWITS came out with such a strong recommendation that would affect women in the military and so soon after the Persian Gulf war was very obvious," she later recalled.

In her office on Capitol Hill, Congresswoman Pat Schroeder was getting ready to launch the political offensive. Armed with the DACOWITS recommendation and a *Newsweek* poll showing that 79 percent of Americans approved of women volunteering for combat, she was about to seize the moment and introduce legislation to repeal the combat exclusion laws for female pilots.

It would be Schroeder's second attempt to challenge the restrictive laws. Her first and more cautious legislation less than a year before, also linked to a DACOWITS recommendation, had followed Operation Just Cause in Panama. Intended to build on the combat roles Army women had played in the invasion, Schroeder and DACOWITS had proposed that the Army open all its jobs to women for an experimental four years.

Schroeder's bill had fallen flat and, like the 1979 legislation to overturn the combat exclusion laws, had never gotten out of committee. Rather than test women's capabilities in the combat roles they had just performed in Panama, the Army moved instead to systematically discredit them. In the year to come, women's performance in the Gulf would again be discredited. Every physical characteristic that differentiated women from men would be blown into epic proportion. Women would be cast as a greater threat to the national defense than Saddam Hussein and Manuel Noriega combined. Panama had been a dress rehearsal. And it had been ugly.

2

PANAMA, THE PRESS
AND ARMY POLITICS

The Sacrificing of Captain Linda Bray

JUST AFTER midnight on December 20, 1989, the first explosions fractured the early morning stillness around Panama City. Operation Just Cause, George Bush's last-ditch attempt to bring Panamanian dictator Manuel Noriega to heel, had begun. In the chaos and violence that followed, a pivotal moment for women in the military also began.

Close to eight hundred military women took part in the brief and furious invasion of Panama as integral members of the largest deployment of U.S. troops since Vietnam. Army women already stationed in Panama or deployed from Fort Ord, California, and Fort Bragg, North Carolina, participated as unit members of the infantry, Military Police, intelligence, Signal Corps, airborne, financial and Special Operations. Air Force women participated as aircraft commanders, pilots, navigators, flight engineers, loadmasters, logistics, maintenance and administrative support of Strategic Air Command tankers and Military Airlift Command transport aircraft.[1] Women made up 4 percent of the 18,400-strong U.S. invasion force and gave the public its first glimpse of the new and dangerous roles played by women in the modern military.

In the early hours of the invasion, Warrant Officer Debra Mann ferried combat troops through a barrage of enemy fire into Panamá Vieja. After her UH-60A Black Hawk helicopter took three hits, she flew the disabled aircraft to Tocumen Airport, a Panamanian Defense Forces stronghold under siege by U.S. Army Rangers. Aloft in another Black Hawk, First Lieutenant Lisa Kutschera flew three air assaults through sporadic enemy fire ferrying U.S. combat soldiers. Both women would be awarded the coveted Air Medal.[2]

Women in ground units were also coming under fire. For over nine hours, two truck drivers assigned to the 193rd Support Battalion delivered infantry troops into the downtown area around the heavily defended Panamanian Defense Forces headquarters. At times the fire was so thick around twenty-year-old Private First Class Melissa Smith's truck that she drove hunched way down in the driver's seat. "Sometimes you could have just reached out and grabbed the tracer rounds as they went by," Smith later told *Soldiers Magazine*.[3]

Captain Marie Bezubic, a supply officer for the 154th Signal Battalion, used up two of her lives in Panama, the first under mortar fire the night of the invasion, the second when she later transported 150 gallons of fuel through the streets of Panama City and came within arm's length of a Panamanian about to light a Molotov cocktail. "I didn't really want to shoot him because there were noncombatants around," says Bezubic. "So I grabbed my canteen cup and threw it at him. It stopped him."[4]

Members of the Military Police were having their own war with the Panamanians. Sniper fire and drive-by shootings were frequent at the roadblocks set up near the Cuban, Libyan and Nicaraguan embassies to prevent Noriega from achieving asylum. The fire was particularly intense from the buildings surrounding the roadblock near the Cuban embassy. One platoon led by Lieutenant Kimberly Thompson exchanged fire with the snipers in the buildings, then shot and killed three men when the speeding van they were in refused orders to halt and crashed through the roadblock. "I've been confronted with situations here that I thought I couldn't handle," Thompson said later to Scripps Howard correspondent Peter Copeland. "As you go through things, you get tougher."[5]

The ferocity of the U.S. air assault on the Comandancia, the stronghold of Noriega's Panamanian Defense Forces on the 4th of July Avenue, ignited the surrounding wooden tenements of El Chorrillo and forced the population into the night streets.[6] One woman fled her burning shanty naked and was pinned down in the street by sniper fire. Private First Class Felicia Featherstone, nineteen, ran out under fire to get her.[7]

Other Military Police operations in Panama were hardly distinguishable from infantry missions. Under the pressure of troop reduction through budget cuts and the increased utilization of each member of the Army, the mission of the Military Police had been expanded to include the assault capabilities of civilian police SWAT teams.

The orders of the 209th Military Police Company commanded by Captain Mary McCullough were to provide security for U.S. bases, set up roadblocks and attack and secure PDF outposts minutes before the U.S. assault was scheduled to begin at 1 a.m. Her briefing to her mobile patrols did not sound like the stuff of female support roles. "I felt a lump in my throat as I realized that for the first time in my military career I was about to tell soldiers, if necessary, to take a human life," McCullough wrote later. "It felt like an eternity to gather myself and say the word 'kill,' but I know it was a matter of seconds."[8]

A similar assault mission fell to the commander of the 988th Military Police Company, twenty-nine-year-old Army Captain Linda Bray. With over a hundred troops under her command, two deuce-and-a-half (two-and-a-half-ton) trucks and twelve Humvees, the Army's low, broad replacement of the jeep, Bray was also directing three simultaneous missions. One of her platoons was to set up a roadblock near the Panamanian Defense Forces headquarters, another to provide security for the headquarters of the U.S. Southern Command, two others to secure a suspected PDF stronghold ringed by a chain-link fence.

The latest intelligence reports estimated anywhere from twelve (a squad) to thirty (a platoon) members of the PDF could be inside the compound whose main building bore the painted crossed sword and rifle insignia of the Panamanian infantry and the head of a German shepherd, designating it a military dog kennel of the PDF's K-9 Corps.

According to Bray, at 1 a.m. on the morning of December 20, she was monitoring her radio at her command post in a junior high school parking lot a mile or so from the K-9 Corps headquarters. One small team from Bray's 988th Military Police Company was supposed to be in place at the front gate of the K-9 compound, another, larger team hidden in the thick underbrush nearby. According to plan, when each platoon radioed its position to Bray using the code word "green," she would launch the operation to secure the compound.

The team at the compound's gate was to call in Spanish for any PDF forces inside the compound to surrender; the second team hiding in the underbrush was to simultaneously cut through the chain-link fence surrounding the compound and take them prisoner. But Bray never heard from the platoon in the woods and the other team was soon radioing frantically for help as they came under fire from the rear. Bray dispatched a backup force from the high school command post with ammunition and flares, but the calls for help continued long after she estimated the reserve force should have arrived. Grabbing more flares and ammo, Bray ordered two other soldiers into her Humvee and ten minutes after 1 a.m., sped to the K-9 compound.

What did or did not happen next set the military and political stage for the controversy to come.

When she arrived at the staging area near the gate of the K-9 compound, Bray says, she was relieved to find her backup soldiers and her original team in place near the compound gate. The unit hiding behind the compound had been unable to contact her, she would find out later, because their radio antennae had been knocked off in the heavy underbrush.

Orangey-yellow bullet trails were crisscrossing the darkness from the M-16s of Bray's company and the Panamanians' AK-47s from the surrounding woods. The thunderous explosion of a U.S. 203 round soon rocked the compound gate while another 203 round fired by the platoon still concealed in the woods scored a direct hit on the building's front door.

Crawling through a drainage ditch, Bray came upon one of her soldiers just as he fired his M-60 machine gun in the direction of the rear sniper fire. Bray grabbed her 9mm pistol and shot in the same direction. Her one shot, out of the thousands of rounds fired in Panama, would reach epic proportions, prompting military sociologist Charles Moskos to describe it in a *Washington Post* editorial "as a shot heard round the world, or at least in the Pentagon."[9]

In the second hour of what had been dubbed "Operation Dogmeat," Bray was relieved that adrenaline was masking the pain in her legs. She had had to have metal pins inserted in both her hips the year before to repair the stress fractures she had suffered from carrying too much weight during her eight years in the Army. Lying on the floor of a Humvee, a gunner's foot planted on her back, she was radioing in the action at the kennel when the Humvee smashed through the front gate of the K-9 compound.

An attack dog leapt out of the darkness. One of her soldiers shot it with his M-16. Six or seven other dogs were killed before the

compound was secured, Bray estimates, two from the explosive impact of the 203 rounds, two or more running loose in the front of the
building, another two who attacked the Military Police as they tried
to enter the main building.

Inside the building, Bray's troops made a startling discovery: a
mini-arsenal of weapons, including more than a dozen AK-47s, 120
M-16 assault rifles, two cases of fragmentation grenades and thousands of rounds of ammunition.[10] The "intelligence" items uncovered, including uniforms and a cache of Cuban money, suggested
that the dog kennel was also a barracks for Special Operations
troops. There were also forty military cots, thirty-nine of which
looked to have been slept in. Assault units are supposed to outnumber their adversaries by three to one, instead of being outnumbered,
as Bray's troops had been. But there were no PDF troops in the
compound. They had all fled.

With the compound secured, Bray returned to the command
post around 4 a.m. to notify the battalion commander. She was
informed by her troops still at the kennel that one of her soldiers
had taken a POW. She had evidently come face-to-face with a PDF
soldier on the edge of the jungle and taken him into custody.

By any measure, Bray's mission had accomplished its goal. Her
soldiers had secured the PDF compound without any loss of human
life or injury, and they had discovered such a trove of weaponry
and intelligence that the Public Affairs Office detailed it in a press
release.[11]

Her soldiers, male and female, had performed well, though at
least one woman was surprised at her baptism by fire. "I knew
MP's broke up fights," said PFC Felicia Featherstone, who had been
stationed at the roadblock near Noreiga's headquarters. "But I never
thought I would have people shooting at me just because I am an
American."[12] In all, Bray estimated later, twelve of the fifteen
women under her command had been in combat.

None of these women were deemed by the Army technically to
have been in combat. It mattered not that Captains Bray, McCullough and Bezubic, Lieutenants Kutschera and Thompson, Warrant
Officer Mann, and Privates First Class Smith and Featherstone had
been fired on by an enemy, and those who were armed had returned
fire. Not even the violent night Specialist Kimberly Herrera of the
549th Military Police Company spent lying prone under a comman-

deered civilian bus in her roadblock and firing at the PDF vehicle which repeatedly came within screeching inches of ramming through the bus was considered combat duty. Women were not in combat in Panama because the Army, the Pentagon and Congress said they couldn't be.

Because of the Army's combat exclusion policy, these women and at least 150 others like them in Operation Just Cause would not receive the combat medals that are the emblem of a soldier's profession. Though Panama was officially a hostile area by perimeter, air, sea, longitude and latitude entitling all service members regardless of gender to draw imminent or probable danger pay, the servicewomen would not get the combat recognition so valued by promotion boards. Instead, they would become embroiled in a political firestorm both inside and outside the military that would spread through the halls of Congress to reach the White House. And the epicenter would be Linda Bray.

The first press reports from Panama did not mention Bray or any of the other women's aggressive military roles. In fact, there were few news reports at all. In a prelude to the military control of the press in Desert Storm a year away, the Pentagon orchestrated the Pentagon press pool as if it were a military unit. Not only did the Pentagon wait to fly members of the press pool into Panama until four hours after the operation began, but it then sequestered them for another six hours at the Joint Information Bureau in the Officers' Club at Quarry Heights, the Southern Command headquarters in Panama City. Instead of supplying the news, the journalists watched George Bush on CNN give his presidential spin on the invasion of Panama from Washington.

The journalists who were already in Panama when Operation Just Cause was launched fared even worse. One group of NMRs, the military acronym for "news media representatives," was forcibly detained by the military at Fort Clayton. Many more journalists, by the U.S. Southern Command's own admission, were held "hostage" in the Marriott Hotel for the first twenty-four hours.[13] So there was no objective observer of U.S. action in Panama, nor would there be.

Determined to advance a positive image of the Panamanian invasion, both the Pentagon in Washington and the Southern Command's Public Affairs personnel in Panama showed the pool reporters what the military wanted them to see and told them what the military wanted them to hear. "We kept explaining to our escorts that we needed to see troops on combat maneuvers, military police on patrol, wounded soldiers, Panamanians being taken prisoner, whatever was happening today that hadn't been reported or photographed," Kevin Merida of the *Dallas Morning News* wrote later. "Officials at the Southern Command were not interested in showing journalists scenes that would detract from what they regarded as a military triumph."

The Pentagon's preoccupation with presenting good news evolved at times into disinformation. Two days after the invasion, with Noriega still at large, U.S. officials took reporters to one of Noriega's residences to see 50 kilos (about 110 pounds) of "cocaine" found in bags in a freezer. The discovery of the cocaine, which made the front pages of most U.S. newspapers, was confirmed by a lieutenant general in the Pentagon as well as by General Maxwell Thurman in Panama. Not until a month later did the Defense Department waffle, first suggesting that the "cocaine" was actually the basis for voodoo spells to be cast on George Bush and members of Congress, then finally admitting that the white powdery substance was a mixture of farina, cornmeal and lard used to make tamales.[14]

The servicewomen involved in Operation Just Cause were presenting a different challenge to the military public opinion machine. At the outset of the operation, Public Affairs personnel offered up women as new and novel story ideas to the reporters under their control. When the women described the combat roles they had played in the invasion, the reporters' stories filed through the Public Affairs Office in Quarry Heights were censored.

The first interview not to be cleared was with one of the female helicopter pilots who had come under fire. "We were told she was not supposed to be ferrying soldiers into a hot zone that was taking fire," says an Army sergeant in Public Affairs who was working with reporters for military publications. "We were told that it was against the law."

The Army truck drivers who had come under fire ferrying troops into Panama City were also put off bounds. "We knew about it, but at the time we couldn't talk about it," says the sergeant. With military practicality, he turned his attention elsewhere. "Once I was told to downplay women in these roles, it became a nonissue," he says. "I sensed the [Public Affairs] command didn't want coverage of women under fire. Nobody came out and said, 'You can't write about women in combat,' but after that I didn't pay attention to what the women were doing."

The story was broken by reporters arriving independently in Panama and outside the control of Public Affairs. Ten days after the invasion, freelance reporter Wilson Ring and Peter Copeland, the Pentagon correspondent for Scripps Howard News Service, both stumbled over the startling new roles women had played in Panama within twenty-four hours of each other. Ironically, their tip-off to the story was the 988th Military Police Company private who had taken the POW at the dog kennel, and who was now pulling guard duty at the gate to Quarry Heights where the Public Affairs Office was simultaneously abandoning any war stories involving women.

Copeland, who had arrived in security-tight Panama on December 23 via a commercial flight to Costa Rica, a chartered flight pooled among other reporters to the Honduras/Panama border, then on to Panama City in a rented bus, was not looking to write an exposé of the Army's combat exclusion policies. He didn't even know at the time that women were excluded from combat units.

He was looking for a story. And he found it through Private First Class Christina Proctor, the tall, blond, twenty-year-old MP from Strawberry, Arizona.

"Seen any action?" Copeland recalls asking the female MP conversationally as she frisked him. "I can't talk about that," Proctor replied in a way that signaled she had. When he pressed her, Proctor requested and got permission from her sergeant to speak to him, the proviso being that she stick to her personal experiences and omit classified operational details.

The story that emerged—of firefights and snipers, attack dogs and a captured Panamanian soldier, even three PDF soldiers later found dead—did not sound like a combat support mission or in keeping with congressional intent. And Private Proctor, whose twin sister was also serving in Panama, knew it. "Congress does not like women in combat, but what they don't know won't hurt them," Proctor told Copeland. "I raised my right hand to defend my country, and I've got a job to do. I was trained just like the guys, and that's what I do."

Intrigued, Copeland asked Proctor for details about her mission, but she refused without permission from her company commander.

"Where can I find him?" Copeland asked. "She's right up the hill," Proctor replied. "She? Your company commander is a 'she'?" Copeland said. "Sure," said Proctor. "Captain Bray. Captain Linda Bray."

The protocol for journalists in Panama seeking interviews with military personnel was to fill out and file a query with the Southern Command's Public Affairs Office, then wait for the PAO to respond. But the operative word "wait" was a luxury few journalists had. The PAO with its staff of only twenty-two was overwhelmed by the number of arriving journalists, which would grow to 855 by the third week in January.[15]

Journalists were also supposed to have someone from Public Affairs sit in on any interview with service personnel. The presenting reason was to translate military jargon into language understandable to lay readers and reporters and to correct inaccuracies or misimpressions before they appeared in print.[16] But the presence of Public Affairs naturally reminded military personnel to speak only about their specific areas of responsibility and never above their rank. Such restrictions, especially with their enforcers present, discouraged any individual from public disagreement with Pentagon policy or personal accounts that contradicted official lines. "Public Affairs puts up clouds of smoke while the truth goes on behind them," says a former PAO representative.

Knowing the pitfalls that lay ahead, Copeland used his own military strategy to get the Bray interview. He took the sergeant from the 988th Military Police Company with him to the PAO. "There was a bunch of harried, overworked public affairs people there," says Copeland. "I asked to talk to Linda Bray and one of them said, 'Sure, here's a request.' I said there's a guy here from her unit who could take me to her office right now and he said, 'OK, go ahead.' I said to the sergeant, 'You heard the PAO say it's OK?' He said, 'Yeah,' and he drove me over to her office."

Bray, who had already been interviewed by Wilson Ring, was responsive to Copeland's questions. She had been instructed to be responsive. The military was still haunted by the "lessons learned" in Vietnam from the negative reaction of the press. The services still blamed the media for turning the American people against the war and the military, undermining the morale of the troops and drastically hampering recruiting. The Army was looking for good public relations to come out of Panama.

"The word to all of us from the PAO was 'talk to the press,' " says Bray. " 'Remember that operations are still classified, so be very careful what you say. But talk to them. Tell them how you feel. Tell them what you think. We don't want to have another Vietnam and have the press against us and attacking us.' "

Bray talked to Copeland for an hour in the parking lot outside her office; he then left to interview other women in her company and others who had taken part in Operation Just Cause. He filed his story to Scripps Howard over the phone from his hotel on January 1 without going through Public Affairs. The *Washington Times* ran Copeland's stories of six women, including Linda Bray, on January 2 under the headline "Army Women Went into Panama with Weapons —and Used Them." "American women participated fully in the invasion of Panama, firing machine guns, taking enemy prisoners and even leading troops into battle," Copeland wrote in his lead.

Wilson Ring's story ran the next day, January 3, in the *Washington Post* and concentrated on Linda Bray. Under the headline "Woman Led U.S. Troops into Battle," Ring's story began: "A female captain led a platoon into battle during last month's U.S. invasion of Panama, the first time that a woman has taken such a combat role for the American military." And the domestic balloon went up.

The complexities of the Army's Direct Combat Probability Coding (DCPC), authored, ironically, by General Maxwell Thurman, understandably escaped the civilian world. Being fired on by an enemy and shooting back seemed a reasonable definition of combat to everyone but the Army and the Defense Department. The nuance lay in the primary mission of Bray's Military Police company as opposed to its secondary mission, which was to provide combat-ready Military Police forces capable of performing tactical operations in the rear of a battlefield.

"We specifically differentiated between the routine—underline the word 'routine'—nature of the duties in direct combat, which is to close with, destroy, defeat the enemy where there is a high probability of injury and/or capture in order to open the number of slots we did to women," Thurman would tell me later.

It was the transition from one mission to another that would so worry male commanders about breaking the DCPC in the Gulf. And it was the transition of Bray's peacetime mission to what certainly appeared to be a combat mission that would worry the Pentagon. Copeland's image of women "firing machine guns" and "leading troops into battle" in the *Washington Times* and Ring's depiction of women "killing three PDF soldiers" in a "three-hour battle" were that of a new generation of women warriors which, by law, policy and military imperative, they could not be.

If Bray and her company had aggressively sought out the male enemy and actually killed three of them, then women had crossed a major cultural line. It was military men who by tradition and law carried the fight to the enemy. Women's proven ability to kill would be both the ultimate equalizer and the ultimate threat to military male power.[17]

Civilians, however, missed such nuances. To many reading the morning newspapers, including White House spokesman Marlin Fitzwater, Bray's blistering assault on a dog kennel was all so— American. Quick to sense a positive spin on the military operation, the White House spokesman seized on the morning's newspapers to embrace military women in general and Bray in particular as popular heroines.

Women had served "with great distinction" in Panama, said Fitzwater at a press conference on January 3, 1990, singling out Linda Bray's assault of the dog kennel as "an important military operation." "It was heavily defended. Three PDF men were killed. Gunshots were fired on both sides. American troops could have been killed. A woman led it and she did an outstanding job." Startled, perhaps, by his impromptu embrace of such modern views, Fitzwater concluded his remarks with a defiant: "So there."[18]

To the Pentagon's consternation, Congresswoman Pat Schroeder was on ABC News that night calling for legislation to open up all jobs in the Army to women, whether combat or not, for four years. Schroeder kept up her assault on *Good Morning America*. On January 5, she blasted the Army's combat exclusion policies as not only failing "to keep women out of combat, as we've well seen down in Panama," but as an "economic issue" which "really keeps women from promotions in certain areas." She argued that it made no sense to restrict the careers of women who voluntarily entered the Army, only to be told, ". . . 'No, you can't do that because of your gender.' "

Just as quick off the mark were conservative opponents of servicewomen whose strategy was to dismiss Operation Just Cause as a test of women in combat. "The sorts of things they were doing [in Panama] could be done by a 12-year-old with a rifle," scoffed Brian Mitchell, author of *Weak Link: The Feminization of the American Military,* who later would join Pat Buchanan's 1992 presidential primary campaign.[19] Schroeder returned the salvo. "The women carried M-16's," she told *Time*, "not dog biscuits."[20]

Schroeder's proposed legislation was as familiar to the Army as it was unwelcome. DACOWITS had forwarded the same recommendation to the secretary of defense in 1989. Though no member of DACOWITS expected the secretary of defense to lean on the Army to change its policies, the path of change, were it ever to occur, would be the easiest in the Army. Repealing the combat exclusion laws that restricted women in the Navy and Air Force would require acts of Congress. In the Army, it would take only a policy directive from the secretary of the Army.

The reawakened debate over women in combat thrust Linda Bray into the spotlight. Requests for interviews with her flooded the Public Affairs Office in Panama and Washington. One Army spokesman called it the hottest issue in her two and a half years at the Pentagon with "massive, massive numbers of calls coming in from all around the country, from little tiny papers out in the heartland of America to major dailies, and even from London."[21]

The Pentagon was taken aback. While the Army had been training women for years in the combat skills they might have to use, it had not anticipated the magnitude of public reaction when the women actually used them. "Certainly it was big news to the American public raised on the myth that women were excluded from military combat," writes retired Air Force Major General Jeanne Holm in *Women in the Military: An Unfinished Revolution*. "And even though Pentagon policymakers knew that women might be exposed to hostile fire and might even have to shoot back, they were not prepared for the deluge of public interest in what happened in Panama."[22]

Everyone wanted—and got—a piece of Linda Bray, served up with enthusiasm by Public Affairs. If the Military Police captain was giving a positive image to the Army, then why not showcase her? That highlighting Bray would be good for the Army outweighed the inevitable harm such exposure would inflict on Bray from a military culture that stressed teamwork over the individual. And so Bray was ordered to the slaughter.

"The PAO never stopped calling me," Bray recalls. "Talk to this one. Talk to that one. I was spending half the day running around talking to the different people they wanted me to talk to. When PAO found out they had a story, it was, 'Let's feed it. Let's keep pumping this, feeding Captain Bray to the press.' "

Bray tried to contain the interviews to the teamwork she had observed among her troops, both male and female, in their first test under fire. But every printed word seemed to advance women as combat equals to men. "Before this all started, I had always wondered what would happen," Bray was quoted in the *Washington Post*. "After this, in my opinion, there is no difference [between men and women]. They worked together as a team, all my soldiers." [23]

Peppered with questions about women in combat, Bray gave answers that implied a radical change in the Army's combat exclusion policies. "It used to be that just because you were a female you would not be able to fight," Bray was quoted in *U.S. News & World Report*. "That is no longer true." [24]

Time slugged its Linda Bray story "Fire When Ready, Ma'am" and pronounced that "for the first time women . . . had engaged hostile troops in modern combat." [25] A front-page story in the *Detroit News* compared her actions "as worthy of a young Douglas MacArthur or George Patton." [26] A *Washington Post* editorial titled "A Combat Soldier Named Linda" used the combat success of the five-foot-one-inch, hundred-pound captain in Panama to debunk the Army's "protective" policies: "In light of the Panama experience, does it make any sense to continue current sex-based rules on military assignments?" [27] And the Pentagon pincers began to close.

"The military got scared," says Carolyn Becraft, a military policy analyst in Washington at the time. "One instinct was to support Bray, which they did initially. But when Bray said that what happened in Panama ought to prove the illogic of the combat exclusion laws, that spooked the military. She was the symbol of change they weren't willing to do. So they deep-sixed her."

The discrediting of Bray began within twenty-four hours of the first news stories in the highest offices in the Pentagon. Major General Patrick Brady, the Army chief of Public Affairs, flew to Panama and walked the compound with her. Brigadier General Bill McClain, the Army deputy chief of Public Affairs, interviewed Bray by phone from Washington. The Army's strategy was to find any errors in the press coverage of Bray, then circulate the new facts to prompt corrective coverage. The Army reasoned that the Bray story and the renewal of interest in the combat issue would then quietly go away.

"We wanted to tone the story down and keep it from being a story as much as we could," said Colonel Bill Mulvey, chief of the Army's media relations division, in a later interview. "We understood why journalists were interested in it, but we didn't want them to be interested in it. Part of it was that we saw the story being used as an argument for the DACOWITS study."[28]

In interviews with Bray in Panama, the Army hit what it considered to be pay dirt. Bray told McClain that she had been misquoted by the *Washington Post* and Marlin Fitzwater about three PDF soldiers killed at the PDF compound. The rumors may have come from her soldiers, she said, but as company commander she could neither confirm nor deny the kills. Three PDF bodies had been found by a cleanup crew in the woods near the kennel, but their deaths could have occurred anytime in the three days following the assault on the kennel and could not be specifically attributed to the night of the invasion or to any U.S. unit, including her own.

The "fierce firefight" at the kennel reported by Peter Copeland was correct, though the "three-hour battle" reported by Ring was exaggerated. Bray reiterated that she had been a mile away at a command post for the first ten minutes of the barrage before arriving on the scene. The heavy fire had continued for another twenty minutes or so before subsiding into intermittent sniper fire.

The Army heard what it wanted to hear and passed it on. "Female's War Exploits Overblown, Army Says" ran the headline in the *Los Angeles Times* on January 6, 1990, four days after Copeland broke the story in the *Washington Times* and three days after Ring's piece had run in the *Washington Post*. Written by Pentagon correspondent John Broder, who hadn't been in Panama or talked to anyone there, the story labeled Linda Bray's "battle exploits" as advanced by the press and Marlin Fitzwater "grossly exaggerated."[29]

Citing an anonymous "Army spokesman," Broder's article reduced the firefight at the kennel to ten minutes, stated no PDF soldiers were killed and removed Bray from any hostile contact with the enemy: what PDF soldiers had been defending the kennel had faded into the woods by the time Bray arrived, leaving the captain and her troops to face only "sporadic" sniper fire. The article's one named source was Brigadier General McClain, the deputy chief of Army Public Affairs.[30]

Broder's article avoided any criticism of the now very public and popular Bray and, by extension, the other servicewomen in Panama, but leveled both barrels at a safer target: Peter Copeland. "The 'in-flated accounts' of Bray's assault on the PDF compound," Broder insinuated, had stemmed from the "original newspaper account of the action, distributed by Scripps Howard News Service, widely repeated by other news organizations."[31]

Peter Copeland, who was called on the carpet by Scripps Howard, was furious. "Broder quoted an anonymous Army official, then compared my story to his 'new truth' based on one interview with an Army General who had not been in Panama," Copeland said. "Broder didn't even back up the charge that Bray's exploits in Panama had been 'grossly exaggerated.' There is no Army person saying that, only the reporter."[32] Still in Panama when Broder's story ran, Copeland "let it be known to McClain's people" in the Pentagon that what the Army's deputy chief of Public Affairs had done "was shitty." McClain's reaction to Copeland relayed back from the Army was world class: "Give Peter my apology and tell him the *LA Times* story was bullshit."

After a year covering the Pentagon, Copeland was not deceived. "The Army wanted it all different ways," he told Captain Joan R. Vallance Whitacre, who was writing a master's thesis on the conflicting media coverage of Panama. "They loved my story at first but when people like Pat Schroeder started waving it at them and saying, 'Why can't women be in the infantry then, why can't women serve in combat?' they panicked. They didn't want to discredit one of their own soldiers who'd performed well and discourage all the women in the military, so they figured out a half-way to do it by throwing cold water on my story."[33]

Broder was unrepentant about his story, but admitted to being "a little used" by the Army "for their purposes." "Brigadier General McClain was more than usually eager to respond to questions about the [Bray] affair," conceded Broder, who also acknowledged he hadn't attempted to check the Army's version of the story with Bray or other members of her company in Panama. "I think there was a concern in the Army and an effort by the senior leadership to try and nip the story in the bud, based not so much on what Captain Bray did or did not do at the kennel, but on the way Pat Schroeder and other advocates of broader female participation in the military were using it."[34]

The military strategy worked. The *New York Times,* whose first Bray story had been headlined "For First Time, a Woman Leads G.I.'s in Combat," was followed five days later by a more muted story, slugged "U.S. Tells Calmer Story of Woman's Role in Commanding Attack."[35] This time the Southern Command Public Affairs Office in Panama had sent out a new press release to correct previous errors or exaggerations and Brigadier General McClain was again the quoted source.

The new version in the *New York Times*, reported without having talked to Bray in Panama, sounded as if she had taken a walk in the park on the night of the invasion. She had "her driver take her to the kennel" not because her troops had come under heavy fire and were calling for help, but to try to stop the PDF from escaping into the woods. The reason she had "crawled into a ditch" was "to get closer to the building," not to keep her head below the line of enemy fire. She had then "sent teams to capture the kennel" instead of being in the Humvee with them as they crashed through the locked gates of the compound. Again, the "ten-minute" firefight at the kennel found Bray safe at her command post half a mile away and, contrary to prior press reports, no PDF bodies were found.

With one stroke from the military opinion machine, Bray's actions on the night of the invasion had been cleansed of any serious gunfire, any proximity to the enemy, any semblance of combat. And there was no one to contest the Army's story. As of January 9, the day the *Times* story ran, officials in Panama had deemed all female officers "currently unavailable" for comment.[36]

Linda Bray was puzzled by the gag rule. After being run ragged by the Public Affairs Office with interviews for ten days, then doing her own work, which often kept her up past midnight, she had been called into the office of her battalion commander, Lieutenant Colonel Michael Shanahan, and ordered not to give any more interviews.

Bray was relieved by that. "After a week and a half of this stuff, I just wanted to be left alone," she says. "I didn't want any more questions from my superior officers or the media. I just wanted to command my company, do my missions and get on with life." On the other hand, she was furious at the new version of her assault on the PDF compound. "It made me so mad that even the Pentagon couldn't get the story straight," she says. "I told them it was ten minutes into the operation when I went to the kennels. It came back that the whole firefight was ten minutes. In my opinion, the Pentagon was trying to discredit women."

Bray took great exception to the Pentagon's denial of her involvement with any PDF killed. Her company had "three confirmed kills," she says, at the roadblock near the Cuban embassy. And Emergency Operations had confirmed that three other PDF were found dead near the kennels. "They couldn't attribute the other three kills to us or to anyone. But there were PDF bodies found near the kennels who could have been killed any of the three days following the night of assault. So that's how it got worked up to—there were three dead, there weren't three dead, maybe there were three dead."

Bray wanted to set the record straight. All four television networks had requested interviews with her in the new round of media interest set off by the Army's "cold water" campaign. Her battalion commander gave her his reluctant consent since the Public Affairs Office had already scheduled them. "I said to him, 'Sir, I'll agree to do these four and that's it. No more.' And that's what I did."

On January 10, 1990, Bray appeared live from Panama on CNN, *Today, This Morning* and *Good Morning America*. Viewers in Congress, the Pentagon and at home tuning into *Good Morning America* saw a segment featuring a rather tense and nervous Bray sandwiched in between stories about two new inductees into Baseball's Hall of Fame and a twelve-year-old Christmas stowaway who had managed to fly free to Florida to spend the holiday with his father.

Though Joan Lunden tried to set Bray up as the woman "who led male soldiers into combat," Bray wouldn't play. When Lunden asked Bray about the initial reports of PDF soldiers being killed by her unit, Bray dismissed the reports as "uncontrolled rumors" and instead stressed her "praise" for "all the soldiers" in her company. "If it was not for their courage and their professionalism, the mission never would have been accomplished."

Bray was marginally bolder on CBS. When Kathleen Sullivan asked her, "Were you in combat?" Bray didn't say "yes," though she implied it. "Shots were fired. I returned fire. And that's the way it was." When Sullivan asked if there were any casualties at the kennel, Bray replied that there were "no confirmed casualties" at the kennel.

But it was Bray's exact answer on all four networks to the payoff question, should women be in combat? that tipped off military insiders. Instead of challenging the restrictive policies of the Army as she had before, Bray's answer seemed straight out of an Army manual.

"In 1983, coming out of ROTC, I took an oath to support and defend the Constitution and to obey the orders of the President of the United States," she said with a deadpan expression on *Good Morning America.* "I will obey those orders and I will support my chain of command."

"Somebody's gotten to her," an Army captain recalls remarking at the time to her husband. She was right.

In an about-face, the Public Affairs Office had reversed its candor advisory for Bray. "First they tell me to tell the media what you feel, tell them what you think. All of a sudden it was like, 'Whoa. Wait a minute. Stop!' " Bray said later.

This time the Public Affairs Office had given written instructions to Bray detailing what she could not say. "I could not say that what my unit did was a combat mission. I had to say it was a Military Police mission, which is just a twist of terminology."

Bray was not to give her personal opinions, but the Army's opinion. If asked about women in combat units, she was to reroute the answer to say that women could serve in combat support and combat service support units where there was a possibility they could come under fire, but that military opinion held that women should not serve in combat arms units. "I was supposed to support that statement."

To make sure Bray understood the Army's position before the interviews, she had been called in to see Lieutenant General Carl Stiner, the three-star commander of Operation Just Cause. For a junior officer, the weight of Stiner's rank and position was akin to a novitiate meeting one-on-one with the pope.

"General Stiner was very serious and looked me straight in the eye," she recalls. "He sat me down and told me what the military's opinion was, that it was fine for women to be in combat support, but not in combat arms." Bray didn't need to be told the Army policy, of course. Everyone in the Army knew that only males served in combat units. But Stiner repeated it all to her again.

"He told me I didn't necessarily have to agree with the policy, but in order to support my superiors and the military, I should support that statement."

Bray, who was looking forward to a lifetime career in the Army, had understood her orders. When she said, "Yes, sir," Stiner patted her on the knee.

■

In Washington, Pat Schroeder's bill to open an Army combat
unit to women for a four-year trial was running into the same stone
wall Bray was facing in Panama. A week before she introduced the
bill on January 23, Schroeder was conceding that it faced deep trouble. Members of Congress were apprehensive about the political accusations, she said, that "this is the congressman who voted to put
your daughter in combat boots."[37]

Both the chair and ranking minority member of the Senate
Armed Services Committee, Georgia Democrat Sam Nunn and Virginia Republican John Warner, were lining up against it, as was
Maryland Democrat Beverly Byron, chair of the House Armed Services Committee military personnel subcommittee. "I'm not comfortable seeing women on the front lines," Byron said vaguely. "I
just have problems."[38]

Conservative organizations, which had gained muscle under
Ronald Reagan and whose influence was increasing under the Bush
administration, derided Schroeder's proposal. Jane Chastain, a board
member of Concerned Women for America, charged that servicewomen seeking combat assignments were being selfish. "There
are some strong women out there," conceded Chastain, a former
sportscaster. "But to me, if they're really interested in military service, they should ask not what their country can do for them, but
what they can do best for their country." Eagle Forum president
Phyllis Schlafly didn't believe there were any strong women anywhere. "Men soldiers know if they're wounded, the women can't
carry them off the field," she said.[39]

Schroeder persisted. She had been enraged by the Army's announcement on January 9 that the coveted Combat Infantryman
Badge would be issued to men for valor under fire in Panama, but
not to women, including Linda Bray. "Women get everything but the
glory, and that's not fair," she had said the next night on ABC's *World
News Tonight*.[40]

Schroeder and her like-minded colleagues in the Senate had
dismissed the Army's explanation that the badge could be awarded
only to members of the infantry, who, by regulation, were all male.
"We believe it is outrageous that the Army refuses to acknowledge
the service under fire of these female soldiers," wrote Ohio Senator
Howard Metzenbaum and five other senators, including Illinois Senator Paul Simon, to the secretary of the Army. "The contention that

they were assigned to a military police unit rather than an infantry unit is irrelevant given the fact that soldiers from both units were engaged in life-threatening combat situations."[41]

The Army's hasty announcement that Bray would receive the Army's Commendation Medal stirred the waters even more. Not only was the Commendation Medal the lowest in the hierarchy of Army medals, but an Army spokesman admitted that it was given more commonly during peacetime "because it has no combat requirement."[42]

The Army could have waived the infantry restriction on the badge and awarded it to women or, better yet, created a new combat award for the Military Police. There were many precedents for military medal expediency. The thirty-day combat requirement for the Combat Infantryman Badge established in World War II had been waived after the seven-day skirmish in Grenada to accommodate the awarding of the CIB to 3,530 infantrymen, pointed out retired Admiral Elmo Zumwalt Jr. An Arctic Service Ribbon had recently been created to acknowledge those training above a specified ice zone for an arctic war. And a Prisoner of War Medal had been created to honor those who had been held POW in Korea and Vietnam.[43]

Moreover, the criteria for selecting those who qualified for these honors were as creative as they were subjective. During the Grenada operation, the Combat Jump Star designed for those making a jump under combat conditions was awarded to an Army Ranger from the 82nd Airborne who never touched ground. His parachute got fouled in the aircraft, leaving him streaming behind the plane as it flew back over the Caribbean until the aircrew pulled him to safety. But he was awarded the Combat Jump Star anyway: the only requirement for the award was to jump, the Army decided, not to land.[44]

There would be no such expediency for the women of Operation Just Cause. Not only would the awarding of combat medals to women contradict the Pentagon's insistence that women had not faced true combat in Panama, there also weren't enough Combat Infantryman Badges to go around.

The 10,000 badges stockpiled by the Army would be quickly snapped up by infantrymen returning from Panama for 90 cents each and given as proud presents to the men's mothers, wives and girlfriends. The civilian women were entitled to wear the CIBs as proof of their men's bravery under fire, but military women were not allowed to wear them as proof of their own.[45] Nor, with the escalation of the Army's campaign to discredit women in Panama before Schroeder introduced her legislation, would women ever be.

The Army strengthened its case against women in combat with a new round of unattributed news stories out of Panama. "2 Army Women Being Investigated for Disobeying Order in Panama" ran the headline in the *New York Times* on January 21, followed the next day by a similar story in the *Washington Times*, slugged "Army Suspects Women Truckers Ducked Panama Combat." "Unidentified Defense Department sources" in both stories assigned the very un-military emotions of fear, weakness and, worst, cowardice to the two truck drivers for allegedly refusing orders to ferry combat troops through sniper fire into a combat zone. "Tears were involved," said one unnamed Defense Department official who claimed the two drivers had "feared for their lives."[46] The Army was considering bringing charges against the women for disobeying orders, which could result in courts-martial.

When an Army investigation three days later concluded that the women had not been derelict in their duties but were simply exhausted—one driver straight from her basic training had been driving for sixteen hours without a break—all talk of charges was dropped.[47] But the Army's public opinion machine had won another round. The "crying" incident in Panama as reported secondhand by an anonymous official in Washington would become a center stone in the arguments against women in combat.

"It didn't take long for the truth to come out of Panama," conservative Brian Mitchell would write.[48] Citing first the "grossly exaggerated" story of Linda Bray's assault on the PDF kennel where "the female officer was not present during the shooting," Mitchell then laid waste to the "female truck drivers" who were "accused of tearfully refusing to drive a company of Rangers to the site of the fiercest fighting."

The orchestration of women from combat heroines to crybabies in less than a month was a public relations coup for the nameless Washington officials. The Army had successfully fended off both the DACOWITS recommendation and Pat Schroeder's legislation. "It died a real quick death in subcommittee," says Lisa Moreno, Schroeder's legislative assistant. "There were hearings, but everybody laughed at the concept of actually opening up infantry, armor and artillery positions to women. It was just too much for people. And that was the end of it."

In Panama, it was the beginning of the end as well for the Army captain who had followed her orders, completed her missions, followed the Army's directives to talk to the press and was now being hung out to dry.

The euphoria that had followed the U.S. siege in Panama had been replaced among the Military Police companies by bitterness and jealousy. Unit cohesion was shredding between the celebrated females in Operation Just Cause and the ignored males. The Army's determination to categorize all service members as "green," and not as black or white or male or female, had failed in the weight of the media spotlight on the females. Morale sank so low in Bray's company that the chaplain was called in.

"The chaplain tried to explain to the males that the media attention was not meant to degrade them but stemmed from so many females being involved in a conflict for the first time," says Bray. "But it became pretty rough to just continue on a day-to-day basis without the soldiers fighting or morale dropping."

The backlash was roughest on Bray. Emboldened perhaps by the Army's public skepticism about Bray's role in the kennel assault, soldiers in other Military Police units were following suit. Who does she think she is? the muttering went. She's nothing special. She didn't do anything. "Some claimed I wasn't even at the kennel," Bray says. "It made me feel awful."

Worse was her new label: "Puppy-killer." The day after the firefight she had returned to the K-9 Corps compound where she documented the deaths of six or seven dogs. Still in their kennels were upwards of thirty other dogs. "I went through the runs after it was over," says Bray. "The dogs were there."

Two days later most of the dogs were dead and Bray stood accused of killing them. She had been charged by her battalion commander, Lieutenant Colonel Michael Shanahan, in response to a complaint filed by the Panamanian kennel keeper. "No way it was us," Bray told her commander. She had returned to the kennel the day after the assault, she told him, and seen all the dogs alive in their runs. But Lieutenant Colonel Shanahan was adamant. Her company had laid siege to the dog kennel on the night of the invasion. He had a report of forty-four dogs killed. As company commander, Bray was responsible.

A pattern of professional harassment took hold which Bray was powerless to stop. Ever since her rash of publicity, the 988th had been worked nonstop, seven days a week. Her troops were exhausted. "We were getting mission after mission after mission," says Bray. "The soldiers were hardly getting any sleep." Bray went to her command to get some of the missions released, but was turned down. "It was like, 'OK, you think you're a combat-proven captain. Let's see how much you can handle,' " she says. Bray figured they were trying to punish her soldiers because of her. "I didn't like that at all," she says.

Her troops were also having to double up on workloads. Though Force Command requirements called for her company to have one hundred Military Police in Panama at all times, as Bray's soldiers were sent home no replacements were being sent from Fort Benning, Georgia. She had repeatedly called her colonel in the "rear" at Fort Benning for replacements, but to no avail. Once again Bray was called on the carpet, this time to explain the personnel shortage. " 'Sir, what do you want me to do?' " Bray asked her commander. " 'I've called my colonel at Fort Benning. Here's his phone number. He's got MP replacements but he's not sending them.' " Bray had to watch while other MP companies got replacements. She had left Fort Benning with 103 MPs. She would return in April with only 85.

But it was the continuing accusation about the slaughter of the dogs at the PDF kennels that bothered Bray the most. "I love dogs," she says. "I've never, ever abused dogs in my life. I didn't understand why I was being accused of killing them."

Her distress at the accusation was soon overtaken by a professional concern. A month or so before she left Panama, Lieutenant Colonel Shanahan called her into his office to tell her a lot of "bigwigs" in Washington were "concerned" about what had gone on at the kennels. According to Shanahan, Bray says, there was a "possibility" that she could be hearing from them "at some future time."

The possibility became reality after Bray returned to Fort Benning in April. The warm welcome afforded Bray and the 988th was reversed two months later by investigators from the Army's Criminal Investigation Command.

For weeks Bray and her soldiers were grilled about the deaths of the dogs in Panama. Though Bray kept insisting that her MP company had been replaced by another at the kennel after the night of the assault, the investigators were so hard on her soldiers that she took one of them to get a lawyer.

Instead of the command atmosphere improving at Fort Benning now that she was out of the pressure cooker of Panama, her harassment by some of her superiors got worse. "It was like they ganged up on me to prove that I wasn't anything special, or I hadn't accomplished anything special, and I was a nobody," she told Peter Copeland, who felt somewhat responsible for Bray's now destructive celebrity and had kept in touch with her.[49]

To Bray, it seemed as if she got "a butt-chewing" nearly every day. "I came home crying almost every night," she says. One encounter was particularly humiliating. Ordered to drop everything by a superior officer in her command and to see him immediately, Bray found him sprawled in his desk chair, his feet on the desk. Bray, who didn't know why she had been summoned, was immediately dressed down for not having brought her first sergeant with her. When she told the officer she didn't understand, he said scornfully, "Oh, come on, captain. Use your brain. One of your soldiers has made a congressional complaint. It's command policy that the company commander and the first sergeant pick these things up."

Bray's explanation that the policy had changed while she was in Panama was met with more derision. "So you don't even know your own command policies?" the officer said. Tapping the "complaint" rhythmically on the desk, he asked her how she was going to answer it. "Sir, if you'll let me read it and see who the soldier is, then I can probably come up with my answer," Bray replied.

"Oh, come on, captain, use your brain," the officer said. "Who do you think it is?"

Bray had three soldiers who had recently been disciplined. One of them, she suggested, must have complained to his congressional representative.

"Oh, very, very smart, captain," the officer drawled, handing her the congressional inquiry. Normally, company commanders have five days to gather information about a congressional complaint and write a written response. Bray says she was given five hours to research and present the response to the battalion commander and the whole chain of command. She managed to hold back her tears until she left his office.

Bray and her company were exonerated in the deaths of the dogs after a six-month investigation by the Criminal Investigation Command. The CIC report found that the dogs had been killed by a soldier in another MP company on a cleanup mission the day after the assault on the PDF compound. Under orders to resecure the area, and seeing that the dogs hadn't been fed or watered since the assault, the soldier had "shot an undetermined number of dogs in their kennel runs, claiming to have been putting them out of their misery," the report concluded.[50]

But even Bray's relief at being officially cleared in the incident was tainted. "No one said a word. No one said, 'We're sorry you went through this.' Nothing," says Bray. "My colonel simply said, 'Did you see this report?' 'Yes, sir,' I told him." The colonel then turned to his secretary, told her to file the report—and dismissed Bray without a word.

Bitter and disillusioned, Bray struggled to keep her Army career on track, but it had become no-win. Her company, which had become close after the return from Panama and the Army investigation, was breaking up. Many had left after three months. Others were being transferred out. There was conjecture that the Army was trying to break it up.

Bray's attitude about the Army had turned south. The young woman who had joined her college ROTC program as a ticket out of the tiny tobacco town of Butner, North Carolina, and whose fast-track success in the Army had culminated in her selection as company commander of the 988th Military Police Company in 1989, was watching her future turn to dust. Bray and her husband, a West Point graduate and Army Ranger whom she had met in Germany, had planned tandem careers in the Army. What had begun as a career enhancer for Bray when her company was deployed to Panama on a normal rotation from Fort Benning just two weeks before the launching of Operation Just Cause had turned into a career crusher. "I was so frustrated and had so much hate in me, I wasn't doing myself or anybody else any good," Bray says.

She considered bringing charges of harassment against her superiors by jumping the chain of command or by going through the Equal Opportunity Office or the inspector general. But Bray knew there would be an even steeper price to pay. "I knew that was just going to make them madder and then they would just do more things to you," she says. "And I didn't want to get into that."

After eight years in the Army it was all over. "Once the tide turned against me, I'd really had it," she says. "There are some people who will stay in and fight and fight and fight to beat the system, but I was just worn out."

In August 1990, Bray submitted her resignation. "I want out," she told her colonel. When her Military Police company was put on alert for deployment to the Gulf shortly thereafter, she withdrew her resignation. When her company was taken off alert in October without being deployed, Bray entered the hospital for another operation on her hips. Her right hip didn't heal properly, and the doctors asked if she wanted to go for a medical discharge. "Sure," said Bray. She was officially discharged with a 10 percent disability in April 1991.[51]

Bray and her husband, who would leave the Army after the Gulf war, continued to live in Georgia just a few miles from Fort Benning. Two years after Bray performed the duties required of a company commander she still hadn't found work. The former Army captain described herself as a housewife.

Her legacy, however, remained. While the Army would continue to invoke the "sensational stories concerning women" whenever the subject of Panama came up and specifically blame "a Scripps Howard News Service reporter" for his exaggerated story about women in combat,[52] the flurry of publicity about Bray put servicewomen—and combat—on the map.

Public opinion was growing in support of women in combat. In 1980, 52 percent of respondents to a Gallup poll had said "no" to the question "Should women be eligible for combat roles?" and 44 percent had said "yes." In a January 1990, CBS/*New York Times* poll taken just ten days after the Linda Bray story broke, public opinion had reversed. In response to the question "Do you think women members of the armed forces should be allowed to serve in combat if they want to?" 72 percent of the respondents now answered "yes" and only 26 percent "no."[53]

By any definition, including the Pentagon's, women had been in combat. "Due to the nature of the Panama invasion, women soldiers quickly found themselves in the 'front line' of the conflict doing battle with the enemy," Air Force Colonel Ronald Sconyers wrote in an internal memo to Southern Command personnel working in Public Affairs. "In fact, there were no 'front lines' during the hostilities. What was considered to be a relatively secure area one minute would come under sniper or mortar fire the next. These circumstances placed women soldiers, for the first time, in direct contact with enemy forces."[54]

Even General Maxwell Thurman, the head of Southern Command and one of the authors of the Army's Direct Combat Probability Coding, was hard-pressed to defend the Army's position that the women MPs, helicopter pilots and truck drivers who were shot at and who, in many cases, returned fire were noncombatants.

"How many women did you have in your command in Panama?" Thurman was asked later by Chicago attorney Newton Minow.

"Eight hundred," Thurman replied.

"How many were in combat?" Minow asked.

"Eight hundred," said Thurman.

In the debate to come about women in combat, their performance in Panama wouldn't count because the services didn't want it to. The Army's "corrections" of Linda Bray's firefight at the PDF dog kennel would cast just the right cloud of confusion. "Inaccurate media coverage," not the reality of women's combat roles, would be cited by an Army historian in an information paper issued on "Lessons Learned in Operation Just Cause" as the trigger for the "heated congressional, media and public 1990 debate on the subject of women in combat."[55]

A presidential commission studying women's roles after the Gulf war would learn nothing from Panama. "The Services report that they did not uncover significant lessons learned about the utilization of women, presumably because of the small number involved," one report about Operation Just Cause would conclude.[56]

Media coverage wasn't the answer. Nor was the number of women involved. To women's critics, the deployment of over 40,000 women to Saudi Arabia beginning seven months after Operation Just Cause in Panama would not count either. Though two women would be taken prisoners of war and over a dozen killed, the Gulf war, too, would be discounted as any test of women in combat. The military culture would not accept women as warriors in life or in death.

3

PUBLIC VICTORY,
PRIVATE LOSSES

The Price of Progress in the Gulf

STAFF SERGEANT Tatiana Khaghani Dees, a member of the 92nd Military Police Company, 93rd Battalion from Baumholder, Germany, was the first woman to die in the Gulf. She drowned on January 7, 1991, after she backed off a pier at the King Abdul Aziz port in Dammam, Saudi Arabia, as she kept her gun trained on a suspected terrorist. Weighed down by her equipment, Dees, the divorced mother of two young children, slipped under the surface before she could be rescued. Her body was recovered by Navy divers.

Dees's local newspaper in New York, the *Rockland News Journal,* carried the news of her death, but it received little national attention. According to the official history of the Gulf war prepared by the Army's Center of Military History, Dees's accidental drowning was a "non-battle fatality."[1] In the tense countdown from Operation Desert Shield to Desert Storm just ten days away, the Pentagon was relieved that Dees's death went virtually unnoticed.

Women were a wild card in the deployment of the All-Volunteer Force to Saudi Arabia. There was no precedent for the number of American women sent to the Gulf, over 40,000, no advance reading on the potential political fallout from their deaths or capture on a foreign battlefield. Though the public had had a glimpse of women's expanded military roles in Panama, there had been no female casualties.

The Army, which sent the most women by far, nearly 31,000, to the Gulf, had long recognized that women faced a high degree of risk on the modern battlefield. Combat scenarios built around a

Soviet attack in Europe had always envisioned the targeting of non-combat supply and communication units in the rear. The complicated coding formulas that supposedly kept women out of the most dangerous, front-line combat and combat support jobs would not shield them from the fluidity of the modern battlefield or sophisticated long-range weapons.

Early predictions in the war against Iraq suggested the casualty rate would be higher among the support troops in the rear than the all-male combat units poised on the border of Kuwait. Not only would the concentration of support troops in the rear make a more productive target for Iraq's maverick Scuds, but it would also be the target of choice for any missile armed with chemical or nerve agents. In the storms and winds of the desert, the commander of the Marine Expeditionary Force reasoned, the nerve gas would be too dangerous for the Iraqis to use near their own front-line troops.[2]

Though Iraq evidently never used its arsenal of chemical and biological weapons, the predictions would become reality. More than half (56 percent) of the 375 U.S. deaths in the Gulf were among noncombat support personnel.[3] According to official casualty records, fifteen were women, including Major Marie Rossi and Staff Sergeant Tatiana Dees.[4]

A small network of military and civilian women tracked the female casualties. With history traditionally written by men about men, they were concerned there would be no record of the first female officers to die in a combat theater since the Vietnam War and the first enlisted women to die in action since World War II.[5] Their research raised the unofficial tally of servicewomen's deaths to nineteen.

The first woman to die as a result of the U.S. deployment to the Gulf was killed before she left the United States. Thirty-six-year-old Missouri National Guard pilot Carol McKinney, a ten-year Army veteran, died along with two other crew members on December 15, 1990, four months into Operation Desert Shield, when the UH-1 helicopter they were ferrying from Jefferson City, Missouri, to Houston, Texas, for shipment to the Gulf, crashed in thick fog fifty miles north of Houston.[6]

Three women whose California National Guard unit was activated to replace regular Army units deployed to the Middle East died in a helicopter crash in Honduras on May 13, 1991. The all-woman crew had been en route to a remote radar site to evacuate a sick soldier when their UH-1 Huey crashed in the mountains.[7]

Two deaths in the Gulf were shrouded in mystery. Shirley Marie Cross, the only Navy woman casualty in the war, was reported to have died from a heart attack. The lack of any other information about her made the "network" suspicious that the Navy was covering up a more sinister cause of Cross's death. The death of Second Lieutenant Kathleen Sherry, the first female West Point graduate to die in a war theater, was also suspect. Fueled by front-page stories in the *Buffalo News* in upstate New York ("Mystery surrounds death in Kuwait of area servicewoman," and "Details of servicewoman's death might not be known for two months"),[8] rumors were circulating that Sherry had been raped and murdered. The different rumor circulating around West Point was that the former cadet had been involved in a love triangle and killed herself. The West Point version was supported by the investigative report of Sherry's death obtained in August 1993 from the U.S. Army Crime Records Center under the Freedom of Information Act, making Sherry's death one of ten suicides in the Gulf.

Death under any circumstances is not an issue on which the military likes to dwell. Though such a risk is inherent in military service, the language of denial reached an art form during the Gulf war. Allied casualties were deemed "KIAs," the acronym for "killed in action"; Iraqi soldiers were not killed, but "attrited." There was no mention of civilian deaths, but of "collateral damage," and those deaths were not caused by bombs or missiles but by "incontinent ordnance." Iraq's infrastructure of bridges, power stations and roads which vanished in puffs of talcum on military videos was not bombed but "serviced" or "degraded."[9]

Instead of issuing a daily "body count" of enemy dead, a practice that had backfired badly in Vietnam, the Gulf policy drew from the British Army's more successful war jargon in the Falkland Islands conflict and substituted the count of Iraqi weapons destroyed. In the antiseptic presentation of the high-tech conflict which never showed the Iraqi body parts strewn around the desert, only weapons were said to be "killed."[10]

There were to be no images of male or female U.S. soldiers arriving home in body bags. On January 21, 1991, five days after the air war began, Pentagon spokesman Pete Williams declared the mortuary at Dover Air Force Base off bounds to the press. The Pentagon even canceled the military ceremonies that traditionally honor returned war dead, citing the "hardship" on families who might feel obligated to travel to Dover for the ceremonies.[11]

Beyond the unknown effects of female deaths in the Gulf, a high number of African-American deaths could also have presented a problem. The "poverty draft" of the 1960s, which was widely believed to have sent a disproportionate number of black soldiers to their deaths in Vietnam, could be replayed in Saudi Arabia. Though African-Americans made up just over 11 percent of the U.S. population in 1990, they made up 28 percent of the troops deployed to the Gulf.[12]

Racial percentages were even more skewed among military women. Minority women accounted for 56.4 percent of the enlisted women in the Army, of whom a full 49 percent were African-American, four times their proportion in civilian society. In the high-risk Gulf, African-American women made up over half of the Army force in supply and services (55 percent), petroleum and water (58 percent), administration (52 percent) and food services (54 percent).[13]

Perhaps that is why the daily release of Gulf casualties contained only the service member's name, hometown of record and age. "There were no sex or race indications," says a Pentagon spokesman. An argument could be made that such spartan casualty descriptives rightfully treated the dead as equal members of the armed forces and not as "black" soldiers or "female" soldiers; nonetheless, these descriptives provided a useful smoke screen for the Pentagon.

"It was a transitional time for the military," says Alice Booher, an attorney with the Department of Veterans Affairs who tracked Gulf casualties for veterans' benefits. "They were very uptight and concerned about what might happen. Women might raise a hue and cry. Or blacks, Hispanics, any subgroup. If there's any one group whose constituency or background might precipitate problems, it's on their minds in Washington. The Republican mentality was paranoid at the very least."

At least eight servicewomen died and many more were injured in "nonhostile" traffic accidents. The auto accident rate in Saudi Arabia was officially attributed to the rapid movement of troops and equipment along the only desert road, often in blinding sandstorms. Unofficially, the accident rate was laid to the "rules are off" atmosphere permeating the combat zone. "We cleaned up forty bodies in three days that were speed violations," says a female officer in the Military Police. "Lives were lost because leaders disregarded directives on safety. There was this feeling that I am God and I can do whatever I want."

Private Pamela Gay died when her truck collided with an armored vehicle, Private Dorothy Fails when her truck was hit by a bus. Sergeant Tracey Brogdon was killed when the driver of her Humvee fell asleep and rammed a dump truck, Private Candace Daniel when her truck overturned in Kuwait, Private Cindy Bridges when her truck flipped off the road in Iraq. More women—and more men—died in accidents in the Gulf than were killed in action,[14] including Lieutenant Lorraine Lawton, the last woman on record to die in the Gulf, when the military vehicle she was traveling in crashed into the back of a parked bus on July 10, 1991.[15] Her husband, Benjamin, an associate professor of Italian at Purdue University who was traveling in the same large convoy several miles behind her, joined Marie Rossi's husband in a new and growing phenomenon: the military widower.

Five other women died in combat as a result of "hostile fire," in Defense Department parlance, including nineteen-year-old reservist Cindy Beaudoin, a medical technician and freshman at the University of Connecticut. The designation of her death as a combat fatality proved to be highly controversial. Beaudoin's "combat" death was first attributed to a land mine she had stepped on while going to the aid of an Army doctor whose jeep had detonated another land mine.[16] After an Army criminal investigation found that three other soldiers in Beaudoin's unit had been accidentally injured by exploding "bomblets" scattered around the desert and mistakenly handed out as souvenirs, her death was officially downgraded to a "nonbattle" fatality.[17] Beaudoin's father, however, made such a forceful protest about the reclassifying of his daughter's death as a noncombat accident eight months after the fact that the Army would reinstate Beaudoin as a combat fatality in 1993.[18]

Beaudoin's death, as well as the deaths of the four other women who died from "hostile fire," would have a profound effect on public attitudes toward servicewomen. Eight hundred people attended Beaudoin's funeral mass on March 11, 1991, following a memorial mass at the University of Connecticut at Storrs. On the same day flags were flown at half-mast in Racine County, Wisconsin, to honor

twenty-four-year-old Army Sergeant Cheryl LaBeau-O'Brien, a helicopter technician whose Black Hawk helicopter was shot down over
Iraq while ferrying U.S. troops.

The three other women killed in combat drew national attention. The Iraqi Scud which slammed into a corrugated metal ware-
house in Al Khobar on February 25, 1991, killing twenty-five
servicemen and three servicewomen, etched the new reality of the
military into American consciousness.[19] The pictures of the victims
crowding newspapers over the next few days intermingled stern-
faced young men posed military-style in front of the American flag
and the smiling faces of Specialists Beverly Clark and Christine
Mayes, both twenty-three, from western Pennsylvania and twenty-
year-old Private Adrienne Mitchell from Moreno Valley, California.

The Pentagon was both surprised and relieved that Americans
voiced no more sorrow or outrage at the deaths of the young women
than they did for the men, and coast to coast simply added more
yellow ribbons to the national displays of support for the troops. The
apprehensive military was well behind the public, which had been
exposed to women's more aggressive roles in Panama the year before
and had accepted the inevitability of female casualties in the Gulf.

"The military totally misread for years how the public would
respond to women dying in combat," says correspondent Fred Francis, who covered the Pentagon for NBC for nine years. "I did more
stories on women in combat and women's role in the military over
the years than any other reporter in this town and it never ceased to
amaze me how badly they'd misread the whole thing. It's the male
culture, it's the warrior mentality. God forbid a warrior should be of
another gender. The public was ready for it years ago."

Timid members of Congress who had resisted the repeal of the
combat exclusion laws took heart. "There hasn't been any national
hue and cry over the deaths of the women," admitted Congresswoman Beverly Byron, then chair of the House Armed Services
Committee military personnel subcommittee, who had fought
Schroeder's bill to overturn the Army's combat exclusion policies
just seven months before.

Other politicians from the commander in chief on down reinforced the acceptability of women on a battlefield. George Bush,
whose performance ratings jumped 20 percentage points during the
war to a thirty-year presidential high of 86 percent, sent his condo-

lences to the Greensburg, Pennsylvania, community that had lost thirteen male and female reservists from its 14th Quartermaster Corps to the Scud attack. Pennsylvania Governor Robert Casey eulogized them as "salt of the earth people" at a memorial on March 2, singling out a male and female reservist as "a former high school football star and a Future Homemaker of America." By making the "ultimate sacrifice," which had formerly been reserved for America's sons, America's uniformed daughters were catapulted up the ladder of social acceptability.

Seemingly overnight, the stereotype of servicewomen as either tough-talking lesbians or the desperate poor who had no other option than to join the military was being replaced by images of the college girl next door, especially in the Army Reserve, where fully 17 percent of the reservists deployed to the Gulf were women.[20] "Everybody knew them. Even congressmen knew people who went. They were their daughters, their friends, their lovers, their wives, their mothers," says Carolyn Becraft, a military policy analyst at the time. "Military people are from everywhere and nowhere, but reservists are from *towns.*" Governor Casey bore out her point in his eulogies for the dead in Pennsylvania. "The roll reads like a list of the family next door," he said. "They were us."[21]

The new image of women in uniform was further implanted on the public consciousness by the disproportionate media attention showered on women in the Gulf, who, overall, made up only 7 percent of the troops. The change was startling to long-term military observers. "The Gulf war [drew] attention to servicewomen as never before," write the authors of *Sound Off! American Military Women Speak Out,* citing the paucity of coverage of women in Grenada in 1983, the 1986 air strike against Libya and the confusion in 1990 surrounding women's roles in Panama. "During Desert Shield, almost every time the news cameras focused on our troops in the desert, they zeroed in on a woman. What a switch!"[22]

The nightly television images of women in their desert BDUs (battle dress uniforms) doing "men's work" were a running documentary of women's modern military roles. Though the majority of servicewomen still served in such traditional roles as administration, medical and supply, the public became accustomed to women operating forklifts, working on ships, flying military aircraft. "Throughout the buildup, you had the education of the American people," says Becraft. "The interview with Marie Rossi captured the nation's attention absolutely. She was so professional, so competent, and she was going in with the invasion. It was just riveting."

Members of the media who played into the disproportionate coverage of women claimed they had no choice: women were often the only story they could get. Just as Army Public Affairs had exploited Linda Bray in Panama, the Army exploited women in the Gulf. "The PAO guys were always saying, 'Hey, let's go talk to the female officer in charge of the traffic pool' or 'Hey, we've got a female battalion commander in charge of supply,' as if that would make up for the fact that we were being kept from covering whatever action there was," says Cabell Bruce, a television producer for *Inside Edition*. It was this kind of trade-off that resulted in ABC's interview with Major Marie Rossi. "I threw a tantrum," recalls veteran cameraman Ken Kay, who flew into Iraq with Rossi. "I wanted a gunship."

Nonetheless, servicewomen's status soared. No longer were women the protected benefactors of U.S. citizenship. They were demonstrably sharing the national responsibility and the burden. To the surprise of the Pentagon, not even the taking of two female prisoners of war, the first since Navy and Army nurses were captured by the Japanese in World War II, slowed the public's embrace of uniformed women. Before the Gulf war, the services had considered female POWs an even greater risk to public support than female deaths. "The argument was," says Pete Williams, " 'One reason you can't have women in combat is that they'll be taken prisoner of war and the public would never support that and the people will go nuts.' "

The services had quietly prepared for the eventuality of female prisoners of war. The forty-year-old Code of Conduct developed by Eisenhower for U.S. combatants and captives after the Korean War had been gender neutralized by Ronald Reagan in 1988. The six standards of conduct remained the same, but the opening sentence, "I am an American fighting man," became "I am an American"; the command pledge to "never surrender my men while they still have the means to resist" substituted "the members of my command" for the word "men." [23]

The prisoner-of-war training and instruction in the Code of Conduct for "each member of the armed forces liable to capture" [24] had also been extended to women. By the end of the Gulf war nearly four thousand women serving in high-risk, or Level C, aviation jobs had completed POW training at one of the Defense Department's five survival, evasion, resistance and escape (SERE) schools. Though women were technically deemed noncombatants, female pilots and flight officers in mixed-gender aircrews were as vulnerable as all-male crews to their aircraft going down behind enemy lines by accident or, to a lesser degree, by enemy fire.

It was a pilot's transition from air to potentially hostile ground which drove the curriculum at the SERE schools and the anxiety about female prisoners of war. The survival and evasion sections of the course before "capture" by the enemy were gender neutral. The phases dedicated to resistance and escape after capture were not.

By the time the students were captured at SERE school, they had spent over a week learning every survival and evasion skill Captain Scott O'Grady would use in 1995 to survive and evade capture after he was shot down over enemy territory in Bosnia. At an Air Force SERE school in the mountains of Washington, the hundred or so students had learned to make shelters out of their parachutes, to recognize what berries were edible and which trees change color if they are near a creek, to stuff dry lichen called goatsbeard in their pockets anytime they saw it as tinder for starting a fire.

The SERE students had spent six days climbing up and down mountains carrying fifty pounds of equipment, moving camp every night, pushing through brambles and creeks and mud. "If there was a meadow, we avoided it," says Lieutenant Grace Tiscareno, an Air Force KC-135 navigator who spent two weeks at the SERE school outside Spokane. The students took turns carrying heavy water bags to stem dehydration and lived off the land, killing and eating a rabbit one night, ants and wild strawberries on other nights. The least amount of weight lost in Tiscareno's group in which she was the only woman was ten pounds.

There was no allowance for gender differences at SERE school. There couldn't be. But both the men and the women qualifying to attend the schools as pilots, navigators and aircrews were already a self-selecting elite. "Level C people are, by nature of what they are, extroverted, aggressive, self-confident, hard-charging people," Colonel John D. Graham, director of the joint-service agency, would tell a post–Gulf war commission.[25] "The women do as well as the men, adjusting mentally to the stress and enduring physically." The only disadvantage the women had was urinating on the move. "For the first time in my life I had penis envy," says an Air Force pilot, who learned to jam her backpack into a tree and quickly lower her pants as she slid down the tree into a semisquat.

The SERE instructors turned "enemy" during the "evasion" phase and pursued their student prey. The SERE students moved through the woods in groups of two or three, trying to elude them. Using maps, compasses and landmarks for navigation, their faces painted with camouflage, the student groups traveled about two and a half miles a day in silence, using hand signals to communicate. "You just move slowly and deliberately to your next hiding slot," says Tiscareno. "It's motion that's going to catch the peripheral vision in the human eye. Put one hand over the log, one leg, lower yourself down, very slowly."

They slept four or five hours a night under evasion shelters they had fashioned a foot and a half off the ground out of their dark rain ponchos. "I hid my shelter so well I couldn't find it," says Tiscareno. "You're supposed to use your compass to shoot a heading to the fire circle from your site, then count your paces to the fire. But I kept having to go back and forth to the fire circle in the rain at eleven-thirty at night looking for my shelter. Eventually, I fell over it."

And then the students were captured.

The 1949 Geneva Conventions governing the treatment of prisoners of war provide that "women shall be treated with all the regard due their sex," a "regard" that allowed for women's "weakness" in terms of forced labor and diet and their "honour and modesty" in providing separate housing and bathrooms. All bets were off about the treatment of potential female prisoners in modern warfare.[26]

While chaplains and medical personnel were deemed separate entities under the Geneva Conventions, and if captured by an enemy become "retained personnel" rather than POWs, all other uniformed personnel were considered to be "combatants." The term "noncombatant" applied only to civilians and injured prisoners, not to the distinctions made by U.S. law and Army policy between men's combat roles and women's noncombat roles. "If you had a woman flying an F-16 on a close air support mission who takes a hit and has to eject and is captured, she might be viewed differently from a nurse who is captured on the battlefield," Hays Parks, chief of the Army's International Law Branch, told a government commission.[27]

The prisoner-of-war training at the SERE schools drew on the experiences of past U.S. POWs, from the servicemen and servicewomen captured by the Japanese and Germans in World War II to the exploitation techniques used by the North Koreans in the 50s and the debriefing of POWs in Vietnam. The coping mechanisms of the sixty-seven Army and sixteen Navy nurses during their three years of internment in the Philippines by the Japanese were of particular interest to SERE. A study of five hundred men and women imprisoned for thirty-eight months or more at the Santo Tomás Internment Camp in Manila found that in terms of weight loss, stress, mental breakdowns and deaths due to disease or suicide, the women did better across the board than men.[28] "Except for complications from surgery, not one woman died," said Parks. "All the nurses came home."

The Army had approached at least one of the World War II nurses, the youngest of whom were in their early seventies, during the buildup of U.S. forces in Desert Shield. "They were trying to find out my opinion about women as potential prisoners of war," says Mary Nelson, a former Navy nurse and POW. "The only thing I could say is that there are circumstances that are different, you don't know what type of people you're dealing with, but you have to have hope. Just don't lose that."

The nurses, fourteen of whom would gather in Washington in March 1992 for a two-day commemoration of the fiftieth anniversary of their capture in the Philippines, also downplayed any applicable lessons from their captivity. "Our experience isn't going to teach future nurses anything that would benefit them, except that they can endure a lot of things they don't think they can endure," says Sally Blaine Millett, an Army nurse who had arrived at Fort Stotsenburg near Clark Field in Luzon in June 1941 to find herself under the concrete floor of the hospital's pharmacy being bombed and strafed by the Japanese on December 7, nine hours after the attack on Pearl Harbor.

The casualty list grew so high in the intense bombing raids in the two weeks following Pearl Harbor that both the hospital patients and their young military nurses were evacuated to Manila. "I took my high-heeled plastic shoes, my dancing skirt and everything that was going to make my life gay in Manila," says Millett, who was then in her early twenties. "I'd heard all the stories about World War I and Paris, which was such a wonderful place to be. I was completely wrong, of course."

On Christmas Eve, Millett and the other nurses were evacuated under fire to Bataan, where, under intensifying Japanese bombardment, she and the other nurses set up three-tiered bed wards under the natural camouflage of the acacia trees. "We lay on the ground during air raids," says Millett, who had traded her easily targeted white nurse's uniform for Army fatigues on the first day of the war.

For four months the nurses on Bataan worked around the clock, caring for the mounting casualties among U.S. and Filipino troops and two of their own who were injured by shrapnel when a Japanese bomb hit an ammunition truck near the hospital. On January 7 they went on half field rations. In March they went on one-third field rations. "There wasn't anything—ammunition, guns, supplies, clothing, food—you can just go down the line," says Madeline Ullom, an Army nurse. "There just wasn't enough of anything."

Hours before Bataan fell to the Japanese in April 1942, the nurses were ordered to evacuate again, this time to the vast, underground Malinta Tunnel complex on Corregidor, which had been stocked years before with military equipment and hospital supplies. "We had to wear wet masks in order to breathe, especially after the shelling and bombing because of the dust and the little stones that would just fall down through the cracks and cover everything," says Army nurse Helen Nester.

The nurses who had worked in the outdoor hospital on Bataan were in particularly bad health. Millett, who was suffering from her fifteenth bout of malaria, was one of ten nurses the Navy tried, but failed, to evacuate three weeks after she arrived in Corregidor. The Navy seaplane hit a submerged log when it stopped to refuel in Mindanao and had to return to shore after the cabin filled with water while taxiing for takeoff. "For ten days we had hopes another plane would come, but it never did," says Millett, who was taken prisoner by the Japanese and held in a Catholic convent.

The nurses in the Malinta Tunnel were captured on May 6, 1942, the day Corregidor fell, by Japanese troops who entered the tunnel wearing asbestos suits and carrying flamethrowers. They were held in the suffocating, airless tunnel for the next seven weeks. Already suffering from malaria, many of the nurses also developed bacillary dysentery from the green flies buzzing around the unburied corpses of U.S. soldiers outside the tunnel. "I don't know how you could train anyone for what happened to us," says Peggy Walcher, an Army nurse who spent nine months in the tunnel on Corregidor.

But there was much to be learned from the captivity of the nurses both on Corregidor, then, for the next three years, in a civilian internment camp in Manila. From the beginning of their captivity on Corregidor, the nurses decided to stay in a group, thus minimizing the risk of sexual assault. "We discussed the possibility of rape, but it was just one of those things," says Hattie Brantley, an Army nurse who would retire with the rank of lieutenant colonel in 1969.

On their first night of captivity, most of the nurses moved into a tunnel lateral which had only one entry and took turns standing guard. "We had a tin plate and a spoon to sound the alarm," laughs Walcher. Two nurses who opted to set themselves apart in another section that branched off to the outdoors soon realized their folly. "They were attacked by a Japanese coming in from the outside," says Walcher. The would-be assailant was driven off by the screams of the two nurses, which drew the other nurses. "We scared him away," says Walcher.

The nurses also maintained their chain of command, headed by a particularly feisty head nurse in her fifties, Captain Maud Davison. Only she dealt directly with the Japanese—and very effectively. "The head nurse raised Cain the day after the attempted assault, and the Japanese immediately announced the death notice for anybody caught molesting a nurse," says Walcher. "And that was the end of that."

The Japanese culture, which reveres age, played to Davison's and the nurses' advantage as well. "A short, stocky, white-haired lady, Captain Davison commanded a certain respect from the Japanese for her age and her no-nonsense attitude," Hays Parks would say about the nurses' experience in the Pacific. "She kept them together, and the Japanese did give her respect."

The novelty of finding women officers among the captured U.S. forces puzzled the Japanese. "I think they thought we were there for the convenience of the officers until they saw us taking care of the patients," recalls Walcher. The women's status as medical officers would not have spared them, however. Under the Geneva Conventions, medical personnel could be retained by an enemy captor to take care of sick or injured POWs, which could have sent the nurses on the Bataan Death March. Ten thousand of the 68,000 U.S. and Filipino troops who surrendered to the Japanese on Bataan would die on the sixty-five-mile forced march toward the infamous Japanese prisoner-of-war camps where many more would die of disease or starvation. Roughly one-third of the American men captured on Bataan did not survive. After talking to Captain Davison, however, the Japanese on Corregidor decided to classify the female military officers as civilian Red Cross workers because so many of the nurses had been recruited by the Army and Navy from the Red Cross's national emergency registry. "This placed the American women in civilian internment camps rather than in military prisons," says Hays Parks.

In September 1942 the nurses were trucked under armed guard into the Santo Tomás Internment Camp in Manila, sick with malaria, dengue fever, beriberi and amoebic dysentery. "The only time I didn't want to live was on the Japanese boat going over," says Millett, whose weight dropped to ninety pounds in the prison camp. The nurses were the only military personnel among 3,500 to 5,000 civilians in the camp, a three hundred–year-old Dominican university.

They remained disciplined, setting up a hospital to treat the other internees. Because of the nurses' poor health, Captain Davison scheduled them to work only four-hour shifts. They maintained their morale by writing and performing plays and knitting stockings and underwear out of string which the Pentagon now displays in its one corridor dedicated to women.

The nurses "resisted" the enemy, one of the tenets of captivity that would be articulated thirteen years later in the Code of Conduct. Forced to bow to the Japanese guards, the nurses took great pleasure in muttering obscenities under their breath as they bowed or seeing how many guards they could get by without bowing or lowering their eyes. Getting to and from the hospital provided a gratifying harassment game for the nurses. "We'd wait together and cross over one at a time so the guards would have to keep bowing over and over again," says Evelyn "Blackie" Harding, an Army nurse who suffered from constant diarrhea and such severe anemia that she stopped menstruating.

The nurses never lost hope, even after their rations were cut to 500 calories a day following the American bombing of Manila in September 1944. "The men that were determined to live, and reconciled themselves that they were prisoners, were fine," says Walcher. "The men who didn't and suffered from dysentery and beriberi and malnutrition—a lot of them just gave up and they died."

Santo Tomás was liberated on February 3, 1945, by the U.S. Army's 1st Cavalry Division—and just in time. The starvation rate of one death a day had escalated to seven deaths in the last twenty-four hours. "What a bunch of emaciated human beings they were," says

Woods Thomas, who at nineteen was one of the liberating force and fifty years later had come to commemorate the nurses in Washington. "It was pretty certain that they would not have lasted much longer." Even the nurses, who averaged thirty-two pounds less than their weight when they were captured, were beginning to have some doubts. "If it had gone on much longer, we would have lost some of our nurses," says Walcher, who had to have a heart valve replaced from malnutrition. "It was the last year that we nearly starved to death. We were really getting in bad shape."

But the nurses did survive, an accomplishment which both the SERE schools and a former prisoner of war in Vietnam attributed less to their gender than to their backgrounds. "The nurses were trained, they were educated, they were volunteers, they were officers," says Giles Norrington, a Navy combat reconnaissance pilot who spent five years as a POW in North Vietnam and was the keynote speaker at the Washington salute to the World War II nurses. "We had more in common with the nurses in the Philippines than we did with the soldiers in the Korea situation who had gotten through the tenth or eleventh grades, were draftees, who didn't understand the war and hated being there." Of the 566 prisoners held in North Vietnam, only four were enlisted. Of the thirteen who died, Norrington says, most were killed in captivity.

The POW training for men and women at SERE school in the 1990s was as realistic as it could be, though well short of the ordeal faced by former POWs from World War II to Vietnam. "We try to replicate what they might expect if they were held as a POW," Colonel Graham, director of the joint-service agency, would say to a post–Gulf war commission. "We can't do that across the board, especially when it comes to the physical things that we are allowed to put these people through, but we try to put them at least in as much mental stress as we possibly can."[29]

SERE's POW training had been classified since 1955. "They feel you'll compromise the training if people show up knowing what to expect, but they simulate very accurately what it's like to be in solitary confinement and other things that happened in the 'Hanoi Hilton,' " says Tiscareno. Other graduates of the POW training were not as reticent.

The norms of civilized behavior were reversed during the students' captivity. For many women "POWs," the Defense Department's definition of acceptable physical abuse included the women's first experience of being hit. "That was my biggest fear going into SERE because I didn't come from an abusive family," says a Navy helicopter pilot who went through SERE training in Brunswick, Maine. "I learned I could take a lot of physical punishment. The first time I got hit in the face, I thought, Hmmmmm, that wasn't so bad."

Women and men were blindfolded and strip-searched to condition both genders for the projected sexual humiliation and exploitation of female POWs. But in another nod to social acceptability, female "guards" strip-searched the female "prisoners" in one room while male "guards" stripped the male students in another.

The SERE instructors would have preferred to run the more realistic British training program for POWs which did not segregate the sexes. Male and females were strip-searched together and no distinction was made between the genders of the "prisoners" and "captors." "The British believe that is what will happen in real captivity," Air Force Major John Bruce Jessen, a SERE psychologist, told a commission on women in combat.[30]

But just as the Defense Department schools were wary about going too far in physically abusing the students, they also worried about the political fallout from mixing naked students and their mock captors. "If individuals outside the military found out about it and misinterpreted what we were doing, perhaps we might run the risk of losing the opportunity to train altogether," says Major Jessen.

The DOD schools got around the public relations threat by simulating mixed-gender contact in the POW compound. The female "guards" tipped off the male "guards" to the specific characteristics of the naked and hooded female "prisoners" who couldn't see anything but their feet. "One gal had a lot of freckles," says an officer attached to SERE. "She was behind a wall, but she didn't know it because she was blindfolded. All she heard were these guys laughing at her and making snide remarks about her body. They want to humiliate you." The "captor" charade proved effective. "I heard these guys talking about a butterfly tattoo I have on a body part my mother hasn't seen for years," recalls an Air Force pilot. "How do they know that? I kept asking myself."

The students were forced into little claustrophobic boxes—"It gets pretty cold in those cement boxes," says an Air Force officer—

and subjected to the same song being played over and over again. The double dose of psychological warfare and sensory deprivation was very effective. "There are no shadows, no way of knowing the time," says another Air Force officer. "When they took me out the next morning, I was completely disoriented. But so was everyone else."

It was the potential for the sexual exploitation of women prisoners by the enemy to gain information from the men that proved the most troublesome at SERE school and marked the gender divide. A survey of both male and female students showed that it was not the women who were overly concerned about their being sexually assaulted by the enemy. It was the men. "The male students are very, very concerned," testified Major Jessen, who conducted the survey.

The women recognized the danger in the men's reaction to their sexual exploitation. If the enemy technique worked, the women prisoners would be subject to repetitive abuse. "The female students basically say, 'I want you to treat it like any other exploitation situation because if you concede information, the next time this man wants information he is going to drag me back in here and exploit me again,' " says Jessen. " 'Sexual exploitation is just like any other exploitation. It needs to be resisted. So let's not make as big a thing of it.' "

Such male discomfort was familiar to female pilots. In Korea during the tense early 80s, helicopter pilot Marsha Filtrante had gone out of her way to defuse male angst over her possible capture before she even left the ground. "Our psychology says the guys have to protect the gals and that's why I was very careful in Korea to make sure the pilots I flew with knew that I had already considered all the possibilities of being taken POW," says Filtrante, the first female platoon leader in her Army aviation company. "In fact, I stood a much better chance of survival as an escapee. A five-foot eight-inch woman in a flight suit walking up to a house would be far less threatening to the Koreans than a six-foot-two-inch guy, and I could sit down and talk to the kids. By the time I finished talking to all twenty-three of my assigned pilots, they were comfortable."

The concern about women was so extensive among the male students at SERE school, however, that the instructors felt it posed a potential threat to national security. Faced with the enemy abuse of female POWs, overprotective men in a true POW setting could compromise the Code of Conduct by disregarding the orders of a superior, signing confessions, putting their fellow prisoners at risk or providing information to the enemy.

Former POWs weren't so sure. "Hypothetically, I don't think a woman being singled out for torture would make any difference," says Giles Norrington. "But we had 566 people in prison in North Vietnam, so there would have been 566 potential responses to the situation. I'd like to think that it wouldn't have had any more effect than if a man were being tortured."

To Norrington, who spent 1,775 days in captivity, abuse was gender neutral: "Torture and rape are two different names for the same thing. Rape is torture. So is being beaten, kicked, deprived of sleep, kept on your knees for hours on end, having heavy nylon cords strapped around the upper arms until the circulation is cut off, your arms drawn together at the back until the elbows touch and your head lowered under your crotch until you're looking at your own buns. You feel brutalized, you feel ugly, you have many of the feelings rape victims have of helplessness, of being dirtied, of fruitless rage. The central issue is to retain your human dignity. The central issue is resistance."

To Norrington, the greater threat to national security was posed by women's cultural conditioning toward male authority. "The relationship to the enemy is the tough one, not rape," he says. "Our culture tells us that when women are asked questions by men, by golly, they're supposed to answer them. And who do you think the interrogators are going to be? A woman POW might very well find herself emotionally charged to answer questions because it is an insistent man demanding the answers. If he knows what our culture is like, that interrogator is already going to have a leg up simply because he was born male."

Norrington also discounted the projection that women would be abused in the presence of their fellow male captives. In North Vietnam, the POWs had always been interrogated—and tortured— alone. "Torture was a very solitary thing and very, very deliberate," he says. "If you put two Americans in the same room and tortured one, the guy who is being tortured will be supported morally by the other, and will probably tend to give up less. The guy being tortured knows the other is sharing the pain."

The SERE schools, however, were preparing their male and female students for any contingency as POWs and considered sexual

exploitation as high risk. To counter the hazard male chivalry potentially posed to national security, the SERE schools had embarked on
a militarily prudent but culturally jarring course. In direct contrast
to the campaign in the private sector to sensitize men to the seriousness of sexual harassment and abuse, the SERE schools were
campaigning just as hard to *desensitize* men to the sexual assault and
enemy exploitation of women.

At the one school which went so far as to simulate the actual
sexual exploitation of both male and female "captives," the SERE
philosophy seemed to be making headway. "The male students in
that school were much less concerned than male students in other
schools," says Major Jessen. "I believe we can feel confident that we
are not going to put national security at risk in that situation, as
long as we have had the opportunity to properly train and desensitize
these people."

All the speculation and cross-gender training at the SERE
schools would come to naught, however, in the Gulf war. Neither of
the women taken prisoner was a pilot. And neither had been to
SERE school.

On January 30, 1991, almost two weeks into the air war against
Iraq, NBC's Pentagon correspondent Fred Francis made one of his
twice daily calls to Riyadh, Saudi Arabia. Iraqi troops were battling
U.S., Qatari and Saudi troops for control of the Saudi border town of
Khafji. In what would prove to be the fiercest battle of the war, three
hundred Iraqis and eleven Marines would be killed.[31] But the news
tip Francis got from an Army colonel in Riyadh set up the dynamic
the Pentagon feared most. "We've got a white female missing and
probably snatched by the Iraqis," the colonel told Francis. "Holy
shit, do we have problems now."

Francis hurried down the hall in the Pentagon to Defense Department spokesman Pete Williams's office to confirm the tip. "Pete
got on the phone and called Powell's office," recalls Francis. "Powell's office confirmed it and I went on the air with it. It was boom-
boom-boom. There was no hesitation at all." NBC's bombshell led
the evening news: an American servicewoman attached to an Army
transportation company was missing near Khafji in the northern
Saudi desert.

The news was particularly ominous in concert with the Iraqi
announcement shortly thereafter that a "number of male and female

transcripts" had been captured. The Iraqi government's assurance that any female prisoners would receive "good treatment in accordance with the spirit of lofty Islamic laws" was questionable in light of the stories circulating about the Iraqi brutality toward women in Kuwait.

The Pentagon was less concerned about the well-being of the missing servicewoman than it was about the effect of a female prisoner of war on the national psyche. Fifty years had passed since the nurses had been captured by the Japanese and they had been officers. The servicewoman, who was soon identified as Melissa Rathbun-Nealy, a twenty-year-old Army truck driver with the 233rd Transportation Company, would be the first enlisted American woman to be captured by an enemy in history.

If indeed she had been captured, there was concern that the Iraqis would publicly exploit her, potentially eroding public support for the conflict during the buildup to the ground war. Such speculation about the negative effect of female POWs on the "national will" had circulated for years, though there had been no such erosion over the nurses in World War II.

The unanswerable question lay in the potential propaganda visuals of women POWs being marched through the streets of Baghdad, women being among the downed, battered Allied pilots captured by the Iraqis and displayed on Iraqi television in January, a woman's face replacing the swollen, scratched face of captured Navy pilot Jeffrey Zaun which ran on the cover of *Newsweek*. Similar images of blindfolded American diplomatic hostages in Iran had helped bring down Jimmy Carter's presidency in 1980. The political effect of women POWs was incalculable.

"Will it cause such a public outcry that our leaders will be forced to terminate the conflict under less than desirable terms and in spite of any national goals which may not have been attained?" Air Force Major Wayne Dillingham had written the year before the Gulf war. "Or, in the alternative, will the outcry incite us to conduct reprisal-type operations which, in turn, may unnecessarily escalate the conflict?"[32]

Perhaps that is why the Pentagon professed not to know what had happened to Specialist Rathbun-Nealy and her co-driver, Specialist David Lockett, or how they had ended up in Khafji. The scuttlebutt going around the Pentagon involved a sexual tryst. "They thought they'd gotten lost for the purpose of being alone," says a

Pentagon observer. "They still do." And a new round of military gender politics began.

Instead of declaring Rathbun-Nealy and Lockett as POWs or missing in action, the Army's accounting of their disappearance merely classified them as DUSTWUN, or duty status whereabouts unknown, a low-level categorization that simply meant the Army had no idea where they were or what had happened to them. "They found her truck and she and a man in her truck had disappeared," Pentagon spokesman Lieutenant Colonel Douglas Hart would say a year after the fact. "We make no assumptions."

Leo Rathbun, Rathbun-Nealy's father, was convinced the Pentagon was covering up his daughter's capture. All the evidence pointed toward her and her partner being taken prisoner by the Iraqis. Not only had Iraq reported "female transcripts" captured, but on February 10, ten days after Rathbun-Nealy's disappearance, NBC News reported that a captured Iraqi said he had transported two American prisoners—a white woman and a black man—to the city of Basra.

"There was never any doubt that they'd been taken prisoner, never a question among reporters covering the story that she was believed by senior leadership to be missing and a POW," says Fred Francis.

But the Pentagon stuck to its low-level story. "The [rescuers] found the truck she was in and it appeared to be an accident," insisted Lieutenant Colonel Hart. "So we couldn't say what the reasons were. The truck wasn't blown up or anything. It couldn't be proven that they had engaged the enemy, so to speak."

Rathbun hounded the Pentagon to have Melissa declared either MIA or POW. Not only was he worried that his daughter might be left behind when the war ended because she wasn't on an official list, he also wanted her to get whatever benefits were due her. "I told them, if she survives this thing and gets home, she won't receive any MIA or POW benefits because you bastards won't say she is one, even if you know she really is," says Rathbun.

It wasn't until February 14, two weeks after Rathbun-Nealy and Lockett had disappeared, that the Rathbuns got an official accounting of their daughter's disappearance. The bare facts in the Army casualty report noted only that Melissa was "last seen" on January 30, 1991, when the two trucks in her convoy "took a wrong turn." When Melissa's truck "became stuck in the sand trying to turn around," the second truck "went for assistance." A Marine Corps patrol found her 22-wheel vehicle "in the vicinity of Ras Al Khafji, Saudi Arabia," but "could not locate the soldier."[33]

The more telling details were in the Army letter accompanying the casualty report and came from the truck drivers who had been following Rathbun-Nealy and Lockett in the second truck. By their account, the young soldiers had thought they were heading back to their base when they were headed toward the fighting in Khafji. Their error became apparent when the two trucks maneuvered around a freshly destroyed Saudi tank partially blocking the road north of Khafji only to be met by two explosions and "the sound of debris hitting their vehicle." Seeing "what they perceived to be enemy troops" ahead near the archway into Khafji, the soldiers tried to turn their 22-wheel trucks around to escape. The second truck made it, but Rathbun-Nealy and Lockett's lead truck crashed into a wall. The last sight the escaping soldiers had of Rathbun-Nealy and Lockett was of the pair still sitting in their crippled truck as Iraqi soldiers approached. When a rescue party of Marines arrived soon thereafter, they found the truck with a flat tire and its engine still running, but "no trace of Melissa or Specialist Lockett."

More clues to Rathbun-Nealy's status in the Army letter came from Saudi interrogation reports of Iraqi soldiers captured during the battle for Khafji. An Iraqi lieutenant told Saudi interrogators he had "witnessed the capture of an American male and female" and that "both had been injured." The "white female," he reported, had "sustained an injury to her arm." Two other Iraqi prisoners of war told their Saudi interrogators what had already been reported by NBC News: the POWs had seen a "white female and a black male" near the city of Basra in southern Iraq.

Based on these reports, the Army notified the Rathbuns, the Army was changing Melissa's status from duty status whereabouts unknown to missing, which put her under the jurisdiction of the National Prisoner of War Information Center. The Army stopped short, however, of declaring Melissa a POW or even MIA, a designation reserved for personnel missing involuntarily as a result of "hostilities directed against the United States."[34] "While there are indications that Melissa and Specialist Lockett may have been captured, the reports received are unconfirmed and unsubstantiated," read the letter from the Army chief of POW/MIA Affairs.[35]

The Army's letter made Leo Rathbun even more furious. Not only had it taken the Army two weeks to at least declare his daughter missing, he was convinced that the Pentagon was denying her POW or MIA status because of her gender. "Bush was afraid of adverse publicity with a woman captured," he says.

The Defense Department denied the charge of gender politics. "There was a long delay in declaring them MIA and I can't remember exactly the reason," says Pete Williams, who joined NBC News after the war. "I don't recall that it was a sensitivity about women. No one ever told me, 'let's hold off on this because she's a woman.' "

But Rathbun-Nealy's presumed capture was all about gender politics. While the Pentagon was playing down her military status, the civilian sector was playing up her sexual status. Though the International Red Cross had predicted that any U.S. woman taken POW would be treated in accordance with the Geneva Conventions and shown the respect afforded women in the Iraqi culture,[36] Rathbun-Nealy became a presupposed rape victim.

Historically, no U.S. servicewomen had been sexually molested as POWs, including the nurses in the Pacific and Lieutanant Reba Whittle, an Army flight nurse who was captured by the Germans in September 1944 after her hospital plane was shot down. The North Vietnamese had not molested Monika Schwinn, a German nurse who had endured forced marches, disease and near starvation in her three and a half years of captivity in Vietnam, including a stint in 1973 as the only woman prisoner at the infamous "Hanoi Hilton."[37] But Rathbun-Nealy's projected sexual molestation overshadowed all other concerns about her disappearance, including her reported injuries.

"I was asked by a reporter what I thought about that little girl's chances of being mistreated in Iraq," says former World War II POW Sally Millett. "I said I would doubt that. I would be inclined to think that she would be treated quite well. The Muslims aren't that mean. And they don't hate women any more or as much as American men hate women."

Rathbun-Nealy as symbolic rape victim was seized on by both sides of the growing debate about women in combat. The National Organization for Women adopted the position of SERE's female students in trying to preempt any reaction that would jeopardize servicewomen's future roles. "We don't think rape is a problem peculiar to women," said NOW vice president Rosemary Dempsey only four days after Melissa vanished. "Men also are victims of rape and sodomy. We'd strongly hope all POWs would be treated in accord with the Geneva Convention and would consider any kind of brutalization affecting either sex equally horrible."[38]

Conservatives were just as quick to adopt the position of SERE's male students in order to limit the future utilization of servicewomen. "It's not a good idea to try to obliterate concerns about a woman's reproductive system and the kinds of humiliation she could be forced to endure," said Jean Yarborough, a professor at Bowdoin College who used the POW issue to question the combat support jobs women had held for almost twenty years. Phyllis Schlafly, president of the Eagle Forum, added: "It's absolutely ridiculous to have women in combat. It's an embarrassment to our country."[39]

While the debate raged in Washington over her reproductive organs and her official status, the twenty-year-old truck driver was very much a POW in the Gulf. Suffering from shrapnel wounds and a bullet through the upper arm, she had been taken first to a prison cell in Basra, then on to a prison in Baghdad. She was, in fact, safer from sexual abuse in Baghdad than were her fellow female soldiers in the field. At least twenty-five servicewomen were sexually assaulted in the Gulf, while Rathbun-Nealy had only one minor and brief sexual incident as a POW. En route by truck from Khafji to Baghdad, she would tell her father, one of her guards had reached over and touched her breasts. When she slapped him, he stopped and did not try again.

Her guards in Baghdad were sympathetic. One, an Arab Christian, gave her a crucifix and another, an Iraqi with relatives in Detroit, gave her a rosary. An English-speaking officer took a particular shine to her, chasing away the Iraqis who gawked at her in her cell and bringing her food. "I'm probably the only POW who gained weight in prison," she would say after her release. Instead of abusing her, the Iraqi officer ended up proposing to her. "She told him she was already married and that her country didn't allow multiple husbands," says her father.

On March 4, 1991, Melissa Rathbun-Nealy was among the first group of U.S. POWs to be exchanged for Iraqi POWs. She was still officially listed as missing by the Army, though U.S. pilots flying over Baghdad had reported seeing her in her prison compound. The Pentagon's stubbornness, whether calculated or not, would make the first television pictures of Rathbun-Nealy still wearing Iraq's yellow prisoner-of-war uniform doubly sweet to Leo Rathbun. "I called that jackass in the Pentagon at 3 a.m. in the morning," says Rathbun. " 'Now, you asshole, will you declare her a prisoner of war?' "

The World War II nurses, who themselves had still been classified as missing a year and a half into their three-year captivity, were more impressed by Rathbun-Nealy's bearing, regardless of what she had endured. "When she came off the plane, she had her head up and her hair combed and she walked like a real American woman," says former Navy nurse Mary Nelson. "I was so proud of her."

The nurses were equally proud two days later when a civilian jet chartered by the International Red Cross flew the last load of fifteen U.S. POWs from Baghdad to Riyadh. Among them, with both her arms in slings, was Army Flight Surgeon Major Rhonda Cornum. No one knew yet that Cornum's weeklong experience as a POW would be reduced to a single incident and prove pivotal in the debate over women in combat.

On February 27, 1991, the last day of the four-day ground war, "Doc" Cornum and seven other crew members were flying low and fast over the Iraqi desert in a Black Hawk search-and-rescue helicopter. Accompanied by two Apache attack helicopters and directed by an AWACS radar plane overhead, they were answering an emergency call to retrieve a downed and injured Air Force pilot. "He was worth getting before the Iraqis got to him," says Cornum, who was planning to jump out of the helicopter to quickly stabilize the pilot on the ground before he was loaded and whisked away. "He was flying a mission for the Army. He was the highest decorated guy in the Air Force. And he was my husband's classmate at the Air Force Academy."

The Black Hawk crew was startled when the seemingly empty desert suddenly erupted into flashes of green light and the crack of anti-aircraft guns. "It was as if we were a lawn mower that had run over a beehive, and the bees were coming up to sting," Cornum wrote later in her Gulf war memoir.[40] While the door gunners sprayed return machine-gun fire, the protective infantrymen aboard the Black Hawk pushed Cornum to the floor. In misguided chivalry they covered her body with theirs, thus pinning Cornum in a direct line with the Iraqi fire coming from below.

The last words Cornum heard after the Black Hawk took a

thunderous hit came from a pilot yelling, "We're going in." By the
time she regained consciousness on the desert floor and saw five
Iraqi officers looking down at her, both her arms had been broken
between the elbow and the shoulder, a bone in her little finger had
been shot away, the ligaments in her right knee were torn beyond
repair and she had lost half the blood in her body from a bullet
lodged in her shoulder. Even at that, Cornum was lucky. She was
one of three crew members to be taken prisoner. The other five crew
members—the two pilots, one of the door gunners and two of the
infantrymen—died in the crash.

As Cornum's Iraqi captors led her by the hair from one command bunker to the next in their desert compound, she was well
aware she had not had any prisoner-of-war training. SERE school
was reserved primarily for high-flying aircraft crews whose return to
earth by parachute made them prime targets for enemy capture.
Army helicopters flew so fast and low in combat that the crews
didn't even wear parachutes and were more or less expected to die if
their helicopters went down.[41]

The Code of Conduct was also just a dim thirteen-year-old mem-
ory to Cornum from Officer Basic Course. What little she remem-
bered came from old war movies and from her husband, Kory, who
had been a SERE instructor at the Air Force Academy. She did know
that under the terms of the Geneva Conventions, a flight surgeon
shouldn't be taken prisoner of war at all. But she had purposely left
her medical identity card behind. Not only did she think it would do
her little good if she were captured on a combat search-and-rescue
mission, she also didn't want to be treated any differently from the
rest of the crew. Forced to kneel on her one good leg in the enemy
compound with a gun pressed into the back of her head, Cornum,
thirty-six, was as much a POW as the surviving twenty-year-old
infantryman kneeling beside her.

For the next seven days Cornum was shuttled blindfolded between Iraqi bunkers in the desert, the Baath Party office and a health
clinic in Basra, a military hospital and a final cell in Baghdad. Like
Melissa Rathbun-Nealy, she had only one, though very unpleasant,
sexual incident. On her first night of captivity, as she and the young
infantryman, Troy Dunlap, were being transported to Basra in the
back of a truck, an Iraqi guard suddenly unzipped her flight suit and
started kissing and mauling her. "I was manually molested, anally

and vaginally," Cornum would tell me later. While Dunlap sat help-
lessly on the other side of the truck, only Cornum's broken arms and
screams of pain kept the Iraqi from consummating the assault. "I
would have gotten raped but he couldn't get my flight suit off," says
Cornum.

Cornum was not physically molested again. Indeed, her experience in captivity seems a benchmark in international cross-gender
sensitivity. With her broken arms dangling and tied in front of her,
Cornum persuaded her next Iraqi guards to cut off her flight suit
with a knife and pull down her underpants so she could go to the
bathroom. They then voluntarily reclothed her in a blue wool bath-
robe. "All three of them averted their eyes, or looked me straight
in the eye, so I would know they weren't leering," Cornum wrote
later.[42]

In Basra, she depended on Dunlap and, later, other male POWs
not only to feed and clothe her, but also for the most intimate help.
"I had my period and they helped me go to the bathroom and
remove the tampons and all that stuff," says Cornum. "It was bad
planning to have my period. I'm not sure what good planning would
be, but it just happened that way. I didn't want to die of toxic shock
out there. I wanted to make it home."

On the fifteen-hour bus ride with other blindfolded POWs to
Baghdad on her fourth day of captivity, Cornum developed chills and
a fever from blood poisoning and had to manipulate her broken
finger to drain the pus. She was cheered, however, when she looked
out from under her blindfold and saw the name tag on a fellow
prisoner with a broken leg: it was the Air Force pilot she and her
crew had been on their way to save.

At home, Cornum's father was as worried about his daughter as
Leo Rathbun was about his. In the brave new world of role reversals,
Cornum's father was sending furious telegrams to George Bush and
Norman Schwarzkopf saying, "You've lost my daughter. What are
you going to do about it?"[43] while his daughter was in Baghdad
listening to Troy Dunlap being interrogated and beaten. "Shouting.
Silence. Whap, the sound of a hand across Troy's face," Cornum
writes. "I felt terrible, helpless."[44]

But Norrington's prognosis turned out to be correct. While the
U.S. prisoners in Cornum's group could hear each other's interrogation, they were interrogated separately. Cornum braced for the worst

when she was brought in for her interrogation and saw Dunlap sitting on a chair with his head between his knees and tied with a rope to his boots before he was led away. But whether it was her obvious injuries, her status as a medical officer or her gender, she was not beaten.

Norrington was also correct in predicting that a woman would be more apt to answer the interrogator's questions. But Cornum deliberately gave the wrong answers. After lying about such inquiries as to what direction her helicopter had been headed when it was shot down (straight north, she had answered, instead of due east), she was abruptly dismissed by the interrogating officer. "Was that it? Was it over?" Cornum would write. "The officer said nothing."[45]

Her release came just as abruptly. On March 5, day 7 of her captivity, Cornum was awakened at 3 a.m. in her military hospital room, blindfolded and taken by bus to a cement block of cells somewhere in Baghdad. A guard threw a pair of sneakers and a plastic bag into her cell containing a yellow suit with the words PW stenciled on the pocket. She was then reblindfolded and bused to another location. But this time when the blindfolds were removed, she and at least twenty other yellow-suited prisoners were in the lobby of a luxury hotel. "You are safe. You are now in the custody of the International Committee of the Red Cross," someone called out. "It's over and you are going home."[46] Not until the Red Cross plane left Iraqi airspace the next day, however, and entered the air over Saudi Arabia, did the POWs erupt into cheers.

Cornum and Rathbun-Nealy came home to the same disproportionate attention which was showered on all servicewomen in the Gulf. Rathbun-Nealy, who had been missing for over a month, had become an international celebrity. In France, a photograph of the twenty-year-old truck driver ran on the cover of *Paris-Match*. The president of Italy sent her a huge bouquet of flowers and she was declared an honorary citizen of an Italian town named Melissa. Newspapers around the world carried her photo on the front page and a special edition of *Life* magazine ran a cover photograph of Norman Schwarzkopf hugging her in Riyadh. "Survivor of 32 Too Many Arabian Nights, Melissa Rathbun-Nealy Heads Home from Baghdad" ran a story in *People*.

The attention upset Rathbun-Nealy, who was just one of the ten prisoners of war released on March 4. "She was very embarrassed that she was considered a hero. 'I just got stuck in the sand,'" she told her father. "She literally disappeared as much as she could. She didn't want publicity."

But Saddam Hussein and his armed forces had given U.S. servicewomen a gift. By taking Rathbun-Nealy and Cornum prisoners of war, by not exploiting them for propaganda as they had the captured male pilots, by returning Rathbun-Nealy in apparent good health and Cornum in better shape than she was when she was shot down, the Iraqi forces had reassured the American public about the viability of women in combat.

For all the trepidation at the Pentagon over women POWs, the public had not overreacted. "Women did get captured," says Pete Williams, "but I don't recall at the time any more great public outrage about that other than the general mistreatment of American POWs by the Iraqis."

Cornum did not reveal the groping episode in her press interviews. Both she and Rathbun-Nealy did tell the SERE agency about their respective incidents in their POW debriefings, but no one else. Like her female counterparts at SERE school, Cornum resented the issue of sexual abuse being seen solely as a woman's issue. "None of the male POWs asked me whether I got molested. I didn't ask any of the guys, either," says Cornum. "The only people who asked were inquisitive reporters." Cornum insisted her feelings of helplessness listening to Troy Dunlap being beaten were no different from his feelings when she was being molested on the truck. "I don't think Troy liked it," she says. "But I didn't like it when they beat him up, either."

It was religion, Cornum told me, that was far more of a danger to her fellow male POWs in Iraq than her gender was to her. "If we're going to pick people to send to war based on cultures, we should have taken out all the Jewish soldiers and left them home," she says. "The Iraqis asked me my religion, but they made all the male POWs drop their pants so they could see if they were circumcised. These guys had to do a lot of talking to convince the Iraqis that circumcision was an American tradition, not Jewish, or they would have shot them. No question of that."

It would be another year before Cornum's episode in the back of the truck would become public knowledge and deemed so explosive in the debate over women in combat that it merited a front-page story in the *New York Times*. Lost in the public frenzy over the sexual groping was the far greater slight to Cornum.

For her voluntary participation in the search for the downed pilot, for all the injuries she suffered in the downing of the Black Hawk, she alone among the surviving crew did not get a medal for the search-and-rescue mission in Iraq. The Army refused to admit she had been in combat. "I got put in for a Distinguished Flying Cross and a Bronze Star," says Cornum. "Everyone else on my mission got a DFC. I got nothing."

The World War II nurses were not surprised. For their service under constant shelling in the Pacific and their three years of internment by the Japanese, the nurses, too, had come home to public, but not military recognition. "The eighty-four women were all but ignored when they came back," says Giles Norrington, the ex-Vietnam POW. "There were press things, to be sure. But the military ignored them. The history books, and that's what really counts, ignored them."

Many servicewomen didn't even know women had been prisoners of war in World War II. "It just isn't taught," says Navy chaplain Eileen O'Hickey, Norrington's wife. "The military writes its own history and talks about the great battles and the great men and we go into the Pentagon and hear about MacArthur. And there's one little corridor for women. Isn't that nice."

The ceremonies honoring women military prisoners of war in Washington, for which Cornum wrote a tribute, were the first and only formal recognition the POW nurses had ever received. "These women were lost for fifty years," says Alice Booher, a member of the southeast chapter of Business and Professional Women which sponsored the 1992 salute.

The Gulf war marked the end of women's invisibility in the military. The women who died or were taken prisoners of war, combined with the seemingly painless rout of the enemy, elevated women's military contribution and cemented their new public status. Though students of military history cautioned that the Gulf conflict was a "distorted model of warfare"[47] and should not instruct public attitudes toward servicewomen, it did.

"The image that came out of the Gulf War was of the professionalized woman militarized patriot," wrote Cynthia Enloe in a paper delivered at a 1991 conference on "Women at War: Images of Women Soldiers" held in Florence. "This was an image that liberal women's advocates in the Congress, in DACOWITS, in the officer corps and in Washington lobbying organizations had been constructing and promoting for the past two decades."[48]

The meteoric rise in servicewomen's status would be met by a determined counterforce both inside and outside the military to reverse that status. With women poised to breach the last barrier of combat, it was incumbent on their opponents to discredit them. As fast as the media and the public embraced the similarities between the military sexes, the more servicewomen's opponents would emphasize the differences. And as hard as servicewomen like Rhonda Cornum fought to keep their reproductive organs out of the debate, they would fail.

4

THE PREGNANCY WARS

Conspiracies, Myths and Propaganda

THE RUMORS about pregnancy started as the first troops landed in Saudi Arabia in August 1990. Units were being sent off without half their female members, one went, because the women were pregnant. Women were getting pregnant on purpose to get out of being deployed. Women already in the Gulf were trying to get pregnant so they could be sent home. Instead of a fighting force, the troops were being made out to be more akin to rabbits.

The mere activation of obstetricians and gynecologists in the reserves led *New York* magazine to run an item on its gossip page titled "U.S. Soldiers Make Babies, Not War."[1] The return of the USS *Acadia* from an eight-month deployment to the Gulf minus twenty-nine, or 8 percent, of the 360 women on board who had been transferred off the ship for pregnancy, branded the destroyer tender "The Love Boat" and a "floating maternity wing."[2]

In the rush to titillation, no mention was made of the 92 percent of the female crew who didn't get pregnant or where the pregnancies occurred. "Nine of the women were pregnant but didn't know it when the ship left San Diego. Five were transferred to the ship in the Gulf," a Navy spokeswoman said at the time. "The ship made liberty calls in Hawaii, the Philippines and other ports." But nobody cared. "The guys loved the Love Boat story," says a male sailor who was aboard another ship in the Gulf. "The news spread like wildfire."

Pregnancy has been the weapon of choice against women since 1975, when the Defense Department directed the services to reverse their long-standing policies of involuntarily separating women for pregnancy. No other issue has spawned such a wealth of legend. And no other issue has played a more negative role in women's assimilation. "If you're a woman and you get pregnant, you've just become a whole other species," says former Army Corporal Jeanne Kelser, who left the service in 1990. "You're immediately ostracized from the social, political and structural framework. Pregnant women are the most victimized minority in the Army."

The case against accommodating military pregnancy has not changed since the 1970s, when virtually every senior officer, including female officers, argued against it. "It is the greatest mistake in the world," Colonel Mary Hallaren, the WAC staff director in the European theater during World War II, told an Army historian in 1977. "I feel very strongly that the military has got to be a ready and mobile force, and I can't see that it's a ready force with women who are pregnant or have small children. I think that is taking away something that the military has always stood for."[3]

The case for keeping pregnant servicewomen, or any pregnant women, on the job hasn't changed either. Without the accommodation of pregnancy as a temporary disability which simply accompanies women into whatever career fields they choose, there can be no equal opportunity. "The structure has to deal with pregnancy for women to achieve equality in the workplace," says Betty Friedan. "Career structures based on men's lives have to be readjusted for women to be successfully integrated into the mainstream. The argument in the military that pregnancy interferes with performance requirements may be right, but pregnancy has to be tolerated if women are to be assimilated."

The services fought to protect their ranks from pregnant women during the wave of equal opportunity legislation in the 70s and the anticipated ratification of the Equal Rights Amendment. The Navy and the Air Force successfully dodged one legal challenge after another to their involuntary discharge policy for pregnancy by granting individual waivers to the plaintiffs and mooting their suits by allowing them to remain in uniform.

But the Navy and every other institution that discriminated against women were bucking the tide of support for women's rights. Pregnancy discrimination was a major issue. While employers regularly awarded male employees medical leave for temporary health conditions with no loss of benefits, pregnant women were often fired or suspended with no benefits or guarantees of reemployment.

Establishing pregnancy as a temporary medical disability was an early priority of the National Organization for Women. In 1972, NOW's efforts succeeded with the Equal Employment Opportunity Commission, which issued federal guidelines stating that pregnancy had to be treated the same as other temporary disabilities: employers were enjoined to grant leaves of absence to pregnant employees and entitle them to reinstatement with no loss of benefits or seniority when they returned to work.[4]

Codifying pregnancy discrimination as sex discrimination became an early crusade for such activist groups as the National Women's Law Center, founded in Washington in 1972, and the Women's Rights Project, established by the American Civil Liberties Union the same year in New York. Leading the legal charge at the Women's Rights Project from 1972 to 1980 was the project's general counsel and a future Supreme Court justice, Ruth Bader Ginsburg. She found the perfect vehicle in the military.

Captain Susan R. Struck, an Air Force nurse, became pregnant while stationed at McChord Air Force Base in Washington and was offered two options by the Air Force: terminate the pregnancy by abortion or accept involuntary discharge. The twenty-six-year-old officer, a Catholic, refused both options. Instead, she sued, lost and appealed, represented by Ginsburg.

In her brief for the Supreme Court's October 1972 term, Ginsburg refuted the arguments the military still uses against pregnancy.[5] To the Air Force claim that pregnancy would hamper the service's ability "to maintain the required pool of men and women ready and available for all military assignments," Ginsburg countered that readiness was similarly impaired by "other temporary physical conditions," from sports injuries to car accidents. The Air Force managed "to tolerate these disabilities," Ginsburg argued, "although additional precautions might have prevented them."

Indeed, she pointed out, the Air Force was already tolerating the disability of pregnancy—for men. Under 1972 Air Force regulations, officers whose wives became pregnant were entitled to a three-month deferment from overseas duty.

Ginsburg made short order as well of the Air Force's hastily assembled pro-contraception policy, which Struck had failed to observe, as another rationale for her discharge. While the Air Force argued that there was a "compelling government interest" to "deter planned pregnancies" or to "prevent unplanned pregnancies" through contraception, Ginsburg countered that the application of the "eleventh hour" contraception policy was the essence of gender inequity.

"If a serviceman and servicewoman conceive a child, the serviceman is not even disciplined; on the other hand, the servicewoman is discharged, regardless of who is responsible for the failure of contraception," Ginsburg argued. "If this is not discrimination, then nothing is."

Ginsburg's arguments seemed compelling but the Supreme Court never heard them. To avoid risking a court decision which would apply to all Air Force women, the Air Force "mooted" Captain Struck's suit by reversing its ultimatum and granting her a waiver to remain on active duty.[6] The "moot and run" strategy would serve the Air Force well in two subsequent pregnancy discrimination suits.

The judicial axe would finally fall when the stubborn Marine Corps refused to play the litigation-avoidance game. Stephanie Cushman took the Marines to court after she was involuntarily discharged in 1970 for becoming pregnant and then denied reenlistment because she had a child. Cushman lost the case in 1974 on the grounds that the Marines had unique requirements for "ready and mobile" personnel.[7] Evidently convinced any higher court would also support such military judgment, the Marines did not move to moot the case when Cushman appealed.

In 1976 a federal circuit court overturned the lower court in *Crawford v. Cushman* and, under the Fifth Amendment's due process provisions, ruled that the Marine Corps regulation was unconstitutional. Following the EEOC guidelines, the court's rationale centered on the Marines' inability to show that the temporary disability caused by pregnancy was different from any other temporary disability in terms of military readiness and, in any case, did not make a pregnant Marine permanently unfit for duty.[8]

The Defense Department was well ahead of the court decision on pregnancy, however. The Judge Advocate General's Office knew that the time when discriminatory laws based solely on gender was coming to an end. The Equal Rights Amendment, though stalled in 1975, had been ratified by thirty-four states. More important, the fledgling All-Volunteer Force was in trouble.

The services needed more, not fewer, women to offset the manpower shortages following the end of the draft. Even though the services were already approving 60 to 86 percent of waiver requests from pregnant women, women were still leaving the All-Volunteer Force at an alarming rate.[9] In the Navy alone, over 90 percent of enlisted women in the preceding decade had failed to complete their first enlistment.[10] Bowing to military pragmatism as well as to the anticipated political realities of the Equal Rights Amendment, the DOD ordered the services to rescind their bans on pregnancy effective May 1975.

The Air Force and the Navy complied, but the Army balked. "We apparently have become the victims of the ERA without the benefit of properly assessing the impact," the assistant secretary of the Army wrote the secretary of the Army, Howard "Bo" Callaway. Callaway forwarded his official resistance up the civilian chain of command. "I am concerned that we are overreacting to special interest social pressures and are failing to recognize Army defense requirements," the Army secretary wrote William Brehm, Gerald Ford's assistant secretary of defense.[11]

Brehm stood firm. "The determination . . . that we will not separate women for pregnancy or parenthood is one which we have accepted in order to best apply the concepts of equal opportunity for our people," Brehm responded to the Army's objections.[12] The Army finally capitulated in November 1975, seven months after the DOD directive.[13] While the ERA would fail in 1982, three states short of ratification, the amendment's ten-year trajectory across the social and political landscape had transformed the military.

"Having opened the barn door on the surge of the ERA, the Army let women come up to a certain level, from which now they cannot comfortably retreat," says Russell Parkinson, a historian at the Army's Center of Military History. "Even though the ERA didn't go through, the Army can never go back and close the barn door again and say, 'We've given women too many rights.' "

No military force in the world allowed pregnant women to remain in uniform in the 1970s. Until 1990, the British military would discharge women at about four months, when they grew out of their uniforms.[14] Even Israel's compulsory two-year service requirement for women exempted pregnant as well as married women. From the moment the civilian bureaucracy in the Pentagon forced pregnancy on the services, the services were determined to prove the civilians wrong.

"Lost time" off the job became a military mantra against pregnant women. That a 1975 study of "lost time" in the Navy found that men lost 190,000 days to drug rehabilitation and another 196,000 days to alcohol rehabilitation, almost twice the absentee rate of Navy women including time lost to pregnancy, did nothing to dissuade the fleet perception that pregnant women were shirkers.[15]

The Army's case against women and pregnancy didn't even bother with comparative statistics. An entire chapter of a 1976 study of Army women was devoted to pregnancy and "lost time."[16] Women lost a stunning 105 days, or 29 percent "of a manyear" for an "average" pregnancy, the Army claimed. Women who chose to end their pregnancies by abortion lost ten to twelve days off the job, including 4.8 days of hospitalization.[17] Even allowing for medical complications, the figure seemed grossly inflated compared to the average stay of four *hours* civilian women spent not in hospitals but in abortion clinics.

The civilians in the Pentagon, who by 1976 had more than tripled the number of enlisted women in the services and during the Carter presidency were planning to double the number again by 1983, were skeptical about the Army's arguments against pregnancy. Because the Army had not considered a single plus about women's service nor evaluated men's "time lost" off the job identified by the Navy, the Defense Department suggested that the resistance to women was based more on "emotionalism" and "unsubstantiated generalities" than "factual information."[18]

The chief of Navy personnel tried to make the same distinction to Navy men by wiring the results of his time-loss gender comparisons to the entire Pacific, Atlantic and European fleets. "These statistics should help defuse the emotionalism associated with the incorrectly perceived imbalance of lost time attributed to our Navy women because of pregnancy," read the fleetwide memo from Vice Admiral James Watkins.[19] But the pregnancy wars only intensified.

The perception took hold in all the services that pregnant women had an unfair advantage over men. And indeed, in one critical area, they did. Because the services placed little value on the military worth of pregnant women, pregnancy became the only "temporary disability" that allowed an enlisted service member to break the contract of service and resign at will. Whereas the services had always been the judge of who joined or left their ranks, pregnant enlisted women could simply quit. No such option existed for men or for female officers.

Pregnancy also played into what was instantly deemed a benefits scam. With the shorter terms of enlistment in the 70s, a woman who became pregnant could spend a significant part of her military commitment on light duty at full pay, reap the rewards of free health care and paid maternity leave—and then quit. "They think they got the gal to stay and she isn't staying," an Air Force officer remarked at the time. "She is still getting out, only after she gives birth rather than before."[20] Almost half of the approximately 8 percent of Army enlisted women who gave birth in 1978 left the service after their six-week maternity leave.[21]

By 1980, pregnancy had become such a divisive issue within the military that even liberal civilian activists were worried. Instead of women being assimilated into the services, pregnancy was ostracizing them. Worse, many nonpregnant women had joined the male chorus and turned against their own gender. "As with most problems, this issue has two sides," wrote Linda Stern in *Working Woman*.[22] "A liberal pregnancy policy can be seen as an encouragement of family life and a fair health benefit for female employees. . . . But some military women feel that others take advantage of the leave."

Pregnancy was deemed such a problem during the Reagan administration that the Army cited it as one of the reasons for a temporary halt to enlisting any more women; by 1982, there were 65,000 women in the enlisted ranks, marking over a fivefold increase in less than a decade.[23] Though pregnant women accounted for only 1.9 percent of the personnel surveyed in twenty-three units by the Army Audit Agency in 1982, increasing the number of women seemed to imperil the security of the Western world. Army Regulation 220-1 stated that pregnant women could not be deployed overseas. Army Regulation 614-30 stated that women who became pregnant while serving abroad in "hostile areas" had to be brought home at four and a half months. Pregnancy so reduced a servicewoman's military value that in "emergency situations" she was to be evacuated with civilian wives and children.[24]

Army commanders didn't know what to do with pregnant women. They were neither required to go on field exercises nor to participate in physical training. In many cases, pregnant women weren't allowed, or required, to do their jobs. Fearful of breaking the medical regulations that prevented "pregnant soldiers" from being assigned to duties where "nausea, fatigue or sudden light-headedness would be hazardous," cautious commanders put pregnant women on limited duty or reassigned them to desk jobs. Fully 54 percent of the pregnant soldiers reviewed in the 1982 audit had been involuntarily reassigned, usually as clerks.[25]

But that led to another problem. Because pregnancy was deemed a "temporary disability," pregnant women were rarely replaced, leaving their colleagues to pick up their peacetime workloads. While the Army's team spirit rallied around male soldiers with temporary injuries like broken legs, there was no generosity of spirit extended to pregnant women. "Morale problems are reported when the pregnant female soldier is not replaced, and male members must assume the redistributed work load," observed one Army study.[26]

The 1982 Army audit took no notice of time lost by men or indeed of time lost by nonpregnant women. But every minute of "nonproductivity" was factored in for pregnant women, including morning sickness. Factoring in time lost off the job to nausea, periodic medical checkups, twenty-minute rest periods every four hours, forty-hour workweeks during the last trimester and up to six weeks of maternity leave, the Army audit concluded that "pregnant soldiers were excused from [certain] duties from 8 to 9 months."

No wonder the question Do pregnant soldiers receive preferential treatment?, included in a questionnaire sent to 1,083 male and female enlisted soldiers, elicited a response of "yes" from 75 percent of the enlisted males, 53 percent of the officers and senior enlisted, and fully 51 percent of the presumably nonpregnant enlisted females. Pregnant women had become military pariahs at home, abroad and in the field. "If there is an absolute precondition for the effective utilization of women in field duty, it must be the exclusion of pregnant women," reported military sociologist Charles Moskos after observing integrated units on field exercises in Honduras in 1984. "Any avoidance of this stand will reflect negatively on the role of all women in field situations."[27]

By the 90s, pregnancy had bred a whole genre of Army conspiracy theories. Women were accused of getting pregnant on purpose to get out of field duty and deployments, and to leave the barracks for family housing. The more macho the division, the more virulent the theories. "In the 82nd Airborne, the males honestly believe women get pregnant just so they won't have to go on the morning runs," says Captain Kathleen Batton, a 1981 graduate of West Point. "They would never say that to their wives or sisters, but they do to women in the Army."

Navy women faced even more accusations. Because pregnant women were not allowed to deploy on ships, women were accused of getting pregnant to avoid going to sea. Because women who got pregnant at sea were put ashore, they were accused of getting pregnant to get off. Because pregnant women were evacuated from isolated posts abroad, they were accused of getting pregnant to come home.

The "personnel turbulence"[28] caused by pregnancy was so persistent that the Navy commissioned a trilogy of pregnancy studies between 1989 and 1992 to separate fact from fiction. And every poison dart circulating about pregnancy in the fleet turned out to be wrong.

While every sailor absolutely knew that pregnancy was epidemic in the Navy, the studies determined that the pregnancy rate of 8.6 percent among married and single enlisted Navy women twenty to twenty-nine was the same as the pregnancy rates among same-aged civilians.[29] While every sailor was just as certain that the Navy was spending a fortune bringing home pregnant women from certain stations abroad, only twenty-five women were returned in 1990 compared to eighty-six men, an overrepresentation of women in terms of relative numbers, but lower in cost because the women had fewer dependents to transport. The average cost of the "early returns" for men was $7,174. The average cost for women due to pregnancy was $2,046. Among medical evacuations, AIDS and substance abuse accounted for up to 8 percent, pregnancy for barely 1 percent.[30]

The charge that women deliberately got pregnant to avoid service was diluted by the finding that most of the youngest women's pregnancies were unplanned.[31] The conspiracy theories rested on the six- to nine-month lead time women had between receiving their sea duty orders and reporting for duty and the biological impossibility of proving that pregnancy wasn't "self-inflicted."

Purposefully avoiding deployment was and is a serious charge in all the services.[32] Young Navy men have been known to try many ruses to avoid going to sea, from taking drugs just before a urinalysis to shooting themselves in the foot. One enlisted woman in 1991 chanced upon the horrific sight of one young sailor trying to get his arm broken by another sailor wielding a cinder block. It was women's lack of accountability for pregnancy under the UCMJ (Uniform Code of Military Justice) which confirmed to Navy sailors that women were getting pregnant on purpose, and getting away with it.

Equally unshakable was the accepted verity that pregnant women who were taken off ships were filling a disproportionate number of shore jobs, thereby forcing men to remain longer at sea. "The charge has never had any truth in fact or numbers at all. It's just perception," says Captain Kathleen Bruyere, the recruit training commander in 1992 at the Navy's former training facility in Orlando, Florida. "We can prove it statistically and tried to for years to those who would listen. . . . Why would we do that? It doesn't make sense. That means you're purposefully going to keep some man or woman at sea for an inordinate amount of time which will make them upset and upset their families and cause them not to re-enlist." [33]

Lost in the universal condemnation of Navy pregnancy was the failure of the Navy to instruct its youngest recruits on sex education and birth control. Though almost two-thirds of Navy pregnancies (64 percent) occurred in the three lowest pay grades, one study found fewer than half the women and men who had been involved in a Navy pregnancy reported receiving any instruction in pregnancy prevention.[34] And fewer than half of the pregnant women and their commands were aware of the Navy's policies governing pregnancy.

When the *Acadia* left San Diego for the Gulf in 1990, Navy policy required pregnant women to be kept on board ship until their twentieth week (the time set by the Navy's Bureau of Medicine when "changes in posture and the woman's center of gravity occur which cause problems with balance and decreased agility"),[35] provided the ship was never more than six hours by medevac from treatment facilities ashore.[36] But many Navy supervisors chose to either ignore the Navy's policies or not bother to learn them. "They just get the women off the ship as fast as they can," says a Navy enlisted woman. Fully 48 percent of Navy first-class and chief petty officers who acted as personnel supervisors in 1990 believed Navy policy *required* pregnant women to be reassigned ashore "as soon as possible." [37]

It was this kind of ignorance and bias toward pregnancy that fanned the flames of conspiracy, not self-serving women. "I got on my hands and knees and begged to stay on board the *Acadia*," said a twenty-five-year-old personnel clerk from the infamous "Love Boat" who had gone on liberty with her twenty-nine-year-old fiancé, a boiler repairman, in Dubai and gotten pregnant. While her fiancé completed the cruise on the *Acadia*, she was involuntarily reassigned to shore duty in San Diego.[38]

Undoubtedly, some women did try to use pregnancy to their own advantage. In keeping with the ignorance supervisors had about Navy policy, fully 61 percent of enlisted Navy women in one Navy study had not been told that they were obligated to remain on board until their twentieth week of pregnancy—an omission that lent itself to their perception that pregnancy was an instant ticket ashore.[39]

The women had not been told, either, that pregnancy was only a temporary reprieve from sea duty. Navy regulations also stated that women whose sea duty had been interrupted by pregnancy were to return to sea duty to complete their tours four months after childbirth. But almost half the enlisted women and 66 percent of their supervisors in one Navy study had never heard of the policy.[40] Such widespread ignorance sometimes led to sad misunderstandings.

"This one young lady absolutely hated Diego Garcia so she got pregnant to get out of there," says a female veteran of the desolate installation in the Indian Ocean. "The Navy flew her to San Francisco to have the baby where she suddenly realized she'd taken on an obligation she was not prepared to meet. She subsequently gave up the baby for adoption and was ordered back to Diego Garcia to finish her tour. That was quite a price she paid. She lost both ways."

And so the war against pregnancy raged on. No allowance was awarded the Navy women who were issued birth control pills whose expiration date had expired[41] or who couldn't replenish their supplies abroad with the same brand they had been taking.[42] "Lost time" to pregnancy remained a mantra, despite the Navy's documentation that the total time lost was one hour a month[43] and the Defense Department's documentation of the time required to travel to the few military medical facilities offering OB/GYN services. "There is no OB/GYN in the two nearest military organizations in my area," an enlisted Marine reported. "The nearest is forty-five miles away from this station and one hundred miles from my home."[44]

There was no recognition of the price servicewomen paid in the pregnancy wars, the harassment they often experienced from their male peers in seeking reproductive health care, the lowered evaluations pregnant women often received from their superiors, the inability of women serving overseas to secure safe abortions. Military funding of abortions for servicewomen had been cut off in 1978 after the congressional passage of the Hyde amendment eliminated federal funding of abortions and in 1988 had been extended to a ban on abortions performed in military hospitals overseas, even if servicewomen paid for them.[45]

Some men resisted taking orders from pregnant women, as if their condition somehow disqualified them from leadership positions. "I didn't command the respect I should have as an officer," says former Army Lieutenant Elizabeth Carey, who had two children in the mid-80s during her posting to Germany with her husband. "The soldiers failed to salute me, little things like that."

Pregnancy cast male doubt on women's judgment, regardless of their seniority. Major Sheryl Rozman was a UH-1 instructor pilot in 1988 with thirteen years of flying experience and the officer in charge of the UH-1 flight simulator, but she faced a credibility gap with her students during her pregnancy. "I was eight months pregnant when I gave this one guy a check ride in the simulator and he failed," she recalls. "I'm sure he went back and said my hormones are all off balance. You get less respect from people who don't know you when you're pregnant. It doesn't sit real well with them."

Pregnancy continued to turn women against women, especially in the Navy. "Some women use pregnancy as 'I can't do this work. I've got to have a sit-down job,' " said an enlisted woman in a Navy aviation squadron in Norfolk, Virginia, in 1994. "They make it bad for the other women because everyone looks at the one who is sitting down not doing her job, not the other two who are out there busting their butts. Amongst the women that creates a lot of hate."

The universal condemnation of pregnancy compelled many women to work right up to the onset of labor. "I was just damned going to show them that pregnancy isn't a weakness," says an Air Force mechanic who stayed on the flight line for all nine months of her pregnancy. Other women disguised their pregnancies or kept the news to themselves so they could continue their training. An Army woman quietly completed her aviation training while she was pregnant. "My daughter has two jumps," she told the authors of *Sound Off!* "When I was pregnant I jumped twice. The Army didn't know I was pregnant. Not by far. I told them after that and they about had a conniption."[46]

Female officers, too, especially Army pilots, hid their pregnancies. As late as 1995 the Army's pregnancy policies not only grounded female pilots starting from the moment their pregnancies were diagnosed to four to six weeks after delivery but threatened to end their flying careers as well. While pregnancy was considered a "temporary disability," the Army deemed *any* disabling condition lasting over six months to be a "permanent disability." That left pilots who reported their pregnancies to their flight surgeons not only immediately grounded but often also permanently disqualified.[47]

Reversing their status as "permanently disabled" was very difficult. "She was advised that, if the permanent disability ended and she were again classified as medically fit, she could apply to the Department of the Army for reinstatement of her occupation specialty," wrote Connie L. Reeves, an eighteen-year Army veteran and mother of two in a newsletter for female pilots. "Approval, however, could not be guaranteed."[48]

Pregnancy policies were more accommodating for pilots in the Navy and Air Force, which, in some cases, allowed female pilots to fly through their sixth month. "It depends on the aircraft," says Air Force Captain Linda Tobin, who flew acceptable "heavy" aircraft like the multi-engine C-141 and the T-43, the Air Force's VIP transport which would crash in Croatia in April 1996, killing Commerce Secretary Ron Brown and thirty-four others. "For the type of aircraft I'm in I could fly up through my sixth month, assuming everything was physically OK, of course."

It was the smaller, faster jets like the supersonic T-38s that the Air Force declared off grounds to pregnant pilots. "You're removed from flying status in the smaller jets as soon as they find out you're pregnant because of the G-forces and other physical stresses," says Tobin. "So the pilots just don't tell."

The Air Force's concern was as much for fetal damage as it was for the health of the pilot. Air Force tests had shown that frog, chick and mouse embryos subjected to very high G-forces in centrifuge tests had caused the rearrangement of their limbs.[49] That such developmental damage if it occurred in human embryos would take place during the first nine days after conception when the pilot didn't know she was pregnant was nonetheless reason enough for the Air Force to keep pregnant pilots out of high-performance jets. "If you're flying an ejection seat aircraft, you're basically sitting on a rocket modem which will get you out of the airplane but puts a tremendous number of Gs on your body," says Navy test pilot Trish Beckman. "They probably would not want a fetus subjected to such stresses. But the ejection rate is very small."

The Air Force was so concerned about fetal protection that the service's first female U-2 pilot, Captain Troy Devine, was required to have a pregnancy test every two weeks to remain on flight status. The Air Force was worried that the radiation levels at the U-2's surveillance altitude of 65,000 feet would be harmful to fetal development. Only after the Supreme Court agreed unanimously in 1991 that employers could not exclude women from jobs in which exposure to toxic substances might harm a developing fetus did the Air Force discontinue Devine's testing.[50]

The labyrinthine pregnancy restrictions on pilots in the hypermasculine community of military aviators added unique performance stress. "I can only think of a few women who did their jobs five times as well as the men, as opposed to the twice as well all women have to do, who didn't get grief for being pregnant," says Beckman.

Faced with such institutional complexities, female pilots went to extraordinary lengths to control their reproductive lives. "Female officers plan their pregnancies down to the minute, the *minute*," says former Army officer Tanya Domi. For nonflying Army officers, the optimal time occurred between field commands and during an assignment to an advanced service school. For pilots, it was time on the ground. "The ideal time is to plan a pregnancy when you're not on operational time—shore duty we call it—when you're doing a job which is not so important," says Beckman.

Waiting for the right moment entailed extraordinary personal sacrifice. Rosemary Mariner, who entered flight training in the first class of Navy female pilots in 1973, flew for nineteen years before she even considered getting pregnant. Her first child, a daughter, would be born in 1994.

Astronaut Eileen Collins, who joined the Air Force in 1978 and seventeen years later became the first woman to pilot the space shuttle, waited to start her family until she had maneuvered the *Discovery* around the Russian space station *Mir* in February 1995. Her first child, Bridget Marie, was born on November 17, exactly nine months later.

The deployment of so many women to the Gulf could have afforded the Pentagon an opportunity to study the effect of pregnancy and separate the myths from the military realities. Pregnancy was either a readiness problem or it wasn't. But the Pentagon did nothing and the internal conspiracy theories became public.

Only two months into the deployment, the *Colorado Springs Gazette Telegraph* reported the suspicions of some male soldiers in an Army transportation company when at least four women of twenty-two in the company turned up pregnant just six days before they would have deployed to the Gulf.[51] There were also anonymous charges from a company commander at Fort Bragg, North Carolina, that thirteen women in his support company of a hundred had to be left home. "Fortunately the enemy gave us six months to fill those holes, or we would have been in a world of hurts," the unnamed commander was quoted in *Newsweek.*[52]

Conspiracy theories gained momentum in the Gulf. There was "no question that pregnancy soared during the war," claimed retired Colonel David Hackworth, a Gulf war correspondent for *Newsweek.* More than 1,200 pregnant women, "the equivalent of two infantry battalions," Hackworth declared flatly, had to be flown home from Saudi Arabia. His informants, "three Pentagon sources," were also unnamed.[53]

Hackworth's defense of his unsubstantiated numbers hinted at another conspiracy. Though he had tried to support his allegations about pregnancies in the Gulf with hard numbers from the Pentagon, he had received no response. "It's hard to get precise numbers, as the Pentagon treats this information with almost as much sensitivity as it devotes to the location of nuclear weapons," he wrote.

Hackworth was correct about the lack of information on pregnancy rates emanating from the Pentagon, but he attributed it to the wrong reason. The Pentagon wasn't concealing the pregnancy rates in the Gulf. They didn't know what they were. No official records were kept on the impact of pregnancy on women's deployability rate to the Gulf or their evacuations from the Gulf.

Whether the omission centered on the services' inclination to avoid the official documentation of the pregnancy issue, or whether the relatively small number of women involved in the Gulf operation was deemed undeserving of special attention, the Pentagon's silence only inflamed the growing speculation about the significance of military pregnancies.

To critics of servicewomen, like right-wing military policy analyst Brian Mitchell, the Pentagon's seeming indifference to the pregnancy issue was a deliberate decision made at the highest levels. "The Defense Department has no interest in answering questions that are going to make present policy look bad," said Mitchell at a spring conference on women in the military held shortly after the war. "Very often, faced with embarrassing questions, they merely respond with, 'Well, we're not tracking that,' or 'There's no evidence.' There's no evidence because they haven't collected the evidence."[54]

What Mitchell evidently didn't know, nor did Hackworth, was that the Pentagon was about to make a retroactive effort to document the effects of pregnancy on the deployability and early returns of servicewomen during the Gulf conflict. The pregnancy innuendo in the press had captured congressional attention even before Iraq launched its first Scud. Anticipating the political reemergence of the women in combat issue, members of Congress wanted the Defense Department to get hard numbers on pregnancy and women's nondeployability rates.

DACOWITS had been looking forward to a Defense Department study of women's historic roles in the Gulf, promised to the committee in the fall of 1990 by Christopher Jehn, assistant secretary of defense for force management and personnel. The DOD's documentation of servicewomen's far-reaching roles on the modern battlefield would give DACOWITS ammunition for congressional repeal of the combat exclusion laws. The committee did not know about the expansion of the study to include pregnancy.

At a Pentagon meeting in late January or February 1991, representatives from the different services had hammered out the information to be collected about women in the Gulf. The supposedly internal study, which became known as the Jehn Report, was expanded at that meeting to include the comparison of male and female nondeployability rates to the Gulf, early returns from the Gulf and, specifically, pregnancy. "The whole purpose of the study was gender differences," recalls Lieutenant Colonel Steve Maurmann, the DOD's deputy defense director of personnel management, who as a major coordinated the project at the Pentagon. " 'Is there a performance difference between males and females; do they deploy and early return differently?' That's what we were looking for."

The DOD project had not begun well. The Pentagon statisticians soon realized that the services did not have the specific information they needed on their data bases. "We discovered that most of the services had no established mechanism to track or report personnel who were deemed nondeployable, who returned early from deployment, or who became pregnant," Maurmann reported to a later commission on women in combat.[55]

The January kickoff of the project had also been a negative. The clock was ticking toward January 16, the "line in the sand" drawn by Bush and the United Nations for Iraq to withdraw from Kuwait. Without reliable data bases from which to easily extract information on nondeployability, the Defense Department realized it would have to gather the information from individual unit commanders on the ground in Saudi Arabia. In light of the commanders' preoccupation with the impending Allied assault on Iraq, the Pentagon had decided to wait until the war was over to find out who hadn't gone—and why.

It wasn't until June, a full ten months after the first troop deployments to the Gulf, that the DOD formally tasked the services to quantify male and female nondeployables, early returns and pregnancy. Getting accurate data, however, proved impossible.

The Air Force turned out to have no idea how many of its male or female "airmen" had been specifically nondeployable to the Gulf or what part, if any, pregnancy had played. In the ten months that had passed since the first troops were deployed to the Gulf, unit rosters in the Air Force had been destroyed. "There were no directions from the Air Force for units to hold their unit call-up rosters and centralize them," said Lieutenant Colonel Mike Lynch.[56]

The Air Force was not trying to cover up its nondeployability rates for men or women. It was simply a nonissue. Relatively few Air Force personnel—60,000 airmen, including 4,000 women—were deployed to the Gulf.[57] And unlike the Army, which deployed its troops in whole units, a system that highlighted the holes left by nondeployable personnel, and the Navy, whose ships acted as seagoing units and therefore also underscored missing personnel, the Air Force put together "packages" of personnel based on a mission demand for "skills needed."

Following the same deployment practice as had been used in Vietnam, the system allowed the Air Force to put together its "packages" from the pools of available personnel in each skill, thereby passing over the nondeployables. "Every one of our units made their manning requirements from the call-up to begin with, so there was no cry to find why somebody didn't go," Lieutenant Colonel Lynch explained to the commission. ". . . What you're looking for, in terms of that data from us, is not there."[58]

But the Defense Department had asked the Air Force for numbers, which the service supplied. The Air Force numbers were not based on nondeployable personnel to the Gulf, but on the servicewide "morning report" of all nondeployable personnel recorded between September and December 1990 and again in March 1991, including key witnesses in courts-martial, AWOLs, prisoners, disqualifying physical profiles, drug or alcohol rehabilitation, HIV-positive personnel and pregnancy. The Air Force then averaged out the percentage of all male and female nondeployables for all reasons servicewide and came up with 1.8 percent of males and 6.4 percent of females.[59]

The Marine Corps had just as much difficulty coming up with pregnancy numbers in the Gulf. Because it had deployed two-thirds of its operating force to the Gulf where the Marines were to be first over the border into Kuwait during the ground war, the corps had made a conscious decision not to burden its commanders with a numbers game. "They had enough to do to get ready to do their mission over there," said Marine Lieutenant Colonel Gene Brindle.[60]

The retroactive search for women's nondeployability rate in the Marines was further complicated by pregnancy being classified as a medical problem like any other in the corps. "There is no way to tell from pulling a report out of the system what the medical problem is," Lieutenant Colonel Brindle reported.[61] Moreover, some units had been organized in the Gulf, then reorganized, leading to the possibility of double-counting.

What numbers the Marines finally did come up with after polling the memories of unit commanders and reviewing eight months of the corps' daily readiness reports on the status of unit readiness and training (SORTS), which did specifically break out pregnancy, was a nondeployability rate for active-duty Marine women of 9.2 percent. Adding in the reserves, the rate rose to 9.8 percent. Out of 3,109 reserve and active-duty Marine women, 306 had been nondeployable because of pregnancy.[62]

The Navy turned out to be equally handicapped in the search for reliable pregnancy statistics and urged "extreme caution" in drawing conclusions from its figures.[63] Because it had no data base on the breakdown of nondeployables in the specific units that deployed to the Gulf, the Navy, too, had been forced to poll the individual units starting in July 1991, almost a year after Desert Shield had begun.[64]

The data returned from the fleet showed that 80,000 men and

2,600 women had deployed while 1,205 men and 155 women had not. Translated into the lopsided percentages caused by the huge differential in gender populations, the Navy's nondeployability rate broke down into 1.5 percent of men and 5.6 percent of women. Pregnancy accounted for 47 percent of women's nondeployability.[65]

The pregnancy factor of 47 percent among the 155 nondeployable women was also more benign than it seemed. Simple arithmetic shows that 47 percent of 155 equals 72. That is the number of Navy women out of a total Navy force of over 82,000 men and women tasked to deploy to the Gulf who were unable to go because of pregnancy. "The bottom line from the Navy standpoint is that personnel readiness was not an issue during the Persian Gulf," said Captain Martha Whitehead, special assistant for women's policy to the chief of naval personnel.[66]

The Army's pregnancy percentages were the least suspect. Alone among the services, the Army had initiated its own and early collection of information on deployability to the Gulf in reaction to the public and congressional furor over single parents. But the Army's data wasn't complete either.

The Army hadn't started collecting nondeployability data from the Central Command overseeing the deployment of troops from the United States until October 1990, two months into the deployment, and until December and January for units deployed from Europe. In the overall urgency of the period, said Colonel Terry Hulin, then chief of Army policy for the assignment of female soldiers, the directive to focus on pregnant women and single mothers had caused "much gnashing of teeth." "Deploying units were extremely busy and were concentrating on deploying and preparing to execute a war against an enemy who had a large, sophisticated, experienced Army and had chemical weapons," Hulin told the commission.[67]

The Army took the reported figures, averaged the total number of nondeployables during the five months of troop deployment to the Gulf and came up with a representative figure of 9,572 nondeployable soldiers at any given time. Of those, slightly over half (53 percent)—5,073 soldiers—were deemed nondeployable for medical reasons, 12 percent specifically for pregnancy. According to the Army, that 12 percent translated to 1,048 nondeployable women a week due to pregnancy, though presumably the same women showed up in the statistics week after week for the duration of their pregnancies and six-week maternity leave. Using those figures, the Army came up with a dramatic gender difference in nondeployability rates: 9.1 percent of women versus 2.43 percent of men.[68]

For months the Defense Department tried to make sense of the nondeployability statistics and pregnancy compiled by the services. Wrenching the numbers into tidy packages was complicated by the latitude many commanders had had with their units. Some commanders of reserve units prescreened their personnel before they were called up, resulting in 100 percent deployability rates. Active duty commanders tasked to deploy only portions of their units also reached 100 percent deployability rates because they could pick and choose the most deployable personnel, most of whom were volunteers. Still other units were patched together with active duty personnel, the individual ready reservists and members of the Selected Reserve who were "cross-assigned" from as many as twenty-nine different reserve units.

"As the services began collecting information, it became apparent that comparison among the services, among the active duty and selective reserve, or even among different units within an individual service was going to be impossible," admitted Major Steve Maurmann.[69]

Even more elusive was an accurate documentation of the early returns from the Gulf for pregnancy—or for any reason. The Army didn't have a central personnel system in the Gulf until late in the war, and even then did not collect data on early returns.[70] Despite David Hackworth's unequivocal claim in *Newsweek* that the equivalent of two battalions of pregnant women had been evacuated, no statistical evidence supported the charge. Zero.

The only hard number on early returns came from the medical evacuation channels, which initially reported that 77 Army women had been medically evacuated from the Gulf for pregnancy. The number of evacuees for "pregnancy associated diagnoses" was later raised to 81, well below the 207 Army women who were medically evacuated for orthopedic injuries, including two amputees.[71] But the low number of documented OB/GYN early returns, which would often be used by servicewomen's advocates to ridicule military concern about pregnancy, was just as incomplete. In fact, no one had any idea how many men or women had returned early from the Gulf.

"There were all sorts of reasons why personnel were leaving —family emergencies, legal issues, pregnancy," confided a Defense

Department spokesman. "Very few field commanders kept records. If a female said she was pregnant and had the medical documentation, they just said, 'Get on the next plane.' We came up with an early return rate of 2 percent for males, 2.5 percent for females. But it's all guestimates."

The Pentagon statisticians were still wrestling with their calculators a full year after the end of the Gulf war. The members of DACOWITS were waiting with increasing impatience for the DOD's promised historical data on women. The murmurs grew louder among the members of DACOWITS that the DOD was suppressing the data. It was too positive toward women, ran the most popular theory. The delay was a high-level conspiracy to withhold evidence during the heightened debate over the repeal of the combat exclusion laws.

The shocker came at the DACOWITS spring meeting in April 1992. The long-awaited DOD report on women was still not ready for release, Major Maurmann explained to the members, because of the difficulty he was having incorporating the pregnancy data, data the members were only vaguely aware of.

A hush fell over the room as Major Maurmann began his preliminary briefing on the comparative rates of male and female nondeployability with an apology for the unscientific manner in which the numbers had been collected. Then he dropped the gender bomb. The figures gathered in the eighteen months since the war showed that women had been over three times as nondeployable to the Gulf as had men in each of the services. The chief cause was pregnancy.

"Our problem is how to present the conclusion of the report so it is not saying more than what the data tells you," Maurmann told the stunned members. "We don't feel comfortable with the data we have. The numbers [on pregnancy] are big enough that it can show you trends, but that is all it can show you."

The Marine representative to DACOWITS added her own apology. The search for hard information on deployability so long after the fact had proved impossible for the Marine Corps. "We went out with a message, in some cases, literally months and months after units had returned from Southwest Asia and we said, 'Count up all your people, tell us who went, who couldn't go, who returned early,'" said Marine Major Karen Heck. "The generals who were actually over there, like General Krulak and General Draude, started taking exception as the reports came in. 'Who said this?' they asked.

'You're asking people who in some cases aren't even still with that unit to now go back and physically find and reconstruct what happened a year ago.' We have very little confidence in the numbers that came back. Our numbers are not good. And we know that."

The servicewomen at the DACOWITS meeting saw through the preoccupation with pregnancy. Though the number of women in uniform had grown steadily since 1973, women, whether pregnant or not, were still a small minority in the overall force. The impact of pregnancy on the military's total readiness was microscopic. "We hit a buzzer every time we hit the pregnancy issue," Lieutenant Colonel Kelly Hamilton told DACOWITS. "The question is: Did pregnancy affect readiness? If it didn't, why are we having this conversation?"

Such logic was lost, however, in the temporary gloom settling over the DACOWITS conference as the word spread about women's nondeployability rates, rumored to be as high as four times that of men in the Navy. More important to Maurmann was damage control.

"How we word the report and how the press takes that information and turns it into something to print, that's what we're really concerned about and that's why it's taken us so long to produce a report that we can release," said Maurmann, who professed to be on his fourth rewrite.

His concern turned out to be well founded. At the height of the debate over women in combat, someone in the Pentagon leaked the damaging report to the most conservative newspaper in Washington. On July 28, 1992, the day the internal report was officially presented to its DOD mentor, Christopher Jehn, the *Washington Times* had the story all ready to go on its front page. The message was not subtle.

"Women Fall Short on Battle Readiness" bannered the headline. "Pregnancy cited as major factor."[72] Instead of providing the platform DACOWITS had counted on to advance women, the pregnancy report in the *Washington Times* article and accompanying front-page chart of women's nondeployability rates in the different services signaled the conservatives' longed-for call to retreat.

There, trumpeted inaccurately by journalist Rowan Scarborough as "the rate at which soldiers, airmen and sailors were not ready to deploy when ordered," were the DOD's nondeployability data, now engraved in stone: 1.5 percent of Navy men compared to 5.6 percent of Navy women; 2.7 percent of Army men compared to 9 percent of Army women; 1.8 percent of Air Force men compared to 6.4 percent of Air Force women. Only the Marines refused to play the shaky numbers game. The article noted that while the Marines sent 952 women to the Gulf, the corps didn't "conduct a gender-based study of deployability."[73]

Pentagon spokesmen scrambled to set the nondeployability figures in context. The number of Army women who actually fell short on battle readiness was "so small," a senior Army officer was quoted, that "it was not a red flag to me. . . . The non-deployable rate is not a war-stopper." A spokesperson for the Navy agreed that pregnancy had not affected that service's readiness, either. "Our data show that and Desert Storm showed that," she said.[74]

Servicewomen's opponents took the same figures and elevated pregnancy to an issue of national security. "If the [services] think this is acceptable, I don't think it is, especially if you're going to put women in combat positions," the *Washington Times* quoted Elaine Donnelly, who had become a one-woman Maginot Line to thwart women's move into combat. "I think it's very significant when commanders have to rely on them [women] being there in times of emergency, but then see unexpected losses."

In the ideological furor over pregnancy, few noticed the General Accounting Office report on deployability, which threw out every pregnancy statistic provided by the Pentagon. Released a month after the completion of the Jehn Report, the GAO dismissed the data on which the Pentagon numbers were based as not only "incomplete" but worse, based on subjective "best recollection." "An accurate total number of nondeployable personnel in Operations Desert Shield and Storm could not be determined because military personnel data bases did not have complete and consistent information," read the GAO report.[75]

More critical to the GAO than women and pregnancy was the agency's identification of three "sizeable problems" of nondeployable personnel. Dental problems, not pregnancy, were cited by the GAO for the nondeployability of 33 percent of personnel mobilized in three National Guard combat brigades. Poor physical condition and insufficient training knocked out fully 42 percent of medical personnel activated by the Army. Lack of training was the major reason as well for the nondeployability of nearly 23 percent of personnel assigned to units in one Army Reserve Command.[76] In the grander scheme of the military mission, pregnancy and women weren't even worth noting.

"The whole issue of pregnancies in the Gulf is a red herring," says General Tom Jones, former director of human resources for the Army. "Pregnancy is really an issue only in forums like DACOWITS and in the press by media people who would like to make a big issue of pregnancies allegedly occurring in the Gulf. Pregnancy did not in any way inhibit our ability to prosecute the war in Southwest Asia. The rate of nondeployables because of pregnancy was what we anticipated it would be. It is not an order of magnitude problem."

The credibility of the Defense Department's figures on women's nondeployability was diminished further by another GAO report released in July 1993. Directed to Defense Secretary Les Aspin and titled *Women in the Military—Deployment in the Persian Gulf War,* the GAO researchers avoided the impossible numbers game and instead convened focus groups from ten military units that had served in the Gulf.[77] The service members' perceptions, the GAO report posited, reflected the perspective of a "broad cross section" of military personnel in all the services on "key issues" related to women in the military.[78]

Sure enough, pregnancy headed the list of service members' reasons for women's nondeployability and early returns from the Gulf.[79] When pressed for details, however, the focus groups were often unable to back up their pregnancy convictions with firsthand knowledge. "Group participants generally identified few actual instances of women that did not deploy because of pregnancy," the GAO report stated.[80]

The focus groups had just as much difficulty justifying their perceptions about pregnancy and the alleged high number of women's early returns. According to the GAO report, ". . . participants in the same or separate groups from the same unit could have been, and often appeared to be, referring to the same case." The report cited six survey participants from one military unit who seemed to agree that two women had returned early due to pregnancy, giving rise to the multiplication factor. "It appeared from the discussion that group participants were referring to the same 2 people and not to 12 separate people," the report stated.[81]

The GAO's investigation of the Gulf pregnancy factor shed no new statistical light but illuminated the weight of military myth. "The groups GAO talked to cited pregnancy as a cause for women returning early from deployment or not deploying at all, but the groups generally identified few actual cases," the report concluded.[82]

The one incontrovertible fact about pregnancy to come out of the Gulf war was its disproportionate importance. The "temporary disability" hardly made a dent on the successful deployment of 541,425 U.S. troops to the Gulf. The overall nondeployability rate for the total force was some 3 percent, well under the 5 percent safety margin set by military guidelines.[83] The 316,000 troops deployed by the Army, over 30,000 of whom were women, reflected a nondeployability rate of only *3.1 percent.*

What amounted to a "witch hunt" for pregnancy in the Gulf ended up straining the unit cohesion so valued by the services. Commanders of some Army units were so nervous about fraternization and pregnancy they relegated women to social isolation, ordering them not to have any interaction with their male colleagues during their off-duty hours. Other commanders sought refuge in the Saudi system of purdah, one insisting that the men and women in his unit be separated in recreational facilities, another counseling a servicewoman "for spending too much time with men, despite the fact that there were no other women in the unit."[84] In at least one Air Force unit, the first sergeant threatened his enlisted female troops with punitive action if they tested positive for pregnancy. "A lot of women were told if they got pregnant, they'd get an Article 15," says Air Force Sergeant Sue Soto.

The pregnancy wars would not abate as a political issue outside the military or as a cultural problem within. Solutions remained elusive, especially in the Navy. A pilot program coming out of the Navy pregnancy studies and a spin-off survey of civilian sex education programs seemed very promising when it was tested among young Navy personnel in 1990 and 1991. Instead of continuing ineffective sex education programs, which did little more than identify body parts and birth control devices, the Navy's pilot program sought to change the behavior of recruits by teaching personal goals and values.

Three years later, however, the Navy's "Personal Values and Relationship Course" was still being tested and had yet to be implemented in the fleet. "There was a lot of concern at the senior level that the Navy was getting into areas they didn't belong in, in terms of saying what was right and what wasn't right," says retired Navy Captain Martha Whitehead. "They have difficulty dealing with pregnancy. It's just not something they're comfortable with."

The admirals seemed paralyzed by pregnancy. As women drew

closer to serving on combat ships after the Gulf war, one Pentagon solution was to get rid of pregnant women altogether. "They want the contract of service to read, 'If I get pregnant, I will be immediately discharged from the U.S. Navy,' " says a senior enlisted woman in the Pentagon.

Short of breaking the pregnancy discrimination law, another Pentagon proposal from a Navy captain was to raise the ages of all female, but not male sailors, assigned to sea duty. "He proposed that no woman should be sent aboard ship under the age of twenty-one," said the Navy's Pentagon representative. " 'Screw it,' he said. 'Let's not send anybody aboard ship until they're a little more mature and won't get pregnant.' "

A proposal from senior Navy women to spread pregnancy accountability to men didn't even make the Pentagon agenda. "If the male were held equally responsible, it would certainly slow down the pregnancy rate," says Captain Whitehead. "We talked about that, but it never got very high in the scheme of things."

Women would remain the target in the military pregnancy wars. Though one of the Navy's own studies had identified over 70 percent of the pregnancies among the most junior, single Navy women to have been caused by military men, and of those pregnancies, 91 percent by Navy men,[85] it would be those same young women who were identified in another Navy study as "the focus of many of the negative attitudes towards pregnancy."[86] The Army, too, would continue to point the finger at women. Though an Army review of 409 "pregnancy incidents" found that "at least" 49 percent occurred among single enlisted women, and the vast majority (87 percent) at their "current unit of assignment," the problem was identified solely as the "pregnant soldier."[87]

It was women alone who would continue to bear the stigma of pregnancy in the services, just as women alone would bear the burden of parenthood.

5

THE POLITICS
OF DIFFERENCES

Military Motherhood, Public Opinion and Congress

THE PICTURES of military mothers kissing their children goodbye were heart wrenching. And during the buildup of U.S. troops in the Gulf, they were everywhere, on the front page of the *New York Times,* the covers of national magazines like *Parade* and *People,* state magazines like *Minnesota Monthly* over the cover line "When Minnesota Moms Go to War."[1] To a nation already absorbing the culture shock of uniformed women being ordered into a potential war zone while able-bodied young men stayed home, the sight of military mothers voluntarily leaving babies as young as six weeks old unveiled a new and disquieting reality in the modern military.

Gone, with the end of the draft, were service exemptions for parents, all of whom, historically, had been male. Defense Secretary Dick Cheney had successfully applied for and received a 3-A draft deferment as a soon-to-be father in 1966 during the Vietnam call-up,[2] but his All-Volunteer Force offered far fewer deployment exemptions for fathers or mothers. The new obligations of volunteer personnel, the Defense Department insisted, were the American way.

"Expecting the same sacrifices of all military members, married or single, with children or without, is the only understandable and fair policy and one which is consistent with the American tradition of equality," Christopher Jehn, the assistant secretary of defense for force management and personnel, would tell Congress.[3]

The public was not so sure. Shortly after the first U.S. troops departed for Saudi Arabia in August 1990, the Pentagon and its congressional overseers unexpectedly found themselves on the defensive in what was dubbed the "Mom's War." And before the first shot was fired five months later, the children of deployed single mothers and married military parents would be known as "Gulf war orphans."

In fact, the number of service parents sent to the Gulf was very low. Of the deployment of over 500,000 service members, only 1,799 were military couples with children.[4] Of the 17,000 active-duty single parents deployed to the Gulf, single fathers outnumbered single mothers three to one.[5] Simply by numbers, the more apt title attached to the full-scale debut of the All-Volunteer Force should have been the "Dad's War." But the spotlight was on mothers. Were mothers going to war the reward of gender equality or the price?

The scales, at first, were tipped toward the reward. An early cover story in *People* was titled "A Mother's Duty" and featured the stories of six service mothers and one fifty-year-old grandmother, in or about to go to the Gulf.[6] The service mothers, among them a Marine weapons system technician and two Air Force pilots, sounded as gung-ho as Norman Schwarzkopf. "I've trained seventeen years to do this," said Lieutenant Colonel Kelly Hamilton, the most senior of the 315 active-duty female pilots in the Air Force. "It's not that people love to go into conflict, but it is rewarding to have your training pay off."[7]

The grandmother, an aircrew nurse in the Air Force Reserve and a Ph.D. from the University of Wisconsin, was as resolute. The photograph of her striding across the tarmac in her flight suit, her posture so determinedly erect she seemed to be leaning backwards, was as empowering to female readers as her no-nonsense message. "I'm a patriot—I was born on Memorial Day—and I love a challenge," said Major Marian Sides, who was flanked by her equally staunch daughter and granddaughter. "I'm ready to go."[8]

For a fleeting moment, women both in and out of the services who had fought the constraints of maternal stereotyping were elated. Instead of service mothers being criticized for leaving their children, they were being praised for having made an equal or even greater sacrifice than service fathers answering the same call to duty. A giant step forward seemed to have been achieved for womankind.

In the early euphoria of the deployment, traditional gender roles merged. Not only were uniformed women going off to do men's work, the men left at home with the kids also were doing women's work. And nobody seemed particularly bothered. The father of two and husband of a Navy nurse deployed to the hospital ship USNS *Comfort* described himself cheerfully as "a survival cook."[9] Another father, whose wife had voluntarily reenlisted in the Army after Operation Desert Shield began, coped alone with the emergency hospitalization of their eleven-month-old daughter while also keeping house, caring for an older child and holding down a full-time job. The experience changed his preconceptions about gender roles. "I guess it all depends on the father," said Gregg Nordin, a twenty-four-year-old robotics operator. "But I know single dads can do as good a job as single moms. I know they can because I am doing it."[10]

To women's advocacy groups, both inside and outside the military, the initial acceptance of male and female role reversals was welcome and critical. Advocates of equal opportunity have long known that interchangeability of father/mother roles is essential to downplay a mother's indispensability to her young children and thereby allow her to pursue a guilt-free life outside the home.

Indeed, paralleling women's move into the labor force, a body of developmental psychology opinion had supported the resiliency of children to bond with any loving and concerned adult. While not discounting the emotional attachment between mother and child, the new theories questioned the exclusivity of that relationship.

The theories, however, had yet to be tested in a modern military conflict. Little research on the effects on children separated from their parents by war had been done since World War II, and at that, the absent service member was almost always the father. There was no research on a child being left by a married service mother, a single parent of either sex or both parents to go off to war.

The media's anecdotal probe of the service mother phenomenon was unsettling. One three-year-old daughter of an Air Force major walked into her father's bedroom just sixteen days after her mother left for the Gulf and threw up on the bed. "I want to call up Mommy and tell her I'm not feeling good," the little girl cried.[11]

Another wave of poignant news stories about children circulated when George Bush authorized the first call-up of units in the Selected Reserve on August 28, 1990. The new round of stories focused on children as old as thirteen being so acutely depressed they refused to get out of bed. And the initial support for service mothers began to erode.

By the time the skies lit up over Baghdad on January 16, 1991, and Operation Desert Shield turned into Operation Desert Storm, military motherhood had become a national crisis. Amidst predictions of chemical and biological warfare, constituent mail demanding the recall of single mothers and one member of married service parents piled up on congressional desks.

On January 18, California Congresswoman Barbara Boxer, a new member of the Armed Services Committee, wrote Defense Secretary Dick Cheney "with the utmost urgency" to plead that he issue an immediate Defense Department directive or regulation permitting single parents or one parent in a dual-career couple the option of returning home "to prevent their children from also becoming victims of the war." Cheney didn't respond.

Cheney knew, as did the generals along the E-ring at the Pentagon, that the U.S. forces in the Gulf couldn't afford to lose any service members. Despite the Army's "stop-loss" deployment policies at the outset of the operation that saw leaves canceled and retirements postponed, the Army still had a critical shortage of trained truck drivers, helicopter pilots, medical personnel and Arabic speakers. As many as 1,500 civilians were already in the Gulf filling in as air traffic safety controllers, engineers, electricians and communication specialists.[12] The Pentagon needed more personnel, not fewer, in the Gulf.

On the day Boxer wrote her letter to Cheney, Bush authorized the Pentagon to mobilize more units in the Ready Reserve and, more significantly, access to the Individual Ready Reserve. In this as yet untapped pool of inactive, backup reservists, who were neither attached to any units nor on any military payroll, were many with the skills the services urgently needed. As military computers began to print out the names fitting those skills, concentrating on the 70 percent who had left active duty within the last twelve months and therefore requiring the least retraining, the military ran head-on into a public relations disaster.

In widely circulated news stories, two Pennsylvania women in the Individual Ready Reserve whose husbands were already serving in the Gulf were involuntarily recalled to active duty under impossible circumstances. One woman who was about to give birth was given only ten days' leave to report for active duty or face charges of going AWOL. The other woman, who received notice of her activation while she was in the hospital recovering from a caesarean section, was granted only a fifteen-day delay.[13] Though subsequently both women were granted six weeks' maternity leave, the country was stunned.

But the computer continued to print lists of individual ready reservists, of whom a far higher percentage sought deferment, delay, deletion or exception from recall to active duty than did their Selected Reserve counterparts. Over eight hunded requests from individual ready reservists were logged in at the Army Reserve Personnel Center, most based on pregnancy or parental responsibility. Though 750 would be considered documented hardship cases,[14] the military procedure was to evaluate each request on a case-to-case basis, a laborious process given the volume, which left involuntarily recalled women in limbo for up to four weeks. Knowing the effect public embarrassment had on the military, some of the mothers took their case directly to the media, with sometimes unintended results.

Sara Davis Waters, a recalled Army aircraft electrician with a two-year-old daughter and a husband already serving in Saudi Arabia, was making her high-profile plea either for an exemption or a Stateside assignment on Larry King Live when the eighth caller turned out to be Prince Fahd Bin Salman from Saudi Arabia.[15] Prince Fahd, the vice governor of Saudi Arabia's Eastern Province, offered to take care of Waters's daughter at his Saudi compound if the Army sent her to the Gulf or, if she preferred, to pay the expenses for a "nanny." "This is a crazy show," King said, before going to the ninth caller.

But the involuntary separation of mothers and children, especially those whose husbands were already scattered around the Saudi desert, upped the ante a critical notch. Where the first women to go voluntarily to Saudi Arabia had been cast as heroines, the involuntary recall of mothers cast whole families as victims.

"Before we knew it, there was legislation on the floor saying mothers couldn't go to war," says Nancy Duff Campbell, co-president of the Women's National Law Center in Washington. Spearheaded by Congresswoman Boxer, no fewer than six House and Senate bills were introduced into the 102nd Congress by the end of January 1991 to bring home single parents and one member of dual-career parents from the Gulf and exempt them from future combat deployments. Sixty-four percent, or two out of three respondents to an Associated Press poll, agreed that it was "unacceptable for the United States to send women with young children to the war zone."[16]

"Our righteous insistence that 'a deal is a deal' is disturbingly reminiscent of the story of Rumpelstiltskin, the dwarf in German folklore, who exacts a terrible price for helping a desperate young woman—her first-born child," said Pennsylvania Senator John Heinz, a bill sponsor whose constituents included the two individual ready reservists recalled to active duty while still in hospital maternity wards.[17]

The members of DACOWITS were alarmed at what could be a serious setback for servicewomen. The news stories about reluctant service mothers culminating in possible legislation sent the executive committee of DACOWITS to the Pentagon for a briefing on deployment policies. Satisfied that the services were dealing more fairly and compassionately with individual cases than the media had reported, the executive committee unanimously adopted a resolution supporting the deployment of parents, including single mothers. "We believe combat readiness cannot be guaranteed without the full complement of forces in time of crisis," the DACOWITS resolution read in part.[18]

The legislative threat to impose a military "Mommy track" and restrict servicewomen's career opportunities drew women in civilian activist groups to a rare meeting with military women held at the Women's Research and Education Institute (WREI) in Washington. "I thought it was important for the women's groups to hear from military women how the deployment policies for mothers worked rather than how they were portrayed in the press," says Carolyn Becraft, then WREI's military policy consultant. "Did the military women favor Boxer's attempt to change the status quo? They did not."

Becraft's original impetus for the educational seminar had been the combat issue highlighted by Linda Bray and Operation Just Cause in Panama. Repealing the laws would require a working alliance between women in the military who did not identify with civilian feminists and civilian women who did not identify with the military. Establishing the gender network, however, was essential for servicewomen who did not have a natural civilian constituency lobbying on their behalf. So was gaining the support of the civilian women, many of whom had come to their activism via the civil rights movement and the antiwar protests of the 1970s. "They were uncomfortable about the military," says Becraft.

The mother issue proved to be the catalyst for NOW, Business and Professional Women (BPW) and the National Women's Law Center. "The women's groups all came motivated by Mommy Goes to War," says Becraft. "The press beat that reluctant mommy story to death, and it was always the same two women from Pennsylvania." To her relief, the women's groups signed on as service mothers' civilian advocates. "Our effort was to keep it from being legislation. Then it's much harder to deal with," says Nancy Duff Campbell.

Servicewomen were incredulous that the legislative debate was taking place at all. The notion of exempting single parents or one member of a military couple or any able-bodied person from deployment worldwide was anathema within the military culture. "There are already avenues for parents to get nondeployable jobs within their career fields if they want them," says Army Captain Laurie Barone, a tactical officer at West Point and married mother of three. "But if you're in deployable jobs, you've both got to be ready to go."

The officers were insulted by the presumption that service mothers needed government protection from the duty they had volunteered for. "Our government trusts us to take responsibility for hundreds of personnel and millions of dollars' worth of equipment, but this legislation is saying we're not capable of making decisions for our own families," says Air Force Lieutenant Colonel Hamilton, who spent close to seven months in the Gulf.

To senior officers like Hamilton, the legislation signaled the beginning of the return to an unwelcome past. Until 1975, women in the military weren't allowed to have families at all. Though they could marry, women were involuntarily discharged for motherhood, even stepmotherhood.

Many senior women who had entered the services in the 50s and 60s and were retiring in the 90s hadn't married at all. "In order to do something about having a family, you had to throw away the career. And for some of us, that was hard to do," says Gail Reals, who joined the Marine Corps enlisted ranks in 1954 and retired as the Marines' only female general in 1990. "For twenty years of my career, it was a sort of separate but not equal environment."

The change in policy came too late as well for retired Brigadier General Evelyn "Pat" Foote, who joined the Women's Army Corps in 1960 at the age of twenty-nine. "I never set out not to marry and not to have children," says Foote. "I just had an all-consuming Army career. By the time the policy changed, I was well beyond what I considered the years that I would want to be the bearer of children."

General Foote and her contemporaries in all the services had been constrained by an executive order signed by Harry Truman in 1951 which decreed that a pregnant servicewoman or mother should not remain in uniform, but "devote herself to the responsibilities which she has assumed, remaining with her husband and child as a family unit."[19] The services were authorized to discharge any woman who had a natural or adopted child under eighteen, was the step-mother of a child who lived in her household for more than thirty days a year or was pregnant.

Women, even senior officers, who wanted to marry a divorced father or a widower with children and keep their jobs had to prove to military authorities they could handle both their domestic and military obligations before being granted waivers to the mandatory discharge policy. Fathers, whether married or single, faced no institutional inquiry into their ability to balance work and care for their biological or acquired children, including many Vietnamese orphans.

Civilian mothers who wanted to enter the services faced particularly severe restrictions. In order to qualify for enlistment, the women had to give up legal custody of their children; once in the military, they could visit their children but not live with them. For two decades, Truman's thirty-day-a-year limitation on servicewomen "domiciling" children was a lawsuit waiting to happen. In 1970 it did.

To Captain Tommie Sue Smith, a lawyer in the Air Force Judge Advocates Corps and the divorced mother of an eight-year-old boy, her orders to relocate to the Philippines but to leave her son behind were "blatantly inequitable." Based then at Andrews Air Force Base, near Washington, D.C., where, the Air Force captain told the press, "We have a general . . . with eight kids and his wife isn't with him,"[20] Smith had already undergone considerable personal sacrifice to satisfy Air Force regulations.

She had followed the customary smoke screen for military motherhood by giving up legal custody of her son in order to join the Air Force's legal branch in 1966. She had also placed her then four-year-old son in a nearby boarding school to fulfill the thirty-day-a-year maternal-housing restriction. When the Air Force cited the thirty-day restriction again as the reason she couldn't take her son with her to the Philippines, though widowed or divorced fathers regularly took their families, Smith filed suit in September 1970, claiming the restriction violated her equal protection under the Fourteenth Amendment. But Smith wouldn't get her day in court.

The Air Force, which retired Air Force Major General and military historian Jeanne Holm claims was already on the verge of lifting the restrictions against mothers with minor children, changed its policy against Air Force motherhood the day after Smith filed her suit.[21] The other services capitulated to motherhood in 1975 when the services lifted the ban on pregnancy.

The hard-won right for women in uniform to enjoy the same family lives as men moved the services from the traditional bachelor force to a married force with children. By the onset of the Gulf war, the armed forces were home to 70,456 service members married to each other, 46,888 with children.[22] The active duty military was also home to 76,238 single or divorced parents,[23] though it was not clear from the Pentagon's statistics how many divorced parents actually had physical custody of their children or were responsible for child-support payments; the Pentagon's cost-conscious figures merely reflected those who were eligible for dependents' benefits.[24]

The transition to a family force was inevitable because the longer tours of duty required of highly trained modern military personnel coincided with their childbearing years. While male draftees in the Vietnam era served two-year tours of duty, the All-Volunteer Force signed up personnel for three-, four- or even six-year tours in advanced technical skills and paid them bonuses to reenlist. The force aged dramatically as a result. The average age of enlisted military volunteers had risen to 26.7 by the onset of the Gulf war in contrast to nineteen among draftees of the Vietnam era. Over half (55 percent) of modern enlisted personnel were married. So were 75 percent of male officers and 50 percent of female officers.[25]

It was to the advantage of the All-Volunteer Force to encourage marriage, especially for men. A married force was more stable than a bachelor force and less prone to disciplinary problems and drug and alcohol abuse. A serviceman whose family was happy with military life and satisfied with military support systems was also more likely to reenlist.

And so the pro-marriage and pro-family programs flowed out of the Pentagon to sweeten the incentives for long-term service. "To keep the morale high and the force operating at peak efficiency, the Department of Defense developed programs to meet family needs that, in the past, were never considered," read a 1991 DOD information paper. "The Department was meeting the competition of the private sector."

The housing benefits, combined with family medical care and travel expenses for dependents, made the All-Volunteer Force a mecca for very young families. Forty-five percent of Army men twenty-two years old or younger were married by 1985, compared to 22 percent of their civilian counterparts. Army women married at twenty, their civilian counterparts at twenty-three. Almost half the 1.6 million children of personnel throughout the services were under six. "Either the military attracts persons already prone to getting married and having children early or the military compensation package induces such behavior," wrote Lieutenant Colonel Connie Reeves in a study of dual-service and single parents after the Gulf war.[26]

The family benefits made the services a particular mecca for single parents; in 1989 there were proportionately twice as many single parents in the Navy as in the civilian population.[27] Unlike their civilian counterparts, single parents in the military received free prenatal, obstetrical and pediatric care along with a plethora of other support systems including subsidized child care, schooling, housing and dependents allowances. Their children benefited as well. Service children could join on-base youth, summer, after-school and summer job programs as "baggers" in base commissaries, and church retreats.

Single fathers were especially drawn to the services by the family support programs, creating a sociological phenomenon. While single parents in the civilian sector were overwhelmingly female, male single parents in the military considerably outnumbered female single parents.[28]

The discovery of this phenomenon in the Navy during the congressional upheaval over the deployment of single mothers created a bit of theater during a DACOWITS meeting in the fall of 1991. The young male Navy staffer setting up charts for a briefing on single parenthood was excited to the point of stuttering over the facts about to be revealed. "Ladies, you're going to love this, love this, love this," he said. "We've found there are twice as many single *fathers* in the Navy as there are single mothers!" The numbers masked the reality, however, that since men greatly outnumbered women in the military, there were proportionately many more single mothers than single fathers: 12.5 percent of women serving on active duty were single parents in 1992 compared to 2.9 percent of men.[29]

The Navy had tried to stall the influx of single parents in the late

80s by declaring custodial parents ineligible for enlistment. Single parents without custody recruited for the Navy were required to sign a statement that if they regained custody of their children, they would be "discharged for fraudulent enlistment." But recruiters either ignored the directive or the enlistees lied. A 1992 Navy study found that virtually all the recently enlisted single parents interviewed for the study had their children living with them.[30]

It was the single mothers, not the fathers, who drew attention within the military. And it was all negative. In an extension of the war against pregnancy, single enlisted mothers were blamed for every military sin from "lost time," their projected inability to deploy to the perceived burden they placed on job detailers. Though detailers spent over six times as much time trying to find joint assignments for the 24,000 enlisted personnel married to each other, single mothers remained close to untouchables in the military caste system.[31]

Army commanders didn't want them in their companies. Navy chiefs didn't want them in their work details. Single mothers trained in specific skills were often assigned instead to insignificant desk jobs or other non–career-enhancing jobs, then watched like hawks. While 50 percent of civilian service wives were working by the time of the Gulf war and sharing time-consuming child chores with their active duty husbands, nobody noticed. "This guy in my unit takes time off to take his kid to the doctor and everyone says, 'Oh, isn't he wonderful,' " says one single mother. "I take my kid to the doctor and my supervisor marks it down as time lost off the job."

While single fathers tended to have more than one child, including stepchildren and adopted children, and cost the services more in terms of benefits and services, those same benefits were universally criticized when received by single mothers. Echoing the sentiment that marks the debate over single welfare mothers in civilian society, single military mothers, too, were accused of scamming the system.

Little or no credit was awarded single mothers for making a better life for themselves and their children in the military than they could in the civilian world. The services provided a strong family environment for children to grow up in and, in contrast to most civilian employers, gave their single parents job training, education and financial stability. Single mothers in the military were very proud of their ability to support their children. "I have all the love and more to give my child," says an Army sergeant and mother of an eleven-year-old boy. "I have a job. I'm taking care of myself and I can take care of him."

The bias against single mothers added intense pressure on them to do well. In the Army Reserve, such pressure often translated to greater motivation and performance. "We have more and more competent women in the reserves, especially single mothers," says Colonel Darrald Hert, an Army chaplain now retired who was activated during the Gulf war. "They're not just weekend soldiers. They need the money and they really want to be there and make it work."

Making it work was increasingly difficult for service parents. Though the Defense Department provided subsidized child care for 154,152 children under five in 1992 at close to 400 preschool programs on military bases, there were still over 60,000 children on the waiting lists. The Pentagon estimated that even with the reduction in forces, the number of eligible children could more than double by 1997.[32]

Parents lucky enough to get their children into on-base centers faced a catch-22. Army parents in one division were expected to report for physical training at 5:30 a.m., but the child care center didn't open until 6:30 a.m. The center closed at 6:30 p.m., well before the division workday ended. And there was no day care on weekends when many personnel were required to work. "The centers are still gauged toward normal civilian workdays and are inadequate for military schedules," says Captain Laurie Barone, whose three children were in day care at West Point. "The centers aren't funded to meet military needs. It's all about money."

The waiting list for child care was so long in the Navy for babies between six weeks and a year—an average of twelve months—that the babies were often pretoddlers (twelve to twenty-four months) by the time of admission. Older children fared no better. As the buildup of troops in the Gulf began in 1990, there were twice as many children on waiting lists at the Navy's child development centers than there were children being cared for.[33] "The famous quote is: 'If you were meant to have children, they'd have been issued in your sea bag,' " says former Marine Barbara Alt.

Such family frustrations were driving both enlisted women and officers out of the military. For all that the services had hoped to stem the flight of women in the "manpower" crisis of the 70s by granting waivers to pregnant women and mothers to stay in uniform, support systems lagged behind. Both enlisted women and female officers cited family concerns as one of the primary reasons they left the services at higher rates than men, especially after their second tour of duty. The reenlistment rate among women dropped by 69 percent once they became mothers.[34]

Though the difference in the attrition rate was much smaller among male and female officers, it was still higher for women.[35] "Many women leave midcareer between major and captain," says Army Captain Dee Weeder. "They want to marry and have babies. And they're tired of fighting the male attitude that 'you don't belong here. We'll tolerate you but we don't have to like you.'"

The women who chose to combine military careers and motherhood went to extraordinary lengths to make it work. In Germany, one Army mother on a Reforger field exercise in the 80s nonetheless kept her baby supplied with breast milk. "She somehow got her milk back from the field to her baby-sitter," says Liz Carey, a former Army officer and West Point graduate who had two children herself while in Germany. "That takes courage."

Other service mothers accepted the most difficult assignments to disprove the assumption they wouldn't. Navy Captain Jane O'Dea, the senior woman in Navy aviation and the mother of two, spent only two weeks at home the year her children were four and seven, and during the next two and a half years was gone twenty days a month. "It's been very, very difficult," says the twenty-one-year Navy career officer who spent the Gulf war in Washington assigned to the Directorate of Space and Electronic Warfare. "But I'm not sure it's that different from other career women who chose to be mothers. But it was very, very tough to deploy like I have."

The pressure was greatest on service couples. "When you have military married to military, there's always a tension," says former Air Force Captain Deborah Gill. "Can you be stationed together or will you be geographic bachelors? What will happen to the children if you both deploy? How realistic are your child care arrangements?"

On paper, the military seemed to have provided a workable policy for the rapid deployment of service parents. Military couples and single parents were required to file both short- and long-term family care plans (FCPs) in the Army, or dependent care certificates in the Navy, for their children or dependent parents with their unit commanders. The certified package included temporary transfer of custody, powers of attorney for a named legal guardian and the guardians' notarized certificates of acceptance, ID cards, escort designation and financial instructions. In the Army, the short-term plans took care of field training exercises. The long-term plans were open-ended.

The Gulf war exposed the depth of the family fault lines in all the services. Air Force parents who were given only a few days' deployment notice or, at best, a few weeks turned out to have their short-term plans in order, but not their long-term ones. Many Navy parents didn't have plans at all. The same Navy study that identified the lack of adequate child care for Navy parents found that 89 percent of single and dual-military enlisted parents serving overseas and 82 percent stationed in the United States did not have valid child care forms in September 1990, one month *after* the U.S. troop buildup in the Gulf began. Only 28 percent had any dependent care certificates in their service records at all, a finding the study found "disturbingly low."[36]

The fault lines were deeper in the reserves and the National Guard, in which barely 20 percent of activated parents had completed the paperwork for their children to receive free medical care.[37] Almost forty years had passed since the last major call-up of the reserves for the Korean War. Many modern reservists had been born after the Korean conflict and had not seriously considered that they would be activated. Like the Navy supervisors, Army Reserve commanders had put family care plans for single and military couples at the bottom of their priority lists. "The lack of preparation was widespread," says retired Colonel Hert, who was assigned to the 63rd U.S. Army Reserve Command covering southern California, Arizona and Nevada. "In our region, less than one-third of reservist parents had family support plans in order. We got them in order."

Activated parents on the West Coast scrambled to find caretakers for their children, some of whom were on the East Coast. Parents, children and caretakers crisscrossed the United States during the call-up. Unit commanders and parents made deals. The mother in one activated reserve couple ended up going to the Gulf after a substitute was found for the father. In the end, only two or three parents under Hert's purview were held back from deployment because they couldn't fulfill their family support programs. But the debut of the family force was chaotic.

Had the crisis required the immediate deployment of the reserves, Hert says, the outcome might not have been as positive as it was in the Gulf. "Mercifully, we had a five- to six-month lead time before Desert Storm. We got everybody prepared to go. But it was a real heads up."

The fault lines showed as well in the military support systems for the families left behind. The services' primary concern was less for the well-being of the children than for the ability to "work" any family problems at home and thereby keep up the morale and job performance of the parents in the field. "Soldiers perform better when they know their families are being taken care of," said Captain Barbara Goodno, an Army spokesman during the Gulf war.

Since the Civil War the annals of military psychology had targeted families as a significant factor in the will and competence of soldiers to fight. What became known in World War II as "combat fatigue" was called "nostalgia" during the Civil War, evoking the overriding feeling of homesickness which led "nostalgia" sufferers to either fight less effectively or, in the extreme, to desert.[38]

The Israelis had found that troops with high levels of concern for their families increased their chances of becoming casualties; even homesick soldiers without families were thought to increase their vulnerability. Aboard Navy submarines the condition was called "Channel Fever," though the consequences weren't as dire. Thoughts about home and family were believed to contribute to feelings of fatigue and depression.[39]

The unprecedented number of single and dual-military parents leaving their families to go to the Gulf added an urgency to the first combat-related test of family support systems. "It was a command concern from the beginning," says Hert. Hours were lengthened and volunteers recruited to man the Defense Department family centers on nearly four hundred installations worldwide. On individual bases, youth groups held letter-writing sessions and developed family videos to send to the Gulf, while church groups organized dinners and supplied free baby-sitting and a network of volunteers to clean houses.

Unit-based groups like the Marine Key Wives and the Navy Ombudsmen supplied support to families, while on-base mental health clinics provided counseling for children and the parent left behind. Service members who weren't deployed set up telephone chains and organized other forms of help to the families in their units and squadrons. "There was one young mother whose car broke down and we got it fixed, and another who couldn't make her car payments and we took care of that," says an Air Force flight officer who was pregnant and couldn't deploy with her squadron. "We had picnics for the kids, drove them where they needed to go. We turned ourselves inside out. When the guys came back, they hugged us. Their wives had told them what we'd done."

The family support systems broke down, however, for the many children scattered among caretakers not on military installations and therefore out of the loop. More than half of the single and dual-military parents in one postwar Air Force study were found to have sent their children to caregivers more than 150 miles from the base. Though the family centers estimated that they responded to 3.3 million phone requests for information and gave help to 8,240 of the temporary guardians during the deployment, the centers were solicited by only one-third of the caregivers. Two-thirds of the guardians didn't know what help was available.[40]

Family support systems were as uneven for parents in the Gulf. Army regulations declared the telephone the first and sometimes successful route for resolving family emergencies. "We arranged a phone call between one eight-year-old girl who needed an appendectomy and her mother in the Middle East," says Hert. "The daughter told her mother she didn't need to come home, that she'd be fine."

It was the arbitrary and capricious power wielded by commanders in granting up to thirty days of emergency leave to personnel to cope with family crises that left some servicewomen embittered. "Messages for women from the Red Cross were not acted on," says Victoria Hudson of her Army Military Police battalion. "One woman who was married to a Vietnam vet was notified he had had such violent flashbacks watching the war on television that he'd been admitted to a VA hospital on a suicide watch. But her commanders wouldn't let her even call for two weeks. Another woman whose ex-husband had taken her children out of state was so worried she spent a lot of time crying. But instead of getting counseling, she was told she'd have to leave the unit. Still another woman whose children were essentially kidnapped and taken to Puerto Rico was denied emergency leave. But a command sergeant major was given emergency leave because his ex-wife died. And the token soldier the commanders chose to send home early was a male sergeant who wanted to go to a wedding."

The bias against women was no different in the Army's Combat

Aviation Brigade. To the disgust of the personnel sergeant who handled all the Red Cross messages and requests for emergency leaves for the entire brigade, emergency leave was granted to a male sergeant whose teenage daughter had run away from home but was denied to a mother whose intact family care plan had deteriorated during the deployment. "The female had documentation that her mother had to have surgery and that her aunt, who took the children, had to have back surgery as well," says the sergeant first class. "But while they let the first sergeant go home based on a phone call from his wife, they wouldn't let the mother go back on emergency leave to take care of her documented child care problem." Instead, the battalion commander initiated action to involuntarily discharge the mother for having an inadequate child care plan.

The few female commanders in the Gulf tended to be more sympathetic. When a Minnesota mother received word through the Red Cross that her eleven-month-old daughter had been hospitalized and was in an oxygen tent, she was given emergency leave by her commander, who also had an eleven-month-old daughter. The Army mother spent a week with her recovering daughter, then, over the protests of her husband, voluntarily returned to active duty in the Gulf.[41]

Other mothers, too, returned briefly to the United States to settle family emergencies. One divorced Army mother of three found herself in an unexpected custody fight for her children with her ex-husband's family during her deployment. "She was notified her mother-in-law was trying to get permanent custody of the kids on the grounds she was an unfit mother by abandoning her kids to go to war," says an Army lieutenant. Because she was facing legal action, her commander allowed her emergency leave to return to the States. She, too, returned to the Gulf after winning the case and making other arrangements for child care.

In the end, the military concern over the nondeployability of single and married parents turned out to be unfounded. Despite the public perception that vast numbers were either unable or unwilling to deploy, *less than one-half of one percent* of the 23,000 single parents and 5,700 service couples with children detailed to the Gulf were unable to go because of family reasons.[42] Indeed, a postwar GAO study of readiness in the reserves found that single parents had a *better* record on deployment than the yearned-for bachelors without children.[43]

Activated doctors and lawyers kept the fax lines humming between Saudi Arabia and the Army's 63rd Reserve Command. "They had a lot of financial problems," says Hert. "Many couldn't make their rent payments. Some had to let their staffs go." Few of the faxes involved mothers. "We got a call from one soldier at 3 a.m. asking us to go check on his wife," says Hert. "He was convinced she was having an affair."

Family care plans held up better than the impression left by news stories. Of all the reasons cited for the early return of women from the Gulf, the least frequent found by congressional investigators was a deficient child care plan. And among the personnel who had to return early from the Gulf for reasons of "family hardship," a far higher percentage were men.[44]

Deployed mothers weren't the problem, either, to the commander of a Navy ship sent to the Gulf; the problem was the "dependents," both male and female, remaining at home. "We were on a ship in Norfolk after the war and the commander told us that he'd received over a hundred messages from the Red Cross the first two weeks they were out at sea," says a military representative to DA-COWITS. "Do you know who the calls were from? They were all from the spouses who had been left behind and couldn't cope. While the public spotlight was on military mothers, it should have been on the military fathers who'd left eighteen-year-old wives with babies at home and foreign wives who couldn't speak English."

"Dependents" were a problem in the Army as well. The Army's own history of the Gulf war documented the young wives left behind who "had never driven a car, paid a bill, or balanced a checkbook." Even if they had mastered such skills, some young wives didn't have access to their husbands' bank accounts—or their cars. "Some soldiers put their cars in unit lock-ups when they left because they did not want their wives to drive them," read the Army's official history. Foreign wives were particularly vulnerable. "One soldier locked his foreign-born wife into their trailer with three weeks of groceries and no plans for a longer deployment," reported the history.[45]

Children, on the other hand, fared far better than expected. Ironically, it was the service children in traditional families, an Air

Force study found, who had more discipline problems and more
trouble sleeping during the deployment than did the children from
either single parent or dual-military families—a reflection, presumably, of the anxiety exhibited by the parent remaining at home. But
even at that, the problem rate was low. The most common problem
among children, trouble sleeping, occurred to only 28 percent.[46]

In contrast, the problems with children in single parent and
dual-military families were greater *after* the war. While children in
traditional families returned to their predeployment problem levels,
the other children continued to have a higher rate of discipline and
sleep problems. Again, the percentages were quite low; 19 percent
of the children in dual-military families continued to have trouble
sleeping, while 17 percent of the children in single parent families
continued to have discipline problems. Some but not many relationships (16 percent) between parent and child were weakened by the
length of the deployment, especially in single parent families.[47]

The new and unexamined factor in children's distress levels was
television. The images of exploding buildings and severed bridges
brought service families at home directly into the combat theater.
"They watched the crisis, then the war unfold; they watched the
rocket attacks as they occurred. And all the while, they knew their
loved one was in harm's way," observed Ellin Bloch, a clinical psychologist in Cincinnati who, together with four colleagues, tracked
active duty and reserve families for ten months during and after
the Gulf war. Psychologically, service family members, too, became
"combatants" and were just as likely to develop the symptoms associated with "combat stress" as were the military veterans, the study
concluded.[48]

The Gulf war took a toll as well on Army parents who were
involuntarily discharged in 1991 at record rates for "parenthood."
More than three times as many enlisted fathers and seven times as
many enlisted mothers were discharged in 1991 as in 1990, the
gender difference undoubtedly reflecting the bias against single
mothers. Other mothers rethought their military obligations after
the Gulf war and voluntarily left the Army at record rates. While
fathers evidently felt little conflict between war and children and
actually resigned in lower numbers at the end of 1991 than they had
the previous year, 982 Army mothers would resign by the end of
1991, an increase of 22 percent over 1990.[49]

Air Force parents, too, were having second thoughts. In an Air

Force study, a "significant" number of single (26 percent) and dual-military parents (30 percent) expressed a "drop in commitment to the military" in the aftermath of the Gulf war. Not surprisingly, modern service parents turned out to be just as susceptible to feelings of "nostalgia" as had their counterparts in the Civil War. The Air Force personnel who missed their children the most were the most likely to feel less committed to their service. So were the parents who felt their squadrons had not been supportive of their families. Overall, the percentage of single parents who had felt very committed to the Air Force before the Gulf war dropped 14 points after the war. Among dual-military parents the drop was 22 percentage points.[50]

The mommy-goes-to-war issue disappeared from public consciousness as quickly as the hundred-hour ground war. Because of the low casualty count overall, little was made of the recorded deaths of single parents, estimated by the Pentagon to be five fathers and one mother. The single mother, presumably, was Army Staff Sergeant Tatiana Dees, the first woman to die in the Gulf.

The legislation restricting the deployment of single parents and one member of married military parents also vanished. Though the House of Representatives passed Congresswoman Beverly Byron's legislation deferring both male and female parents with children under six months, the bill was killed in the Senate Armed Services subcommittee on personnel by Senator John Glenn.[51] Glenn's reason concerned the codification of the exemption rather than the voluntary internal reassessment of deployment policies by the military, but the bottom line was any exemption for fathers. "The parenting issue was never about women," says a congressional staffer. "It was always about men."

On May 26, 1991, a month after the formal cease-fire in the Gulf, Byron quietly resubmitted her legislation, this time dropping men and limiting the deployment exemptions to servicewomen. Offered this more palatable military solution, the Pentagon voluntarily altered its own policies. In new servicewide regulations issued that August, all married or single mothers with babies under four months old were given the option not to deploy to areas that were classified as "dependent restricted." No deferments were offered to the 49,819 single fathers on active duty.[52]

Military observers like Martin Binkin at the Brookings Institution expressed cautious optimism that the issue of military mothers, especially single mothers, was settled. The fact that the public was now aware of the number of single parents and married couples in uniform, combined with "the Pentagon's revisions of assignment regulations, should resolve the issue," Binkin concluded in his postwar tract *Who Will Fight the Next War?*[53]

At the National Women's Law Center, Nancy Duff Campbell was not so sure. "I'm not sanguine about the new policy," says Campbell of the four-month deferment offered to women, but not to men. "The question is: is four months an appropriate 'disability period'? The law in this area has always permitted there to be policies exempting women during the period of 'disability,' but most physicians talk about that period being six weeks."

The possibility of service fathers legally challenging what could be considered a "parenting" period granted exclusively to service mothers and thereby shortening maternal exemptions back to six weeks concerned Campbell. "I think it would be nice if men had the same four-month deferment, too," she says. "But I think there are arguments to defend the policy as it is, even as limited to women."

Congressional unease about military mothers and news accounts of pregnancy as a deployability factor would provide ongoing leverage, however, for women's opponents. While the Coast Guard would demonstrate the value it placed on both mothers and fathers by inaugurating parental leaves of absence in 1991, conservative forces within and without the military services would continue to use pregnancy and motherhood to devalue servicewomen.

In the heat of the debate over women in combat in 1992, a presidential commission would ignore the Pentagon's four-month grace period for deploying service mothers and instead issue recommendations on family policies that effectively ended a woman's career. Pregnant women as well as personnel with debilitating injuries like broken legs would be removed from units with the highest deployability ranking and be temporarily reassigned to a unit with a low deployability probability.[54] But while personnel whose broken legs had mended would resume their normal duties, mothers would not.

One recommendation called for single parents with custodial care of their children to remain in nondeployable positions until the children were "school-age." Another would force one "parent" in a dual-career couple to resign. The most radical option called for the eventual voluntary or involuntary discharge of all single and dual-service parents at the discretion of their commanders.[55]

The commission's purported rationale for the draconian measures was to reduce the number of children "subjected to prolonged separation or the risk of becoming orphans during deployment," but the underlying thrust in the post–Cold War drawdown of the military was to return the services to an all-male force. "They are saying let's just get rid of them," said Pat Schroeder.[56]

The hard-line approach struck a chord in the services. While increasingly dependent on women volunteers, the services did not want the characteristics that distinguished them from men. "If the military needs women, but does not want pregnant women or mothers, and does not allow abortions, about the only alternative left is to accept lesbians," concluded one servicewoman.[57]

Such ambivalence about women put the services on a collision course with the reality of their presence. The wars against pregnancy and motherhood exposed by the Gulf war were just smoke screens for the deeper division between the military genders. At its core, the conservative male culture hated women within its ranks.

6

THE MILITARY CULTURE
OF HARASSMENT

The Dynamics of the Masculine Mystique

" 'HEY, TELL ME about the pussy,' " says a supply sergeant to an Army warrant officer in Nelson DeMille's best-selling 1992 novel, *The General's Daughter*. The warrant officer, who is about to arrest the supply sergeant for trafficking military supplies, gives the sergeant the answer he wants to hear. "Well, I got me a little slopehead 'bout as tall as a pint of piss, and I just pick her up by the ears and stick her on my dick, then slap her upside the head and spin her 'round my cock like the block on a shithouse door.' " The supply sergeant roars with laughter.[1]

Though fictional, DeMille's story of the gang rape of a female cadet at West Point and the investigation of her subsequent murder embodies many of the male attitudes ingrained in the military culture —the institutional promotion of male dominance, the aura of hypermasculinity, the collective male imperative to disparage women in general and specifically women in the military. "They squat to piss. Try doing that with sixty pounds of field gear," grumbles a DeMille colonel at the bar in the officers' club before ambling off to the men's room.[2]

Projecting the fictional colonel's attitudes onto all men in the military would, of course, be a stereotype as inaccurate as it would be sexist. Many individual men in the different services work well with women and respect both their contributions and authority. But individuals don't count in the military. The military culture is driven by a group dynamic centered around male perceptions and sensibilities, male psychology and power, male anxieties and the affirmation of masculinity. Harassment is an inevitable by-product.

If the Freudian observation is true that the tenets of masculinity demand man's self-measure against other men, military service offers the quintessential paradigm. The services revolve around competition and graded contests, the results of which are publicly displayed on servicemen's chests. Servicemen who have proved their measure against a historically male enemy by earning combat ribbons and badges, prisoner-of-war medals and the Purple Heart are the models for military masculinity. Though a study of infantrymen in World War II found that only 15 percent ever fired their weapons in combat[3] and that fewer than 15 percent of the hundreds of thousands of military personnel who served in Vietnam are estimated to have been in a firefight[4] the minority of men set the model for the masses.

Short of experiencing combat, men in the most high-risk specialties define the masculine edge—the Navy SEALs, the 82nd Airborne, the Special Operations forces whose classified missions are shrouded in secrecy. "When you're around the 82nd Airborne or the Rangers, you can smell the macho, feel it, hear it," says Tod Ensign, director of Citizen Soldier, a civil liberties organization based in New York. "To be called 'STRAC' (Straight, Tough and Ready for Action) is a great compliment. That means you're ready to jump out this window, rappel down the side of the building and kill someone with a pencil."[5]

Military aviators are high on the masculine role-model scale. The entire Air Force exists to support the 3 percent who are pilots. In the Navy, fighter pilots fly off nuclear-powered aircraft carriers manned by crews of five thousand. So admired are fighter pilots that their recognition transcends enemy lines. When Germany's World War II Luftwaffe ace Adolf Galland died in 1996, his obituary merited four columns and a photograph in the *New York Times*.[6]

The aviator mystique grew around the early test pilots like Chuck Yeager, who, despite two broken ribs, flew what was little more than a primitive rocket straight up into the heavens in 1947 to become the first man to break the sound barrier. *"Manliness, manhood, manly courage* . . . there was something ancient, primordial, irresistible about the challenge of this stuff, no matter what a sophisticated and rational age one might think he lived in," writes Tom Wolfe about the pilots in *The Right Stuff*.[7]

The legend lingers in the almost erotic male worship between young men, competitive men, daring men. The love affair between the hero of the film *Top Gun*, played by Tom Cruise, and his girlfriend was secondary to the sexual tension between Cruise and a rival pilot vying for the Navy's top flying spot. The sexual payoff of the film was not between Cruise and his girlfriend, but in the clenched fist hug between the two men. Similarly, the payoff in *Independence Day* was the victory cigars shared between a Marine pilot and a computer scientist after they had destroyed an alien spaceship, not the embraces of their wives. "The military is a sexual fantasy built around images of masculinity," observed writer Nancy Chapkis at an international symposium on women and the military system in 1987. "Only other men can pose a sufficient threat and a sufficient challenge to serve as worthy objects of desire."[8]

Images of the ideal male play throughout the military culture, where men spend more time in the company of men than in any other institution save prison. Dress uniforms in the Marines are designed to set off the male body, to accentuate the slimness of the waist, the breadth of shoulder, the length of leg. Male vanity is understood in the military. "I can see why the Defense Department sent you," a retired general remarked matter-of-factly to a young Air Force officer at a 1992 hearing. "You're so handsome."

The image is especially important in the officer corps. During the Pacific campaign in World War II, Douglas MacArthur had his pants custom-pleated below the waist to make him look slimmer, and his hat heightened to six inches above the brim to make him look taller.[9] Army officers stand unflinching, and unprotected, in snow or rain. By policy, male (but not female) officers are not allowed to carry umbrellas. Even ears make the man. Among the disqualifying physical characteristics for candidates to West Point listed in the 1992 admissions catalogue were disfigured or uneven ears as well as "moderately severe acne or resultant scarring" and other "unsightly congenital markings."[10] "There used to be a medical regulation that ruled out ugliness," says Colonel Pierce Rushton Jr., West Point's director of admissions. "Extreme ugliness was a disqualifier."

Arrogance flows naturally from the institutional promotion of the alpha male. The symbolic power inherent in the uniform, in the weaponry and in the national license to resolve conflict by violence encourages military men to cast themselves as superior to their civilian counterparts. "It's very macho the way men see themselves as unique or special," says Tod Ensign. "One of the most important and guarded myths of the military is the necessity to maintain that hyped-up sense of maleness."

Psychiatric literature is steeped in the various passages young men feel they have to take to get away from their mothers and, by extension, all things feminine, to establish a masculine identity. Among militaristic cultures, the passage to manhood can reach epic proportions. In one legendary tribe in South America, young warriors went so far as to cut out their nipples to remove any resemblance to the female form.

The U.S. military practices its own exorcism of men's sexual duality or feminine "negative identity."[11] Thirteen years after women were integrated into the All-Volunteer Force, Marine Corps drill sergeants were still purging male recruits with a "torrent of misogynist and anti-individualist abuse," writes conservative icon George Gilder. "The good things are manly and collective; the despicable are feminine and individual."[12]

Though Gilder and his conservative ilk like sociologist Lionel Tiger are universally debunked by feminists as reactionary misogynists—author Susan Faludi scorns Gilder for "bemoaning the loss of traditional manhood in society"[13] in her 1991 best-seller, *Backlash*—Gilder's description of "the extirpation of feminine ties and sentiments" in the Marine Corps remains a contemporary catechism to many men in uniform. "When you want to create a solidaristic group of male killers, that is what you do: you kill the woman in them," he writes.[14]

The methods were more subtle in the other services, but the underlying premise remained the same: the way to pump up masculinity was to tear down femininity. Army drill sergeants in the early 90s still humiliated lagging male recruits by calling them "sissies," "crybabies" and "girls." "So are we having menstrual cramps this morning?" one drill sergeant at Fort Jackson, South Carolina, derided a male recruit struggling with push-ups.

The same techniques were applied to female recruits to drive out their "femaleness." "You wuss, you baby, you goddamn female," was the 1991 strategy shouted at a company of female recruits, also at Fort Jackson. So antithetical to the military culture is anything feminine that the reverse psychology backfired when practiced on female recruits at the former Naval Recruit Training Center in Orlando, Florida. "You boy!" a female company commander screamed at the occasional female straggler during the 5 a.m. formation run around the paved "Grinder." Against the backdrop of male recruit companies simultaneously jogging around the Grinder, the intended pejorative sounded more like a compliment.

The masculine forces driving the military culture made the enforcement of sexual harassment policies impossible. The systematic denigration of feminine attributes in the making of a military man required the very harassment the directives were supposed to eradicate. If the measure of a man was in his contrast to a woman, then she, by definition, had to display the feminine attributes for which she was derided.

Women could be "militarized," but not so much as to threaten masculine self-confidence. Women in the Army were trained to use weapons, but assigned to support units, not male combat units. Women recruits in the Marines received less training time than the men, as did female pilots in the Navy and Air Force; additional combat training was reserved for men.

The gender line never wavered. While male recruits' heads are ritually shaved in all the services to submerge their individual identities into the male collective, women are required to wear their hair "in an attractive, feminine style,"[15] not longer than their uniform collars, but not so short as to appear mannish. Male Marine recruits are instructed in the application of combat camouflage, female recruits in the application of cosmetics.

"Women Marine recruits receive instruction in hair care, techniques of make-up application, guidance on poise, and etiquette," read a Marine recruit training manual for women in the wake of the Gulf war.[16] The corps even issued an official Marine lipstick to its female recruits in boot camp.

The Marine justification for the cosmetic feminizing of its female recruits underscored the separate roles for the sexes deemed necessary in the military culture. "This program is designed to give you self-confidence *and improve your ability to function as a Marine,*"[17] the section in the woman's manual on "Professional Development" concludes (emphasis added), thereby assigning female Marines the role of feminine standard-bearers by which male Marines could offset their masculinity.

Imperative in all the services was the buttressing of men's real or imagined sense of virility. A Marine platoon graduating from recruit training in 1989 proudly posed with their drill instructors for their formal photograph holding a blown-up picture of a naked woman and a hand-lettered sign reading "kill, rape, pillage, burn." [18] A poster of nude pinup girls plastered the interior wall of a Marine tank gunning down Iraqi tanks in Kuwait.[19] "Male sexual imagery has always been important in combat units," said Dr. David Marlowe, a social anthropologist and chief of combat psychiatry at the Army Institute of Research.[20]

The collective forces at work in the military culture demand women's marginalization. Accepting women as military peers is antithetical to the hypermasculine identity traditionally promoted by the institution and sought by many military men. Only by excluding women or denigrating them could men preserve their superiority.

The accumulating directives from the Defense Department on sexual harassment were supposed to change all that. Taking its lead from the Equal Employment Opportunity Commission, which in 1980 had expanded the definition of gender discrimination to include sexual harassment as a violation of Title VII of the Civil Rights Act of 1964,[21] the Defense Department had issued its first policy declaration that harassment was "unacceptable conduct" that would not be "condoned or tolerated in any way." [22]

By 1981, all the services had issued their first formal definitions of sexual harassment which included "unwelcome sexual advances [and] requests for sexual favors," and creating "an intimidating, hostile, or offensive working environment."[23] Sexual harassment awareness and prevention was added to existing programs on human relations. "For the first time, sexual harassment was treated as a different and separate form of discrimination, just like race, age, religion and national origin," says former Air Force Colonel Mickey Collins

But nothing changed. By 1990, after DACOWITS had finally pressured the Defense Department into documenting the extent of sexual harassment in the services, it was epidemic. Two out of three women in the Defense Department study of 20,000 personnel reported experiencing at least one form of harassment in the past year, including pressure for sexual favors (15 percent) and actual or attempted rape (5 percent).[24] "The results are sobering," said Christopher Jehn, the assistant secretary of defense for force management and personnel.[25]

The Navy had not reached its goals first stated by the 1987 Navy

Women's Study Group and, of necessity, repeated in 1990 to (1) "Eliminate sexual harassment practices in the Navy" and (2) "Create a professional environment predicated on mutual respect,"[26] because it couldn't.

The architects of the All-Volunteer Force had concentrated on the effect women would have on men, not the effect men would have on women. The influential 1977 Binkin-Bach study advocating women as a personnel resource devotes only two paragraphs to what little was known about tokenism, whereas three pages are reserved for warnings about menstruation.[27] Similarly, the study expresses no major concerns about the as yet unexamined behavior of men in groups. "At the outset, it is important to point out that an understanding of the behavior and performance of *men* in groups, particularly under combat or sea-duty conditions, is far from complete . . . and precious little is known about the effects of combining men and women," the authors concede.[28]

Civilian academics and writers studying the group dynamic in the 80s cast a wide net, chronicling the behavior patterns and the perceived demands of "masculinity" in such varied male groups as sports teams, college fraternities and Little League. Virtually every characteristic pinpointed as unique to men in groups was rampant in the military culture. And every one of them fit the definition of sexual harassment.

Crude jokes and sexually demeaning talk about women, a group dynamic observed by Freud as directed *against* women by men in groups, but more sexual and clever when directed *toward* women, was the bonding mechanism among fraternity "brothers" studied on one college campus by Professor Peter Lyman, director of the Center for Scholarly Technology at the University of Southern California.[29] Reducing women to sex objects was considered essential to forging close fraternal bonds. "The group separated intimacy from sex, defining the male bond as intimate but not sexual and relationships with women as sexual but not intimate," observed Lyman.[30]

Talking "dirty" about girls and "faggots" was the group mechanism used by boys on ten Little League teams to prove their budding heterosexual identities.[31] Women, even among this subculture of preadolescent boys, were perceived as a threat to the integrity of the all-male group. "Girls can easily break the bonds of brotherhood among boys," noted Gary Alan Fine, a sociologist at the University of Minnesota.

In a prelude to the sexual exhibitionism of Navy pilots at the Tailhook convention in 1991, the preadolescent boys' aggressive pranks like "mooning" passing cars were always performed in the presence of the male group and, if successful, gave the boys group status.[32] Such male-to-male displays served to wean out the wimps in the male group and establish a leadership hierarchy based on daring. Just a few boys set the behavior standards for all, a group dynamic which would also play out at Tailhook.

The widespread display of pornography in male cultures from locker rooms to military bases was found by other researchers to further reinforce the separate and superior male position sought by men in groups. To many gender analysts in the 80s, pornography represented the greatest barrier to sexual equality by making sexism sexy. "Pornography institutionalizes male supremacy the way segregation institutionalizes white supremacy," writer John Stoltenberg told a 1984 conference on men and masculinity in Washington, D.C.[33]

In the extreme, the male group dynamic crossed the line into criminality. A study of twenty-six gang rapes reported between 1980 and 1990 revealed that men who raped in groups were already members of closely knit male collectives. None of the fifteen reported gang rapes by college athletes between 1989 and 1990 involved athletes in solo sports like swimming or tennis, but rather team sports like football, basketball and lacrosse.[34] The negative group dynamic was no less powerful in the military.

The forces which drove college athletes to rape as teams in 1990 paralleled the forces that had driven U.S. soldiers to rape as platoons in Vietnam. The civilian males were young, as were their military counterparts. Each group spent their time almost exclusively in all-male subcultures—sports teams trained, competed and traveled together; military units patrolled, ate and lived together twenty-four hours a day. The success of each group depended entirely on teamwork: in the case of sports teams, to win; in the case of military units in Vietnam, to survive. Under such intense pressure, the demands of the group often overrode personal morality, individual conscience and the law.

Among the college students and soldiers alike, men who

wouldn't dream of raping a woman on their own raped in a group. "They only do it when there are guys around," Susan Brownmiller quotes a Vietnam veteran in her classic book *Against Our Will: Men, Women and Rape.*[35] In the gang mentality which would play out in the group molestation of women at Tailhook, the victims were incidental to the act. The men in Vietnam were raping for each other.

Even men who didn't take direct part in the sexual assaults were bound by the group dynamic. Some participated by taking photographs, as did soldiers involved in the violence surrounding the My Lai massacre in March 1968, during which over three hundred men, women and children in one village were killed between breakfast and 10:30 a.m.[36] Others practiced passive participation by remaining silent. In a forerunner to the stonewalling of investigators following Tailhook, a sergeant in Vietnam reacted to his squad of nine men raping a woman by going to another part of the village where he sat by himself, staring at the ground.[37]

Whether military or civilian, the grip of brotherhood overrode all. "There has never been a single case, in all the gang rapes we've seen, where one man tried to stop it," reported Gail Abarbanel, director of the Rape Treatment Center at Santa Monica Hospital in California. "It's more important to be part of the group than to be the person who does what's right."[38]

Women were little more than trophies in contests of male dominance. Navy fighter pilots at the Tailhook convention would sport T-shirts reading "Women Are Property," and affix squadron stickers to various parts of women's anatomy. In Vietnam, at least one woman's body was found spread-eagled with a brigade patch between her legs. Other women's bodies were found with their vaginal access blocked by entrenching tools, grease guns or grenades.[39] Sexually assaulting women was such a universally accepted by-product of military male behavior that it would be 1996 before rape was defined as a war crime by the International Criminal Tribunal in The Hague.[40]

In such a group-driven male culture, the sexual harassment directives from the Pentagon were doomed to sink like stones. The group dynamic which in the extreme drove the gang rapes by soldiers in Vietnam and athletic teams on college campuses stepped down only by degrees to the hanging of pornographic pictures of women in locker rooms and barracks and down again to the dirty talk and male initiation rites deemed so essential to bond fraternity brothers and even Little Leaguers. It was a bonding dynamic the military well understood.

While the civilian sector was just beginning to be educated on the dynamic of men in groups, the U.S. military had been exploiting it, unchallenged, for two hundred years. And rather than being seen as negative, the dynamic was positive.

The coarse, sexually demeaning language that bonded men in college fraternity houses multiplied out in the services to bond men in platoons, squadrons, companies, whole divisions and fleets of men. "We find ourselves cursing and swearing every two seconds," says Gloria Johnson, a Navy airman at school in Orlando in 1991. "That's all you really hear out here, instructors, everybody. You just get used to it. My first day at boot camp, our company commander said, 'If my language offends you, fuck it, you're just going to have to put up with it.' "

At the military academies, each service boasted its own repertoire of WUBA jokes, an official Navy acronym for "Working Uniform, Blue Alpha" issued for the first class of female midshipmen at the U.S. Naval Academy, but commonly understood as "Women Used By All." Freud would have delighted in the classic WUBA jokes unabashedly greeting women midshipmen at the Naval Academy as late as 1990.

"How are a WUBA and a bowling ball similar?" Answer: "You pick them up, put three fingers in them, and throw them in the gutter."

"What's the difference between a WUBA and a warthog?" Answer: "About 200 pounds, but the WUBA has more hair."[41]

The verbal denigration of women served a useful military purpose. In times of sharper gender divisions, vulgar language and profanity had been traditionally restricted to men. Its excessive use in the military culture served as both reminder and reinforcement of a separate male society with its own language and rules. And so, despite sexual harassment policies, the language continued.

Equally resistant to the sexual harassment policies were the sexually explicit and aggressive cadence calls which drill sergeants and company commanders had used to motivate their troops on training runs and twelve-mile road marches since the Civil War. The psychology of cadence calls was the timeless essence of male bonding.

In World War II, the cadences had been racist as well as sexual, the twin package of bonding criteria researchers would find in the 80s among all-white male fraternity groups and the members of the Little League. One vintage cadence call began: "LEFT! LEFT! Had a good job when I LEFT!/ LEFT my wife with eight nigger babies,/ Hay foot, straw foot . . . ," the latter referring to the technique drill sergeants used to help rural recruits identify which foot was which —hay tucked into the laces of the left boot, straw on the right.

Sexual aggression was pumped into the young men in 1944 as it would be fifty years later. The World War II regimental song of the 342nd Infantry began: "We're Colonel Heffner's raiders/And we're riders of the night;/ We're horny sonsabitches,/ We'd rather fuck than fight." The message was as collectively inspiring as it was loud. "Imagine three thousand men, 90 percent of us boys under twenty-one and a good many of us still virgins, marching along singing this," recalls Clement Wood, an Army private at the time. "I guess it made us feel tough and manly."

In the less innocent days of the Vietnam era, cadence calls became known in the Army and Marines as "jodies," a generic term defined admiringly by one drill sergeant as "a stud who's sleeping with everybody's girlfriend while they're working." But the basic message of male dominance was the same. "I wish all the ladies were piled on the shelf, and I was a baker—I'd eat 'em all myself," starts "Heybobareba," a classic jody still "called" in 1995 in the Marines.

To the men's great pleasure, jodies derided sentimentality as a hated sign of "feminine" softness and extolled "masculine" aggression. "There's a yellow bird with a yellow bill, sitting on a window sill. I lured it in with a piece of bread, and then I STAMPED its little head," was a West Point favorite in the 70s, accompanied by the synchronized stamping of cadet boots at the matching word.[42]

Midshipmen at the U.S. Naval Academy in Annapolis drilled to particularly graphic cadence calls. One classic extolled the sexual prowess of a downed, but hardly defeated, pilot. "Climbed all out with his dick in his hand/Said, 'Looky here, ladies, I'm a hell of a man.'/Went to his room and lined up a hundred . . . /Swore up and down he'd fuck everyone./Fucked ninety-eight till his balls turned blue/Then he backed off, jacked off, and fucked the other two."[43]

The young men loved the jodies. That servicewomen and female officer candidates did not made the calls even better. The women were kept in their inferior place while the men were maintained in their superior one. So the sexual harassment directives to clean up the jodies and to return to the more formal term of "cadence call," were spotty at best and met in at least one Army unit in the 90s with insurrection.

"The men shouted down the guy calling the politically correct cadence. It got ugly," says a drill sergeant who trained infantry soldiers at Fort Benning, Georgia, in 1992. "They wanted to hear how the man is masculine over the woman and that's what we sung to them and that's what maxed their PT tests. The response was tremendous whether I was running soldiers five miles or walking eighty people in a line down the street singing that or 250 soldiers in a company. The dirtier the better. It got results."

Equally ignored were the Pentagon directives to denude the military workplace of pornographic posters, *Playboy* centerfolds and other prominently displayed sexual erotica. Though the salacious depiction of women clearly fit the service and EEOC definitions of a "hostile work environment" shared by both sexes, men were not about to relinquish their sexual authority. "When I asked my boss to take down the pornography in our office because it was fueling male sexual discourse in the workplace and causing fractionalization, he told me I was too straitlaced," says former Air Force Captain Patricia Gavin, who subsequently filed a complaint about the harassment going on at the Fort Benjamin Harrison Defense Information School in Indiana in 1991. "You would have thought I'd asked for the Red Sea to part."

Go-go dancers and strippers continued to be prime entertainment at on-base service clubs, despite Pentagon directives to end the practice. Not only did the clubs depend on strippers and prostitutes to attract money-spending males, the strippers also reinforced the masculine collective. Unlike the ambiguous roles played by modern servicewomen, there was no end to the positive role played by exotic dancers and prostitutes.

The shared male delight in publicly exhibiting their collective libidos transcended rank, race and ethnic backgrounds, reaffirming the bonds among men. Strippers were also seen as safe. While other women might strike a romantic relationship with one of the men and thereby break the bonds of brotherhood, a paid commodity, especially of another race, was not a threat.

In the Philippines, servicemen at the now defunct Subic Bay

Naval Station regularly sought the services of the "hospitality girls," as government officials called them, or "little brown fucking machines," as Navy sailors called them. For $10, servicemen could simultaneously enjoy lunch, a cold beer, and a blow job performed by a Filipino woman on her hands and knees under the table.[44]

Strippers were no less essential to the male collective in Korea. "When I left Korea in 1992, the whole unit threw a party," says an Army senior personnel specialist. "The commander danced with a stripper. The first sergeant danced with a stripper. I danced with a stripper. That was the top command level in the biggest aviation unit in the Army. There's no way you're going to change the military climate. It's a tradition."

The services had known everything there was to know about sexual harassment, and subsequently failed to control, since 1980. Members of DACOWITS were becoming increasingly convinced at the time that the hostile male atmosphere toward women and attendant sexual harassment were invisible, and unaddressed, factors in servicewomen's high attrition rate.[45] The advisory committee had heard too many stories on too many bases. "Where we experience it [harassment] is when we go out as individuals to visit a military installation and we meet with enlisted personnel," said Sally Richardson, the 1979 chair of DACOWITS. "We are very often seen as a channel for this kind of information."[46]

Congresswoman Marjorie Holt, the ranking minority member and only woman on the House military personnel subcommittee in 1979, was equally suspicious of the unexamined effects of sexual harassment on the morale and retention of servicewomen. As the number of women entering the services multiplied, so did the number of complaints swamping the Maryland Democrat's office from nearby Fort Meade, an Army base in Holt's congressional district.

What neither DACOWITS nor Holt knew was whether sexual harassment was as widespread in the services as their anecdotal evidence suggested or just concentrated in pockets. The services, which had documented everything negative about women from the lesser strength of their handgrips to their inability to do as many push-ups as men, had not expressed the slightest interest in tracking obstacles to their well-being. "Gender discrimination and sexual harassment were not issues in the 70s. Race was," says former Air Force Lt. Col. Mickey Collins, then an equal opportunity officer.

There were no records of harassment or assault in the 70s because virtually every sexual humiliation, great or small, was silenced or condoned by the male chain of command. When Diana Danis, executive director of the National Women Veterans' Conference in Denver, was raped four months after she joined the Army in 1973, her company commander had told her she would ruin the young sergeant's career if she pursued the "issue," and to forget the assault.[47]

Barbara Franco didn't even bother to report her second abduction and rape in August 1975. When she had reported being raped and stabbed in the arm by three men wearing dog tags during a weekend pass from Fort Lee, Virginia, her first sergeant had asked her, "What did you expect? You're not even wearing a bra," and ordered her out of his office.

Reassigned to Fort Hood, Texas, where the rape rate was so high that 6th Air Cavalry assault helicopters flew nightly patrols over the base, Franco had been raped again after the erroneous announcement at morning troop formation that enlisted women could not bring charges of rape against enlisted men because "rape was incidental to military service for women." So Franco didn't tell anyone after she was abducted by two men while walking to the motor pool, taken to a remote area of the base and "repeatedly sexually assaulted and tortured" until she escaped six hours later. Instead, she told a post–Gulf war congressional subcommittee, she tried to kill herself by taking an overdose of Valium.[48]

Women in all-female barracks were easy targets. Though the separate women's branches in the Navy, Army, Air Force and Coast Guard were being phased out in the 70s as women were integrated into the regular force, on most installations servicewomen were still housed separately from their units. "It gave the men one location, one prime area, to do whatever," says Sergeant First Class Vennie Hilton, who joined the Army in 1975. "We had rapes in Hawaii."

The violence was so intense at a "Wacshack" in Germany in 1979 that one Army woman spent her own money to live off base in an apartment. "I came back from flying one day to find the building locked down and MPs in the hallways," says a combat aviation mechanic known as Dragon Lady. "It turned out two women had been murdered and left in the shower, one strangled, the other impaled on a broomstick. I never went back inside. We weren't even safe in our own building."

It had been no different in the continental United States. At Fort

Devens, Massachusetts, in 1975, men from a field artillery company regularly climbed over the fence surrounding the female barracks and into the windows, sometimes accosting the women in their racks while they slept. One night the female barracks sergeant armed the women with baseball bats and positioned them by the windows. "I organized a full-staged combat incident and we bloodied the hell out of those assholes," says former Army Captain Tanya Domi, who used to carry a baseball bat for protection in the motor pool and a butcher knife in the field. "It was no way to live."

Women faced some degree of sexual humiliation every day. In the Navy, female recruits were ordered to dig trenches for their breasts before doing push-ups; their breasts were said to give them an advantage over men in lessening the distance they had to raise themselves on their arms. In the Army, women were forced to wear very short exercise shorts for physical training. Drill instructors calling the cadence for the "leg-spreader," a stomach muscle exercise which requires prone recruits to hold their legs off the ground and open and close them, often held the cadence while the women's legs were spread apart, then stood in front of them and stared. "We asked repeatedly for bigger shorts or the permission to buy them for ourselves. But they said, 'No. These are the only size. Wear them,' " recalls Sergeant First Class Ann Marie Fleming, one of five women among sixty men at an NCO primary leadership course in 1978.

The male chain of command had said no as well to the young women when they reported a male instructor for using his master key to come into the women's rooms. " 'If you want to graduate you will not submit this report,' " the commandant told the young women the day before graduation. The women had withdrawn their written statements.

Instead of protecting servicewomen, male chains of command often exploited them. In Maryland in the late 70s, one private first class listened incredulously as an Air Force colonel offered her as a prize to a group of student pilots. "He said, 'I'll give you an incentive. Anyone who passes their checkride the first time can have a weekend with Smith,' " she recalls. "I thought he was joking at first, but then I realized he meant it."

Recruiters took easy advantage of the Pentagon's long-standing policies against enlisting homosexuals. Barbara Alt was only eighteen in 1976 when she decided to join the armed forces—she didn't care which one—to get money for college. Because the Marines, as opposed to the Navy, could enlist her right away, she opted for the corps. Her recruiter in Port Jefferson, Long Island, rehearsed the answers she should give at the regional military processing center in Fort Hamilton, New York, instructing her to say " 'No, I've never used drugs.' 'No, I'm not a homosexual.' I don't care if you are or not. Just tell them 'no,' " her recruiter told her.

The recruiter called in his sexual chip the night Alt was accepted into the corps. "You know, I could get in serious trouble because I don't really know whether or not you're homosexual," he told Alt as they drove to the recruiting office, ostensibly to pick up some papers. On the bus to the processing center the next day, the young female recruits for all the different services discovered they had a bond. "Who'd you have to have sex with?" they asked each other, then pointed at their various recruiters. When Alt arrived in Parris Island for boot camp, she discovered from other female recruits that the homosexuality scam for heterosexual sex was nationwide.

Female officers, though far less likely to be sexually exploited by their male superiors than enlisted women, were not immune from "rank-rape." One such "rank-rape" in the Marines Corps effectively destroyed the health of a female officer who reported being assaulted by a senior officer. "If this goes beyond this office, you're dead," her commanding officer told her. "You can kiss your career goodbye." Frightened of starting a new life outside the Marine Corps, the young officer kept quiet. The men evidently didn't. The female officer became known among the brass as a safe lay, a good Marine who wouldn't rock the command boat. In the process, she also became a nighttime dependent on drugs. "They pound on the door every night, every night," the officer would whisper to me in 1992. "Sometimes I say, 'Fuck off . . . Sir.' "

The secret world of harassment and sexual abuse in the services intensified with the phasing out of the separate women's components. Until 1978 when the WAC (Women's Army Corps) was dissolved by Congress, women had had the protection of the "Petticoat Connection," the WAC term for its all female chains of command. "We had had WAC staff advisors who advocated for women, particularly enlisted women," says retired Army Sergeant Carol Ogg. "If they had problems within the male ranks, like sexual harassment, the WAC first sergeant would go to the man's sergeant and straighten it out." Losing the Petticoat Connection was a great loss for Army women who had nowhere to turn for help. "Nine times out of ten during integration, the woman was being harassed by the sergeant himself," says Ogg. "Who was going to advocate for that young woman?"

Marine women lost their protection as well after integration. "The Women Marine companies were safe havens," says General Gail Reals, the Marine's most senior woman until her retirement in 1990. "You had a place to live where you didn't have to be constantly on guard. You had a woman Marine company commander who would go to bat for you. With the opening of all the opportunities for women came a price."

It was just that suspected price that had driven Congresswoman Holt to press the services on their knowledge of harassment within their ranks during four consecutive days of congressional hearings on women in the military in November 1979. But the secret had been well kept.

The assistant secretary of defense for manpower, reserve affairs and logistics, Robert Pirie, assured Holt that though Defense Department statistics were "not as good" as he would like, the available data showed that harassment of women "does not constitute a major command problem."[49] The civilian leadership of the Air Force had fallen for the same smoke screen. The small number of "equal opportunity" complaints recorded by the Air Force in 1979—only 152— signaled good news for Antonia Chayes, undersecretary of the Air Force. "I do not think it [sexual harassment] is a very serious problem," Chayes told Holt.[50] The Army, too, denied any problem. Its data on harassment did not support "an area . . . which requires considerably more attention," William Clark, an acting undersecretary of the Army, assured Holt.[51]

The Coast Guard testimony was the most relevant. Unlike the Navy and Air Force, which were bound by the combat exclusion laws, the Coast Guard had dropped all gender-based restrictions on women in 1978. At the time of the 1979 hearings, Coast Guard women were serving as commanders of Coast Guard cutters, as pilots and crew in aviation units, as personnel assigned to isolated loran (radar) stations. But Rear Admiral William Stewart, personnel chief of the U.S. Coast Guard, acknowledged only a few cases of harassment. "I am satisfied from my personal monitoring of the situation that these are isolated instances, there is no pattern to them, and I think they are more a one-on-one type of situation than they are anything else," Stewart told Holt. "We are always concerned but we would be concerned about harassment of our males as well, ma'am."[52]

Within a month of the hearings, Holt's suspicions were confirmed. Blasted across the front pages of the *Baltimore Sun* in December 1979 were a series of articles on the harassment of Army women at nearby Fort Meade which mirrored the harassment complaints in Holt's in-box. In the same pattern the Army would follow in 1996 after accusations of rape and abuse surfaced publicly at the Army Ordnance Center and School in Aberdeen, Maryland, the Army ordered investigations into harassment at Fort Benning, Fort Dix, Fort Bragg and the Presidio in San Francisco.[53] Armed with the ammunition she needed, Holt called for another hearing on women in the military, the first to concentrate on sexual harassment.

On February 11, 1980, seven years after the architects of the All-Volunteer Force had folded women into its male ranks, the tip of the iceberg emerged in Room 2118 of the Rayburn House Office Building. By the end of the day, eleven years before the volcanic scandal of Tailhook and sixteen years before the unfolding of abuse at Aberdeen, both Congress and the services knew everything they needed to know—and would subsequently ignore—about sexual harassment.

The five enlisted women were young, all from the Army base at nearby Fort Meade. They served as ammunition specialists, military policemen and administrative personnel. Three were married.

One had joined the Army for training in law enforcement. Another had followed her brothers and father into the services "because they loved it so much." Another had planned to make the Army her career. But all five of the women were either getting out or had already left. The reason was sexual harassment.

To Private Sarah Tolaro, it was the "several very bad experiences" she'd had in the Army. Beyond the "general outlook on females in the services," beyond being talked to "extremely dirty and nasty," Tolaro most resented "being pushed into a corner by two NCO's and having them expose themselves to me and then laugh."[54]

To Lori Lodinsky, it was the accumulation of being "intimidated" into a relationship with her platoon leader the day she had arrived at Fort Meade, followed by an assault by her supervisor during a night training drive. "He told me to go real fast on the airfield and weave in and out of the lights to test my ability at high speeds in a police sedan," Lodinsky testified. "Then he started grabbing me, while I was going about 60 MPH, all over my body. I screamed. I knocked out a row of lights. . . . That was one of the incidents. There are many more."[55]

According to the women's testimony, virtually every safeguard the Army had established to meld personnel of disparate backgrounds existed only on paper. The Army's required "human relations" training which Specialist Jimi Hernandez had attended in Germany did not follow its syllabus on race relations, gender relations and religious and ethnic differences. Instead, she testified, the twenty men in her discussion group, in which she was the only woman, focused entirely on sex "as far as women do not belong in the service, etcetera."[56]

In keeping with the low number of official complaints registered by the services, none of the women had bothered to report the harassment they had witnessed or experienced, including the woman who had been forced into a sexual relationship by her platoon leader. "I was afraid to," said Lori Lodinsky, who subsequently accepted Chapter 5—the inability to cope with military life—to leave the Army. "He said if I was to tell anyone about this, I would be in serious trouble."[57]

Neither had Private Tolaro reported the men who had exposed themselves to her nor the drill sergeant who had told his male troops to hit on female recruits because "women specifically came in the Army for that reason." "Every time I have brought up anything that I felt was important to me, I have been told 'Do not make waves,' " Tolaro testified. ". . . I have discovered through my time in the service that if I take it any higher than me, I am going to come back with 'I'm sure you deserved it anyway,' so, you know, 'just drop it.' "[58]

There it was, every nuance of the harassment issue which would haunt the services and embarrass the Pentagon for over a decade, recorded in 1980. By any measure, both Congress and the services had enough of a snapshot to start tracking the problem, to collect data, to survey the captive military population to determine the extent and the ramification of sexual harassment and to take the same lead in accomplishing gender integration as the services had with racial integration. But they didn't.

Instead, the cultural roadblocks to the seriousness of the harassment issue in the Pentagon as well as the corridors of Congress were forecast by the subcommittee's response to the chilling testimony of Jacqueline Lose, another member of the Military Police, who had lasted only six months in the Army.

In the most graphic testimony of all, Lose described "several experiences" she'd had with male peers to the congressional subcommittee. "At one time I was held down in a room by one man, with two other men in the room present, telling me he was going to give me what I deserved and I didn't know what I deserved . . . ," she testified. "I had to look to the others for help, but nobody would give me any. I screamed and yelled, but nobody came."[59]

"Were they aware you were married?" asked Antonio Won Pat, the representative from Guam, voicing the commonly held perception of married women as inviolate male property and single women as fair sexual game.[60]

"Yes, they were aware," Lose replied.

"But you never succumbed, of course?" Won Pat pressed, as if a screaming woman pinned to the floor and being molested was still responsible for the outcome of the assault.

"I was held down on the floor and he sat on my chest and held my hands down with his knees while he was touching me and kissing me," Lose explained. "He eventually let me go. It was about forty-five minutes he held me down."

But the congressmen still didn't get it. "Did they try to sexually assault you or was it mainly a feeling maneuver?" asked Congressman Sonny Montgomery, as if anything short of penetration was acceptable male behavior.[61]

The impossibility of moving sexual harassment up the rung of congressional and service priorities played out time and again at the 1980 hearing. When one of the servicewomen testified of her discomfort every afternoon at 4 p.m. when her work supervisor left to watch the go-go dancers during happy hour at an on-base club, one congressman expressed outrage that the military shift ended so early; another suggested equalizing the situation by adding male go-go dancers. And to Tolaro's complaint of being talked to "extremely dirty and nasty," another subcommittee member reminisced almost nostalgically about the "barracks" culture which demanded speaking in "four-letter words."

The solutions to the harassment issue offered by the 1980 congressional subcommittee and by the senior women in the services who also testified would become a familiar mantra in congressional hearing rooms for decades to come. "It is a matter of educating people," concluded Congresswoman Holt. "If they realize the horrible situation, how terrible Mrs. Lose must feel when she has to remember that awful experience . . . then we can overcome it."[62]

The commitment of the chain of command and their congressional overseers to eradicating sexual harassment was the solution to Major General Mary E. Clarke, the last director of the WAC and commander of Fort McClellan, Alabama. "The only way we're going to lick this problem . . . is for all of us to be very concerned about it. It is a leadership problem," said the highest-ranked woman in the Army.[63]

Opening combat jobs to women was the early and constant answer to Congresswoman Pat Schroeder. "Don't you think you all have a difficult role in being treated seriously unless women are allowed to voluntarily go into all slots?" Schroeder asked the senior women present.[64]

The male members of the House subcommittee remained incapable of seeing harassment as a professional problem, as a management problem, as a serious leadership problem affecting both men and women. Whereas racial harassment would have been seen as an institutional problem demanding swift leadership response, sexual harassment was reduced to a woman's issue and hardly worthy of male attention.

Congressman Montgomery was so determined to make harassment a nonissue that he produced nine other servicewomen representing all four services whom he insisted "had been selected totally at random" from computer lists by the subcommittee's staff.[65] Predictably, not one of Montgomery's witnesses admitted to being sexually harassed.

Where Holt's group objected to coarse and sexual language, Montgomery's group testified they "coped" with it. Where some women felt so intimidated and offended by the prurient behavior of servicemen in mess halls that at one point the Marine Corps had had to designate a separate chow line and eating area for women,[66] Montgomery's women paid no mind. Just as men had been mindlessly harassing women since time began, many women continued just as mindlessly to accept it. "The guys whistle, or, if you are going to eat in the chow hall, you will hear people making comments," a Montgomery airman said nonchalantly at the hearing's inconclusive end. "Most of the harassment is not directed at you per se, it's usually directed simply because you are female."[67]

And so harassment soldiered on. The hierarchical command structure would remain the paradigm for harassment it had always been. Forty-three percent of the enlisted women interviewed by Army auditors in 1982 reported that their superiors bartered sex for favoritism, an offer many young women either fell for or felt they couldn't refuse.[68] The 1990 Defense Department survey of sexual harassment came up with almost the same percentage. Forty-two percent of women experiencing some form of sexual coercion or harassment named their military superiors in the chain of command as the "perpetrators."[69]

Navy company commanders and Army drill sergeants would continue to wield the same power over young recruits they had always wielded. When a man identified himself as a drill sergeant to a recruit celebrating her first twelve hours of liberty after graduating from basic training at Fort Jackson, South Carolina, in 1990 and ordered her to produce the military ID she had left in her motel room, she didn't hesitate. She didn't even doubt his identity in the motel room while he raped and sodomized her. "He kept asking me questions and I kept answering, 'Yes, drill sergeant, no drill sergeant,' " she says. She gave the same explanation later to the Military Police who asked why she hadn't fought back. "He said he was a drill sergeant," she kept repeating.

Senior-subordinate abuse would remain entrenched. A twenty-two-year-old Navy seaman never told her alcoholism counselors at a Navy hospital in Florida about the commodore of her first duty station in 1991 who promised career favors if she would come to his office after hours in civilian clothes and sexually arouse him by talking dirty. "He's a damn captain in the Navy and I'm a measly seaman. What else could I do?" said the young woman at the time. "Every time I said, 'People are talking, this isn't a good idea,' he'd say, 'Don't worry about it, just don't worry about it.' "

The backlash began when the Navy captain was transferred to a new duty station. The seaman, the only woman in her squadron, was shunned by her male colleagues and written up for every infraction they could think of, including her increasing reliance on alcohol. "They didn't want me in the squadron anymore, they didn't want me in that building; they wanted me gone," she says. Because she feared even more retaliation, the seaman didn't dare tell the Navy therapists about her destructive relationship with the captain or her "punishment" by the men in her squadron—the very reasons she'd been sent into treatment. "I'm afraid," she says.

Harassment like the seaman's sexual exploitation was kept silenced by the military's reporting mechanism. The proper procedure was for servicewomen to lodge an "equal opportunity" complaint within their chains of command, the very structure that was often doing the abusing. The improbable equation required the complaint against someone in the chain of command to be evaluated, investigated, judged and adjudicated by that same chain of command. Save for jumping the chain of command and lodging the complaint with the inspector general, servicewomen had no other recourse. Whereas the thousands of civilians employed by the military, many of whom worked side by side with servicewomen, are entitled to bring harassment suits against the military under Title VII of the 1964 Civil Rights Act, their counterparts in uniform could not.[70] "The only person you have to be judge and jury is your commander," says Patricia Gavin, a former Air Force captain.

There was no incentive, however, for military supervisors to address or even to acknowledge harassment problems in their commands. In the highly competitive military structure, promotions and perks are awarded on the basis of problem-free leadership records. The mechanism to project seamless perfection depends on denial and deception, even at the company level.

"The officers in the company have people they have to answer to above them," says a former servicewoman. "And they are so worried about answering to those people that they don't want to even admit to themselves that there are any problems, much less try and solve them. They are too afraid somebody is going to find out about them and that puts their career on the line."

Even base commanders were kept in the comforting dark about harassment on their own turf. During Holt's 1980 hearing on sexual harassment, the commander of Fort Meade testified he had first heard about the harassment on his own base from reading the *Baltimore Sun*.[71] In the impetus to paint a rosy picture, harassment complaints were stonewalled at every level, starting at the bottom. "Between a young enlisted woman and the base commander you may have twenty layers of the chain of command that may have been telling her, it is all in your head," says Carolyn Becraft, director of the Women and the Military Project for the Women's Equity Action League in 1992.

Equal opportunity advisors whose job it was to be the vehicle for complaints often contributed to the silence. Save for the Air Force, which offered a permanent career track to equal opportunity advisors, the services treated equal opportunity as temporary, collateral duty. Already pressed by their other responsibilities, personnel assigned to equal opportunity often left the troublesome issues on the lowest rungs of their priority ladders. "They put the regulations in their back pockets, go out to the fleet and forget all about them," says a senior enlisted woman in the Navy.

Even when EO advisors took their roles seriously, they were institutionally handicapped. The advisors were enlisted, giving them little clout in the hierarchy of officers. Moreover, they had no authority to act on equal opportunity complaints, but could only advise their commanders on what action to take. The decision lay entirely in the hands of the commanders, who were more apt to bury the complaint to maintain the appearance of their trouble-free leadership. There was nothing an EO advisor could do without risking his or her career.

"We are taught to be loyal to our boss," says an Army platoon sergeant and EO advisor in 1992. "If we go around him, it's very dangerous. Even as an equal opportunity staff advisor, I can't think of a time I would not be loyal to my boss. I would document any complaint and let him know I was documenting it and how I feel about the situation. But I've been in personnel for seventeen years and I've been to bat for young soldiers who've been discriminated against, who've been assaulted. I know what the command problem is. Hopefully, he'll have a conversion overnight and come in and change his opinion."

The regulatory status of sexual harassment further complicated the reporting process. Harassment was not, and is not, included as a punishable offense under the Uniform Code of Military Justice. Though the UCMJ provides penalties of a bad conduct discharge and one year of imprisonment for dueling (Article 114) and three months of confinement and forfeiture of pay for abusing a public animal (Article 134), there are no such safeguards for abusing women. In the extreme, UCMJ penalties for rape carry the death penalty or life confinement and forced sodomy can put a man or woman away for twenty years, but the subtler forms of harassment are not codified.

To force sexual harassment charges under the UCMJ, servicewomen have to try to link their charges to such recognized offenses as "conduct unbecoming" (Article 133) if the harasser is an
officer, or among enlisted, "maltreatment of subordinate" (Article
93), "Indecent, insulting or obscene language prejudicial to good
order" (Article 134) or "extortion" (Article 127).[72]

The smoke screen made it impossible to track either the number
of harassment incidents or their resolutions. Most complaints were
resolved at the lowest level, and the punishment meted out, if any,
reduced to the nonjudicial Article 15 for minor offenses. "Anecdotal
evidence suggests that a slap on the wrist is much more common
than severe punishment and that significant redress for victims is
unusual," says Nancy Duff Campbell, co-president of the National
Women's Law Center in Washington.

Most women didn't bother to report harassment at all. By reporting a problem in what was supposed to be a trouble-free command, she became the problem. She risked being written up by her
superiors for the most minor infractions or losing seniority by being
moved out of her company to a new company or being shunned by
her peers as the Navy seaman had been and Navy Lieutenant Paula
Coughlin would be after Tailhook. There were so many ways to
backlash women that reporting harassment was just not worth it. In
1984, four years after the Navy established its sexual harassment
programs and policies, only twenty-four sexual harassment cases
were brought up for hearings, and of those, nine were dismissed as
unsubstantiated.[73] In contrast, 31,488 sex discrimination complaints
were lodged with the EEOC in 1984, 5,035 of which were for sexual
harassment.[74]

The Pentagon's policies made it far easier for men to harass
women than for women to defend themselves, especially during the
presidency of Ronald Reagan. In 1981, soon after Reagan and his
conservative entourage moved into the White House, the Defense
Department tightened its policies against homosexuality to close any
loophole from legal challenges in the courts. No longer did individual
commanders have discretionary authority to retain or dismiss enlisted homosexuals. The new policy mandated the administrative
discharge of "a person, regardless of sex, who engages in, desires to
engage in, or intends to engage in homosexual acts."[75] By the time
the policy was extended to cover officers in 1985, what can only be
described as a decade of terror for women had begun.

Sexual blackmail became the order of the day. Service personnel who resented taking orders from women, who had received bad performance reports from women, who'd had their sexual advances turned down by women, could start the rumor mill rolling by dropping hints of lesbianism. Women's only recourse was to have voluntary or involuntary sex with their potential accusers. "Some women have allowed themselves to be raped by male officers, afraid that the alternative would be a charge of lesbianism," the late Randy Shilts writes in his 1993 book, *Conduct Unbecoming: Gays and Lesbians in the U.S. Military*.[76]

Lesbian-baiting became a military art form. At a joint Army and Air Force base in Kaiserslautern, Germany, in 1984, servicewomen gathering at local bars after work dreaded hearing the theme to the film *Ghostbusters* blasting out of the jukebox. The song signaled the arrival of the "Dyke-busters," a predator posse of servicemen sporting T-shirts bearing the word "dyke" with a slash through it who would press them for sex. If the women reported the "Dyke-busters" for sexual harassment, the odds were their superiors would tell them it was just a joke and to lighten up. But if the women refused to have sex with the men, they could be thrown out of the military. The men "reported those who didn't agree to the military investigative services as dykes," said Michelle Benecke, a former Army officer in Germany, Harvard Law School graduate and advocate for servicewomen.[77]

That some women were homosexual goes without saying. An oft-cited study of 1,456 former service personnel in 1984 indicated that while the proportion of homosexual males seemed to be the same both inside and outside the services, homosexual women were more likely than heterosexual women to have had military service.[78] A former Army officer, herself a lesbian, estimated that as many as 20 to 25 percent of the women in the services in the 80s were lesbians. "Lesbians represented a significant population in the military," she says. "They were nontraditional women with high levels of confidence who would have been stigmatized in the private sector. They fit in better in the military."

The "witch-hunts" for lesbians, however, were way out of proportion. Entire bases were swept in the Army and Air Force, as was virtually every Navy ship in the new Women at Sea program. Twenty-nine of the sixty-one women aboard the USS *Norton Sound*, including all but one of the nine black female crew members, were investigated for lesbianism by the Naval Investigative Service. So were five of the thirteen female crew members aboard the USS *Grapple*, the salvage ship which would help raise the remains of TWA 800 off Long Island in the summer of 1996. "It has become the only accepted way, the only legal way to harass women in the Navy," USS *Grapple* petty officer Mary Beth Harrison explained to Connie Chung in 1991.[79]

No woman was immune, whether homosexual or heterosexual, married, single or a mother. The senior enlisted woman in one Army aviation brigade was called in by her sergeant major for taking the young female troops in the brigade to the NCO club. It didn't "look good," he warned her. People "were talking." But she held her ground. "Why deny these young women the same right to a mentor you had growing up in the military?" she challenged the sergeant major, who subsequently backed down. But the suspicion lingered. "Whenever they see more than one or two women together, they think we're either going to take over or we're lesbians," says the sergeant.

Ironically, the very qualities most admired in men—aggressiveness, strength, athleticism—made women suspect. Rosters for the women's softball teams were ready-made launch points for investigations by the Naval Investigative Service. So was the length of a woman's hair. "Sometimes they will call you, or accuse you of being a lesbian because your hair is short," said a crew member of the USS *Yellowstone*. "Well, we cut our hair short for the cruise because they won't let you have curling irons on the ship and [long hair] is too hard to take care of in the summer when it's hot."[80]

In 1988 the Marine Corps weighed in with the most far-reaching "lesbian" purge of all, this one at Parris Island Recruit Training Depot, the only Marine boot camp for women. Prompted by a spurned boyfriend after he kicked in the door to a motel room in 1986 and reported finding his former lover naked with another Marine woman, the investigation snowballed into accusations of homosexuality against seventy women at Parris Island, many of them drill instructors.[81] According to a report in the *Harvard Women's Law Journal*, almost one-half of the post's 246 women were questioned about alleged lesbian activity.[82]

One Marine sergeant was interrogated nonstop for seven hours, during which she was threatened with losing custody of her six-month-old daughter if she didn't cooperate. She finally signed a prepared statement admitting her "guilt" just to end the ordeal. Another sergeant under suspicion also capitulated after the Naval Investigative Service agents threatened to tell her critically ill mother of the lesbian allegations. Rather than defend herself at a hearing, she resigned from the Marine Corps.[83]

The women who did try to defend their careers met a wall of male ignorance. A charge of "indecent assault" against one of the accused stemmed from her putting her arm around the shoulders of a weeping colleague. Charges against another woman reported in *The Progressive,* a liberal Wisconsin magazine, were based on her habit of sending flowers to friends.

"Approximately, how many times have you sent flowers to a fellow Marine?" transcripts from the hearing read.

"About six times, sir," came the reply.

"Are you aware of any other Marines sending flowers?"

"No, sir, I'm not," replied the woman, who subsequently resigned from the corps rather than face further inquisition.[84]

The lesbian purges reached the height of absurdity in the Navy in 1990 when the commander of the surface Atlantic fleet took it upon himself to ferret out lesbians by shifting the Navy's suspicious sights from female athletes to the Navy's best and brightest women. On July 24 the nearly two hundred ships and forty shore installations in Vice Admiral Joseph Donnell's domain received his personal instruction to deal "firmly" with "the stereotypical female homosexual in the Navy," whose characteristics he identified as "hard-working, career-oriented, willing to put in long hours on the job and among the command's top professionals."[85] In short order, a female chief electronics technician was brought up on lesbian charges aboard one Navy ship. So was the first woman to be selected as Sailor of the Year while serving aboard the USS *Yosemite.*[86]

The holy war against lesbians added unique stress to women already bucking male bias in the services. During her thirty-six-year career in the Marine Corps, retired General Gail Reals was locked out of her barracks while agents searched all the women's gear for proof of homosexuality. She was suspect because she played on a softball team which lost 75 percent of its members in a single purge, was pressured for sex by a married senior officer wielding the threat of lesbianism and questioned about her sexuality on several occasions.

The accumulating experiences had a direct and isolating effect on her life. "I gave up playing sports because I couldn't play and not be tarred by the same brush," says Reals, who had several security clearances to protect on her way from private to general. "I had to watch very carefully who I associated with. When I was able to have my own apartment, I certainly never had a roommate. It was a concern how you wore your hair, how you wore your watch, whatever. Everyone talks about the impact on homosexuals and lesbians, but the purges had a far broader impact."

Eighteen Marine women ended up being discharged in the purge at Parris Island, among them eleven drill instructors.[87] Two other women, both drill instructors, were demoted after testifying as character witnesses for the accused. Three other Marine women received criminal convictions for homosexuality and were sent to the brig. "They want women out and this is an easy way to do it," said former Marine Corporal Barbara Baum, who was busted to the rank of private, discharged from the corps and sentenced to a year in the Marine prison in Quantico, Virginia.[88]

No one knows how many other women voluntarily left the services out of fear of being ensnared in the lesbian drift nets. The unofficial total from the Parris Island purge alone was sixty-five Marine women who either resigned or didn't reenlist.[89] Fully 10 percent of the Marines' only-female drill instructors were bullied out of the corps in the Parris Island purge.

The ripple effect spread to other female athletes. At Camp Lejeune, North Carolina, a Marine corporal who had been named 1987 Marine Corps Sportswoman of the Year, a top athlete who had earned a place on the all-Marine female softball team in 1987 and the all-Marine volleyball teams in 1986 and 1987, reacted to the news that she, too, was under investigation by going into her garage, starting her car engine and sitting there until she died.[90]

Short of driving women to suicide, charges of lesbianism proved to be the single most effective weapon in driving women out of the services. In 1979 six times as many Army women as Army men were discharged for homosexuality.[91] The lopsided ratios were even greater in the Navy and Marines. Between 1982 and 1987 eight times as many Marine women as men were discharged for homosexuality.[92] In 1989 the discharge rate for women was ten times that for men.[93]

The tragedy of the lesbian witch-hunts is that they had so little to do with lesbians. In the hyperheterosexual military culture, men are far more threatened by male homosexuality than by female homosexuality. Lesbians wouldn't figure at all in the national furor over gays in the military following the 1992 election of Bill Clinton. The passionate debate about overturning the DOD ban against homosexuals would be led by men about men, without a nod to women. Sam Nunn, then chair of the Senate Armed Services Committee, would choose the cramped living quarters on board an all-male submarine as a photo op to illustrate the impossibility of mixing gay and straight men. Ignored would be the racks in berthing areas for women on Navy ships, stacked three deep and separated by only forty inches.

Male homosexuals in the military would turn out to be just as dismissive of female homosexuals. While women veterans would work tirelessly to overturn the military's discriminatory policies toward both servicemen and servicewomen, male advocates would take notice only of themselves. At a 1993 fund-raiser for the Campaign for Military Service in East Hampton, Long Island, not one lesbian veteran was on the invitation list. "The military is a man's world," campaign director Thomas Stoddard would tell me by way of explanation. "Besides, women can't afford a high-ticket event."

The harassment of women would continue in the military culture. The institutionalized gender discrimination that kept women out of core combat positions and specialized training would cast them as secondary players to men just as the regulations against homosexuality would continue to hold women sexual hostage. A 1997 study by the Servicemembers Legal Defense Network would find evidence of ongoing witch-hunts for lesbians and women's disproportionate discharge rate for homosexuality. While women made up 13 percent of the services in 1995, they made up 29 percent of the discharges. In the Army, women accounted for fully 41 percent of the discharges.[94]

The group dynamics at work in the military culture would make inevitable the collective abuse of women at Tailhook in 1991 just as they would the sexual misconduct uncovered throughout the services in 1996. The Navy men who gang-raped a female helicopter mechanic in a barracks in Coronado, California, in the 90s while other men watched were no different from the Army men who had molested Jacqueline Lose in the barracks in front of a male audience at Fort Meade, Maryland, in 1980; the soldiers in Vietnam who raped for each other in the 60s were no different from the men in the 90s who declared it a multi-service "contest" to "cover" the same woman and "brag about it." "It makes you more of a man in your peers' eyes," admitted an unidentified serviceman on ABC News *20/20* in 1996.[95]

The denigration of women was an integral and, in some opinions, essential part of the military culture. In the underground world at the service academies, it was critical.

7

THE UNDERGROUND WORLD
AT THE ACADEMIES

Token Women and the Rites of Male Passage

GWEN DREYER, a second-year midshipman at the Naval Academy, was studying in her room on December 8, 1989, when two male midshipmen burst through the door, pinned her arms and carried her, struggling, into the hallway. Dreyer thought they were going to dump her outside in a snowbank in retaliation for the snowball she had landed on one of them earlier in the day. Instead, the young men, one a varsity wrestler, forced her into the men's bathroom where, in front of a waiting male audience, they handcuffed her to a urinal. While some of the midshipmen traded sexual taunts about Dreyer and exposed themselves while pretending to urinate, others took her picture. Among them was the Human Relations Council member in Dreyer's company who had supplied the handcuffs.

In good midshipman fashion, Dreyer didn't report the incident to the academy chain of command that Friday night. Nor did her roommates who freed her after an argument with the midshipman holding the handcuff keys. The young women remained silent through the rest of the Army-Navy football game weekend they spent at a hotel with Dreyer's stepmother and her father, a former naval officer and second-generation academy graduate. "We decided they were just tired. They're always tired at the Naval Academy," recalls Dreyer's stepmother, Carolyn. And then, at 2 a.m., the phone rang.

"Gwen was crying so hard she was almost incoherent," says Carolyn Dreyer, as the story poured out. " 'Why did they do this to me?' she kept repeating. 'I thought they were my friends.' " Gregory

Dreyer immediately called the security detail at Bancroft Hall, the massive dormitory where all 4,000 midshipmen lived. He knew the midshipmen culture would target her for telling and for any disciplinary actions the academy would take. "We wanted to make sure there was somebody right by Gwen's door to protect her," says Carolyn Dreyer.

The Dreyers were at the academy by eight the next morning to demand a swift investigation and appropriate punishment. They didn't get it. In what would prove to be a pivotal moment for all the academies, the Naval Academy delayed its investigation into the handcuffing until the academy reconvened after Christmas break and then didn't hand down its verdict until mid-February 1990, two and a half months after the incident. By then, the Dreyers were incensed.

Not only had the varsity wrestler pressured Gwen to testify on his behalf—"You'd better or we're going to make your life miserable," he had warned her, then followed up by slamming his fist into his hand whenever he saw her on campus—he and his co-conspirators were found virtually not guilty.

Wearing the cultural blinders that would lead the Navy through one scandal after another in the 90s, the academy's disciplinary board found that Dreyer's handcuffing was neither premeditated nor hazing, both of which were dismissable offenses. Instead, the two midshipmen who had physically overpowered Dreyer were given the lesser charge of general misconduct, which landed them demerits and the loss of a month's leave time; the six other boys in the bathroom received no reprimands at all. And a toxic cloud began to form over the Naval Academy which would spread to engulf West Point and the Air Force Academy and generate no fewer than nine separate investigations, five of them ordered by Congress.

The Dreyers maintained a public silence about the incident and its handling by the academy out of deference to their daughter, who wanted to finish the school year. But the sexual overtones to the urinal incident, the young men who dropped their towels and exposed themselves to her when she had to go into their rooms on academy business, the arrogant young men who persisted in showing pornographic films in the only recreational rooms for both male and female midshipmen in the dormitory and who referred to female sophomores like Gwen in their "youngster" year as "cuntsters," spoke to a larger and unaddressed cultural problem at the Naval Academy.

The story broke a week after Gwen left the academy in May 1990, to finish her engineering studies at California Polytechnic State Institute.[1] Acting on a tip, a reporter from the local *Annapolis Capital* called the Dreyers to confirm the anonymous phone calls he had gotten from two women midshipmen about the handcuffing. Gregory Dreyer did so. The series of national news stories that followed about harassment and bias at what was inarguably one of the nation's most prestigious institutions sent shock waves through the country and Congress. A national icon was being smashed. "This is just the tip of the iceberg," Carolyn Dreyer told the *Baltimore Sun*.[2]

Dreyer turned out to be just one of many female "middies" to be handcuffed by male midshipmen. " 'We'll keep doing this until you all get a sense of humor,' " she quoted one of her assailants. She had been pressured by academy officers to remain silent. "We're told that sexual harassment is a big deal with those up high, so you're supposed to upkeep the image of the academy and not complain about these problems that really need fixing," she said. Other female midshipmen were muzzled by fear. "A lot of them won't talk about any of this because they know what will happen," said Dreyer, who described her status as an "outcast" among her peers and academy officers alike for reporting the handcuffing, for "breaking an unwritten code."

Academy superintendent Admiral Virgil L. Hill Jr. tried to downplay the story, insisting to every news medium that Dreyer's harassment "was a very, very isolated incident," that the "climate" for women at the academy was not only "improving," but was "overall very good." But parents of other female midshipmen and former mids themselves came forward to disabuse him.

One former female midshipman reported that her mental abuse in 1987 was so intense that she checked into the Bethesda Naval Hospital for a psychiatric evaluation before leaving the academy.[3] Women who had stayed the course at the academy and were now Navy officers in the fleet were no less affected by their experience at Annapolis. "What goes on during your four years, you accept," said Lieutenant Barbette Lowndes, a 1980 graduate. "But once you hit the real world, you say, 'Hey, that shouldn't have happened to me.' "[4]

The complexities within the academy culture began to reveal

themselves when thirty demonstrators from the National Organization for Women started picketing the "sexist" academy outside the main gates, only to be rebuffed by the female midshipmen. In a show of solidarity with their male peers, the young women confronted NOW, insisting they had joined in such academy rituals as stripping, tarring and feathering a male West Point cadet during Army-Navy football game week and handcuffing a male middie to a urinal. "It's not a matter of gender, it's a part of life here," one third-year midshipman hurled at NOW. Added another: "You are doing a lot of damage."[5]

Alumnae of the Naval Academy were just as upset with Dreyer's public exposé of the academy culture and blamed her for setting off such a high-profile ruckus. "She could have done whatever through her chain of command to right the situation, but she chose to leave and go public and all that did was hurt the women who stayed," says a female member of the class of '83. "The guys say, 'Well, the only reason we're getting all this publicity is because we've got women here, so we don't want women here.' "

But the balloon was up on Capitol Hill, where legislators had both a private and public stake in the academies. Aspiring applicants to all the academies were screened and nominated by members of Congress. The midshipmen's and cadets' education, training, room and board, uniforms and allowances of $500 a month were paid for by funds allocated by Congress. Scandal at the academies cut close to the national quick, especially the abuse of America's best and brightest daughters by America's supposedly best and brightest sons.

"Those responsible for sexual harassment were only given demerits and a loss of leave time, while the victim has felt it necessary to resign from the Navy," Senator Richard C. Shelby, chairman of the Senate Armed Services subcommittee on force requirements and personnel, protested in a widely publicized letter to Defense Secretary Dick Cheney and H. Lawrence Garrett III, the secretary of the Navy who would keep his job through this Navy scandal but lose it to Tailhook, just fifteen months away.[6]

Investigations were launched by the Navy. Garrett dispatched the naval inspector general, Rear Admiral M. E. Chang, to the academy to investigate the equal opportunity climate for women. The chief of naval personnel, Vice Admiral Jeremy "Mike" Boorda, who would succeed Admiral Frank B. Kelso II in 1994 as chief of naval operations after the Tailhook scandal and commit suicide in 1996, was assigned to review the academy's Honor Concept and Conduct System. Admiral Hill reconvened the academy's own Women Midshipmen Study Group a full year ahead of schedule; the next gender review had not been scheduled to begin until 1991.

The academy's Board of Visitors formed a special subcommittee on women's issues to review all the other reviews. Among the subcommittee's members was Maryland Senator Barbara Mikulski, who was furious that she and other board members had not been informed about Dreyer's handcuffing or the investigation at the time but had learned about the incident from news accounts five months after the fact.

Sam Nunn, chair of the Senate Armed Services Committee, and two subcommittee chairs, John Glenn and Richard Shelby, went outside the Navy to investigate the stream of harassment and hazing stories coming out of the Naval Academy, including reports of one male midshipman bound and taped to a chair by classmates who thought he had lied and another who had been forced to eat and drink until he vomited.[7] In the most far-reaching probe of all, the General Accounting Office was tasked to prepare separate reports on hazing, sexual harassment and the treatment of women and minorities not only at the Naval Academy, but at West Point and the Air Force Academy as well. The GAO's comprehensive reviews of life inside the academies would result in five separate government reports released between November 1992 and March 1994 and be followed by an update on sexual harassment in 1995.

Never have so many high-powered resources been assigned to review what many suspected but didn't want to believe. The comforting attitude change observed during racial integration in the 60s, which found that increased contact between "whites" and "blacks" produced increasingly positive "white" attitudes, was not proving out in gender relations in the military. In spite of the optimistic hypothesis pursued by researchers in the 70s—"as men become more accustomed to women in the workplace, they will become more accepting of them as well"[8]—women were hardly more assimilated at the Naval Academy in 1990 than they had been in 1976.

Forty-five percent of male midshipmen entering their first year at the Naval Academy felt women did not belong there, the Women Midshipmen Study Group found in its review completed in July 1990. More telling, 38 percent of the male midshipmen in their senior year still felt the same way. "That over one third of graduating male midshipmen believe women should not be at the Academy defines the magnitude of the cultural barriers to the acceptance of women midshipmen," stated the women's issues report.[9]

The "cultural barriers" identified in the Naval Academy's eighty-nine-page internal report compiled by four officers, two midshipmen and an academy psychologist turned out to be a laundry list of the "white male anger" looming on the political horizon. Ignored in the highly touted progress women had made at the academies since the 70s was the parallel resentment festering in men.

Male midshipmen remained convinced that women got preferential treatment in the admissions process, from academic boards, conduct boards, honor boards, from their company officers, in physical fitness standards and their selection as midshipmen leaders, perceptions of reverse discrimination that persisted, the study group found, "even in the face of actual facts that show no favoritism exists."[10]

The bias against women was perpetuated, according to study group findings, by "a persistent, vocal minority of midshipmen, officers, faculty, staff and graduates" whose "negative attitude and inappropriate actions . . . exert such a disproportionate influence on the Naval Academy climate that most midshipmen readily acknowledge women midshipmen are not accepted as equals in the Brigade."[11]

The institution played into the bias by marginalizing all women at the academy. Instead of showcasing or even acknowledging the female officers who by 1990 had been graduating from the Naval Academy for ten years, the few female graduates working at the academy were clustered out of sight in administrative staff jobs.[12] Not one female graduate served either as a company officer or on the faculty. "Many midshipmen have never met a female graduate," noted an academy briefing paper distributed to the astonished members of DACOWITS in the spring of 1991.[13]

The brigade of midshipmen was kept in the dark as well about the military contributions women had made to the Navy since World War I. Neither plebe indoctrination nor the core curriculum mentioned anything about the roles played by Navy or Marine women, including the 4,000 Navy women who had served in the Pacific during World War II[14] or the Marine women and Navy combat nurses who served in Vietnam. There was no recognition either of women's more current roles, including the 248 women among the crew of the USS *Acadia* who had been deployed to the mined waters of the Gulf in 1987 to repair Iraqi missile damage to the crippled USS *Stark*,[15] the female Navy aviators who had flown supplies to besieged Marines in Beirut in 1983, or, in 1986, had trapped on and off aircraft carriers in support of U.S. operations against Libya.[16]

The academy deemed women's value so insignificant to the Navy that their career opportunities weren't even mentioned in plebe indoctrination or during the four mandatory career lectures on the male-only warfare communities in the midshipmen's second year. "Generally, women's career opportunities are covered only in response to specific questions," stated the study group report.[17]

Women in their last year at the academy and on the threshold of entering the fleet as naval officers were just as devalued. While the academy mandated the attendance of all senior midshipmen for the one-hour update on career opportunities for men in the warfare communities, attendance was optional for the tagged-on twenty minutes spent on women's noncombat career opportunities. Naturally, the able-bodied male midshipmen didn't stick around and never did find out what female officers did in the Navy. Only the maimed and ruptured males knew. "Generally, only non-physically qualified male midshipmen attend this lecture with the women," noted the Women Midshipmen Study Group report.[18]

Even the academy's active-duty career counselors, whose job was to advise both male and female midshipmen on their futures in the Navy, paid scant attention to the job opportunities for women. Female graduates like Lieutenant Barbara Bell, '84, the first female instructor at the Navy's elite test pilot school, took it upon themselves to return to the academy to personally counsel the young academy women. Says Bell, who had chosen Navy aviation on her own because it was closest to what her male counterparts were doing, "They were feeding the women the same limited knowledge in 1989 they'd fed me. One woman told me she'd wanted to go into aviation but hadn't because the opportunities were so limited and I thought, You've got to be out of your mind. It turned out her company officer had no idea what was available to women in aviation and had made no effort to find out."

The demeaning environment for women, in which over 60 percent of female midshipmen were ranked by their fellow midshipmen in the bottom half of their companies, was a natural hotbed for sexual harassment.[19] No fewer than ten ongoing contributors to "an intimidating, hostile or offensive environment" in Bancroft Hall were identified by the Women Midshipmen Study Group, from the routine use of WUBA jokes to identify female midshipmen to lewd messages and graphics being sent via electronic mail to female midshipmen's computers.[20] The study group listed nine other contributors which "perpetuate stereotypic male views of women as sex objects or ornaments," including erotic posters hung in dorm rooms and company T-shirts "with lewd acronyms or pictures of nude women."[21]

Fourteen years after gender integration, the only universally accepted role for women at the academy was as photographic pinups in the "Company Cuties" section of *The Log,* the midshipmen magazine, and as the subject of dating gossip on "Tales from the Darkside," a feature on WRNV, the academy's internal radio station.[22] "Despite official policy to the contrary," the report understated, "a climate free of sexual harassment does not exist at the Naval Academy."[23]

The sexual arrogance of the young male midshipmen was, in fact, unparalleled. Even accounting for their youthful fantasies—a West Point officer would refer to the male cadets there as "hormones with legs"—the sexual subjugation of women at the Naval Academy went beyond youthful norms.

The male midshipmen practice of sporting Chiquita banana stickers on the inside of their hats to mark sexual "scores" in their rooms and Dole banana stickers for "scores" elsewhere on campus was probably little different from the sexual bravura fraternity brothers exhibited for each other on civilian campuses.[24] What was chilling in the midshipmen culture were the institutionalized expressions of violence and sadism.

Recorded in the *New Republic* by Carol Burke, a Naval Academy faculty member from 1984 to 1991, the midshipmen's earning of "brown wings," Navy aviation vernacular for anal intercourse, was close to an obsession. The "brown wings" theme ran through the "lewd electronic messages" (noted but not parsed by the Women Midshipmen Study Group) sent to female midshipmen by e-mail and in songs sung by the male glee club on buses en route to concerts to sing patriotic medleys.

Set to the tune of "The Candy Man" and retitled "The S&M Man," the first verse of the glee club favorite ran "Who can take a chain saw/Cut the bitch in two/Fuck the bottom half/and give the upper half to you." The fourth verse ran: "Who can take an ice pick/ Ram it through her ear/Ride her like a Harley,/As you fuck her from the rear."

The same stirring theme ran through the verses female midshipmen were receiving almost nightly on their e-mail. Read one: "I love my woman dearly/We get together yearly/And although she said it stings/I still earned my brown wings."[25]

The various teams investigating the treatment of female midshipmen at the Naval Academy seemed stunned by their findings. The women's issues report described the nine male and female officers on the naval inspector general's team as "almost palpably dismayed" when reporting their finding that incidents of sexual harassment at the academy were neither properly identified nor "punished severely."[26] Similarly, the report noted the "visible distress" of members of the Women Midshipmen Study Group when they delivered their depressing findings on the nonassimilation of women.[27]

What was more surprising than their findings was that their discovery evoked such surprise. Historically, culturally and politically, the academies have been ground zero for the gender wars in the military since the beginning. And the Naval Academy was the least of it.

The GAO's survey of harassment at the academies would find that 50 percent of the female midshipmen at the Naval Academy experienced some form of harassment at least twice a month.[28] The rate rose to 59 percent of female cadets at the Air Force Academy. Leading the pack were female cadets at West Point. Seventy-six percent of the young women at the U.S. Military Academy would report recurring harassment to the GAO, giving the female cadets the dubious but predictable distinction of being the most harassed women on record at any military college campus in America.

Not one academy graduate in the 70s, not one single admiral in the Navy or one single general in the Army, Air Force or Marines or their commander in chief, Richard Nixon, wanted the academies opened to women. Nor did the top echelons of the Department of Defense, the civilian secretaries of the services or the superintendents of West Point, the Naval Academy and the Air Force Academy, all of whom testified as one in front of the military personnel subcommittee of the House Armed Services Committee during nine separate sessions in the spring and summer of 1974 on the issue of admitting women.

To the admirals and generals dug in before Congress, the academies existed only to produce combat officers who, by law and policy, women couldn't be. Tampering with the gender formula at the academies that had produced such proven leaders of men as Dwight David Eisenhower, Douglas MacArthur and five-star Admiral Chester Nimitz, the World War II commander in chief of the U.S. Pacific Fleet, the officers argued, would be tantamount to national suicide. "I urge that we not experiment in this direction with the future defense of the nation," argued Lieutenant General A. P. Clark, a West Point alumnus and superintendent of the Air Force Academy.[29]

Determined members of Congress argued just as vehemently to extend the federally funded education at the academies to America's daughters. The progression seemed only natural to the congressmen who had been felling barriers to women for over a decade: the Equal Pay Act in 1963; Title VII of the Civil Rights Act in 1964; the Equal Employment Opportunity Act, Title IX of the Education Amendment and the grand finale in 1972 of the Equal Rights Amendment; which had been ratified by thirty-three states by the time of the hearings.[30]

At least six bills to integrate the academies had been introduced in the House of Representatives, four by Delaware's Pierre "Pete" du Pont alone.[31] Other congressmen, in partnership with lawyers from the Center for Women Policy Studies, were pursuing gender integration through the courts. The suits brought by two California congressmen in 1973 against James Schlesinger, the secretary of defense, on behalf of their female nominees to the Air Force and Naval Academies were working their way through the courts in the summer of 1974 at the same time the generals and admirals were in Congress mounting their arguments against women.

Ninety-four percent of West Point graduates entered the combat arms, Army Secretary and West Point graduate "Bo" Callaway insisted, leaving only the cadets who were medically disqualified relegated to noncombat jobs. What Callaway left out were his hasty instructions to West Point in the fall of 1973 to cancel the academy's inaugural plan to allow some able-bodied cadets to enter noncombat branches like the Finance Corps, the Signal Corps and the Medical Service Corps.[32]

The Air Force Academy projected a combat profile as well, testifying that 70 percent of academy graduates went into combat fields closed to women. Lest the remaining 30 percent be considered a vulnerability, Lieutenant General Clark warned Congress that the entry of women into a military institution that trained men for air combat would "inevitably erode this vital atmosphere."[33]

The Air Force claim would prove false. The academy's own records showed that fewer than 40 percent of its graduates between 1964 and 1973 participated in combat jobs, writes Major General Jeanne Holm, then director of the WAF (Women in the Air Force), in *Women in the Military: The Unfinished Revolution*. Moreover, she points out, it was academy policy to accept male candidates "who were not qualified to fly and could therefore never qualify as Air Force combat leaders."[34]

Only the Navy's case against women had some merit. Naval Academy graduates automatically became officers in the Navy's Unrestricted Line and were required to go to sea or enter Navy aviation. But the 1948 combat exclusion law did not allow women to serve on Navy ships except for transports and hospital ships, or to fly combat aircraft. Without repealing the law, argued Vice Admiral William P. Mack, the superintendent of the Naval Academy, there would be no way to assign graduating female midshipmen to ships in the fleet or even to train them aboard the academy's ships. He was, however, "philosophically opposed" to the repeal of the law.[35]

As hard as the services fought to make combat the central argument against women, proponents of integration fought as hard to sidestep it. The issue of women in combat and, by extension, women's eligibility for the draft were it to be reinstated, was too divisive, too politically dangerous for Congress to address. Instead of challenging the combat exclusion laws, which was the only possible solution, congressional integrationists chose instead to debunk the academies for their old-fashioned, obstructionist attitudes.

"The overwhelming bulk of the opposition to women in the service academies is based on nothing more than inertia and resistance to change," scoffed New York Congressman Samuel Stratton, chair of the subcommittee on military compensation.[36] California Congressman Don Edwards charged the DOD with "outmoded patterns of thinking."[37]

The 1974 hearings ended inconclusively but with the services believing they had won.[38] Though the Senate had twice passed resolutions supporting the integration of the academies, the services had been assured by the conservative chair of the House Armed Services

Committee that he would block any legislation to open the academies. But the services had underestimated the political commitment
of Congress to equal opportunity. In April 1975, Stratton circum-
vented the House Armed Services Committee and boldly approached
the full House with a proposal to attach an amendment integrating
the academies to a military appropriations bill already on the floor.

In a last-ditch debate, proponents for the Army tried and failed
to have West Point exempted from the amendment. A congressional
bid to establish a separate academy for women also failed. The coming political reality so alarmed West Point's new superintendent,
General Sidney Berry, that he declared he would resign if women
were admitted and enjoined the young male corps of cadets to continue their fight against women because "we can still beat this
thing."[39] But they couldn't.

On May 20, 1975, the House of Representatives approved the
Stratton amendment by a strong vote of 303 to 96. The Senate followed suit on June 6 by voice vote. On October 7, President Gerald
Ford signed the defense appropriations bill and declared women
eligible for appointment to the academies for the academic year
beginning in 1976.

The political fiat would have little impact, however, on the defiant academy cultures. The united stand of the generals and admirals
to not surrender their academies to the political forces of equal opportunity had already doomed women's assimilation. The charge
from Army Secretary Callaway in 1974 that the admission of women
would "lead to the lowering of standards for men,"[40] and from
Air Force Academy Superintendent Clark that the academies would
"inevitably find it necessary to create a modified program to accommodate the female cadet, or, God forbid, be required to water down
the entire program . . . ," would reappear twenty years later in the
GAO's post-Dreyer handcuffing reports as examples of harassment.
Nearly two-thirds of the women at West Point and one-third at the
Naval and Air Force Academies would report being told repeatedly
by their male colleagues that "standards have been lowered."[41]

Similarly, the leadership's insistence that the academies existed
only to produce career combat officers would be swallowed whole by
generations of cadets and midshipmen. Though over one-third of
academy-generated officers resigned within the first eight years of
service and fewer than half stayed in uniform until retirement,[42] the
phrase "you don't belong here" would be leveled at female cadets

and midshipmen for decades to come by their male classmates, especially in the combat arms culture at West Point.[43]

Public law 94-106 opening the academies to women was straightforward. Academy-bound men and women were required to meet the same standards for "appointment, admission, training, graduation, and commissioning." The only nod to gender in the law allowed for "minimum essential adjustments" in physical requirements because of the "physiological differences between male and female individuals."[44]

What the law failed to address was the impact the combat exclusion laws would have on generations of women cadets and midshipmen in the combat cultures at the academies, the consequences of women's tokenism dictated by their necessarily small, noncombat enrollment and their perceived interruption of young male tradition and rites of passage.

Women would be blamed for every change at the academies from the crackdown on hazing following the Dreyer handcuffing to the modernization of the academy's physical training programs. The substitution of running shoes for combat boots after gender integration in the 70s brought young male charges of lowered physical standards, even though men's injury rates had come down along with that of women. The 90s crackdown on the counterproductive hazing of freshmen by upperclassmen, which at the extreme caused such stress symptoms as headaches, stomachaches and depression, grade point averages below 2.4, higher attrition rates and lowered commitment to military service, was also attributed to women and seen by some male cadets as a loss of military manhood. "I feel robbed of the tradition and pride from graduating from here," one Air Force cadet told the GAO investigators chronicling academy hazing in 1990 and 1991. Echoed a male midshipman: "We are the last of a dying breed. Please, leave us alone, look away, and let the tradition continue."[45]

For all that Congress had convinced itself that the academies did not exist to produce combat officers, the combat exclusion laws would prove fatal to women's assimilation. The ethos at the academies revolved around combat. Cadets at West Point drilled on the vast parade grounds called The Plain under the watchful gaze of America's founding combat officer, General George Washington. They went to class past the life-size statues of alumni war heroes MacArthur, Eisenhower, Bradley and Patton. Eighty percent of the male cadets at West Point went into the combat arms branches.[46] "There's a certain mystique about going infantry or armor," said a male cadet in 1992.

Midshipmen at the Naval Academy were surrounded by monuments to naval war victories throughout the "Yard," as the campus is called, by the reverence given to the alumni names inscribed on the honor rolls in Memorial Hall, by the photographs of academy graduates awarded the Congressional Medal of Honor. Every physically qualified male midshipman went into the warfare specialties (aviation, submarines, surface ships or Marine Corps).[47] "They think of themselves as warriors crawling around with daggers in their teeth," a Naval Academy spokesman told DACOWITS in the spring of 1991.

The academies downplayed their combat cultures in the gender turmoil of the 90s. The mission statement at the Naval Academy didn't mention combat,[48] the academy's post-Dreyer report emphasized, but goals of the "highest responsibilities" for leadership and citizenship. West Point's mission statement didn't mention combat, either. A chronology produced by West Point's historian of the military academy's five different mission statements issued since 1925 stressed "a lifetime of service to the nation."[49] But the contradiction remained.

"The academy claims to be a leadership school, but then West Point shoots itself in the foot. 'Combat! Combat! You've got to go combat arms!' " said graduate Captain Mimi Finch in 1993. "Ninety-nine percent of the officers West Point brings back as role models are in the combat arms. And then we say to the women, 'Hey, you can be here and you can be part of this and you're important.' Well, unh-unh."

The contradiction at the Naval Academy was particularly convoluted. While the male midshipmen's assumed "warrior" identity had been a plus at the academy before the admission of women, women's legal inability to assume that same warrior identity had turned the combat image into a negative. The academy's own post-Dreyer study group cited the young men's "combat officer ideal" as a reason a "disturbing percentage" of male midshipmen thought of women as "less effective leaders."[50]

Academy women were further distanced by the young male absorption with their physical prowess. To many of the young male warriors-in-waiting, the prime milestone along the road to military manhood lay in their competitive strength, speed and stamina. The academies fed the need for male-to-male appraisal by grading what were essentially physical fitness tests, by making contests out of scored field exercises. The women who couldn't keep up were not only scorned by the male cadets but were also deemed risks to the national defense.

The academy had reevaluated the physical and military training programs in the 70s which were creating the most tension between men and women, changed some and dropped a few. The Enduro Run, a timed "buddy-team" run up and down steep hills in full field gear, was canceled after the third summer of Cadet Field Training because male cadets bitterly teamed with female cadets got lower scores than all-male teams. "This was the event that sparked the most criticism of the women by the men," wrote Donna Peterson, '81, in her memoir of the second class at West Point. "It's a tough event, and too many women weren't even completing it at all, let alone passing it."

The academy attributed the cancellation of the Enduro Run to the "realization that the run had become an activity which merely emphasized creating a stressful environment for cadets . . . without any educational purpose,"[51] but the young men saw it as a softening of combat training and ruination of a West Point tradition, albeit barely ten years old. "I never heard of the Enduro Run when I was a cadet," says Colonel James L. Anderson, West Point's longtime director of physical education.

With each adjustment, male resentment grew, climaxing in West Point's "Doctrine of Comparable Training." Instead of male and female cadets being held to identical physical standards, the academy developed a formula of "equivalent effort" to equalize the physiological differences between men and women. Male cadets had to complete the academy's required indoor obstacle course in 3:20; women were allotted 5:30.[52] Women received the same grade for completing 48 push-ups in two minutes as men did for 72, for running two miles in 14:46 as men ran in 12:43.[53] Women's abdominal muscles gave them a slight advantage. They had to perform 84 sit-ups within two minutes to get a B grade while men had to do 82.[54]

Though comparable gender standards were provided for by law and policy at the other academies and in the services, they were unforgivable to the male cadets at West Point. ". . . A large minority of men . . . want equal treatment with *no* exceptions," concluded one study of the first class of 1980.[55] The demand was no different twelve years later. "Man to man, woman to man, let's see how many push-ups you can do and let that determine our promotions," said a furious male cadet in 1992.

That proportionately more female than male cadets had been selected as Rhodes and Marshall scholars by 1992,[56] and proportionately more women entering West Point had been National Honor Society members and high school valedictorians and salutatorians in all but two years since integration in 1976,[57] would never translate to leadership qualities in the young male culture. In the 90s as in the 70s, the only criteria were how much weight cadet women could carry and how far and fast they could run. "It's the only way to get their respect," says cadet Karen Roe, '92, who ran a 44-mile race from the George Washington Bridge to the Bear Mountain Bridge in just over seven hours. "They say, 'Hey, look at her. She can run.' "

The reputation and harassment level each female cadet would live with for four years at West Point rested on twelve weeks of physical training, the first six at Cadet Basic Training—or "Beast Barracks"—during freshman summer, the second six at Cadet Field Training during sophomore summer. Academics never entered the lexicon. "Your classmates look at you and remember, 'Oh, that's the one who couldn't carry her rucksack' or 'That's the one who couldn't carry the M-60,' " said a senior "Firstie" in 1992. "It's sad that nothing else counts here but those two summers."

Women's unwelcome participation in the young male rites of physical passage did not seem enough to explain their high rates of harassment at West Point. While some female cadets lagged behind the males, more than a few competed at male levels. In 1995 cadet Rebecca Marier would combine a 3.95 academic average with 70 push-ups, 100 sit-ups and 6-minute miles to become the first woman to graduate at the top of her class.

The answer lay more in the threat all women posed to the most macho of young male cultures, the unique dynamics of tokenism and the political pressure on the academy to resolve the unresolvable. At the uncomfortable epicenter of the military gender wars at West Point were the academy's well-intentioned and beleaguered colonels.

West Point was tense in March 1992. The colonels had been summoned by DACOWITS to a spring meeting of all the academies in the wake of the Dreyer handcuffing at the Naval Academy and the lurid stories emerging about the molesting of women at the 1991 Tailhook convention. The GAO's reports on sexual harassment, hazing and the treatment of women and minorities at West Point were hanging over the academy like the sword of Damocles. Though the GAO's report on sexual harassment at the academies would not be officially released until January 1994, the West Point colonels had the early results and were already practicing damage control.

"I don't attribute any Machiavellian tendencies to the GAO investigators, whom I've got to believe are trying to do their job," says Colonel H. Steven Hammond, West Point's director of the Office of Leader Development Integration. "But I do wish they would send qualified people in here to do their assessments and write their reports. The people they sent up here don't know a thing to begin with. You sit them down and spoon-feed them for weeks and months on end, and they just basically choose to ignore everything they're being told. Some people have come to the conclusion that they have an agenda."

The colonels were already on the anti-feminist agenda of the political far right. Phyllis Schlafly and Elaine Donnelly were building a case against women in combat with excerpts from Colonel Patrick Toffler's 1991 testimony about gender integration changes at West Point as a witness of fact in the legal confrontation between the Justice Department and the Virginia Military Institute over admitting women. West Point stood accused by the political conservatives of falsifying women's physical education scores through "gender-norming" the differences between men and women, of "sex-norming" the unearned advancement of women through affirmative action and gender quotas, then "hiding it from the public."[58]

At the opposite end of the polarized gender debate, the colonels were on the DACOWITS pro-feminist agenda for their policy of requiring female plebes whose roommates were away to move in temporarily with other female plebes to discourage male cadets from making unwanted night visits. Splashed across the pages of the *Army Times* and the *Air Force Times* in December 1991 was an angry confrontation between the executive committee of DACOWITS and the colonels over the academy's "No Sleep Alone" policy and the addition of privacy locks to cadet doors.

Instead of the committee praising the colonels for their policy, which had resulted in no reported incidents of "unauthorized touching" for two years, DACOWITS had accused them of punishing the wrong people by making the women move. "I think one thing this [policy] points out is, who is the burden on?" charged Jean Jackson, the panel's chair designate for 1992. The colonel's target should be the academy culture, which fosters such behavior toward women, held DACOWITS, not the barracks gropers who are merely a symptom. "It's an underneath atmosphere that we're looking for—that we want you to look at," urged DACOWITS chair Becky Costantino.[59]

The colonels were well aware of the ongoing cultural hostility toward women. In every survey of graduating seniors since 1981, only 11 to 37 percent of female cadets reported feeling "totally accepted" by other cadets, compared to 48 to 71 percent of the men.[60] That an ongoing majority of male cadets felt that women's integration had not been successful[61] did not signal a failure to the colonels nor any cause for alarm. To the West Point colonels, the gender disharmony among cadets was just a fact.

"Feelings are important, but we cannot possibly predicate our actions on everybody's feelings," says Colonel Patrick Toffler, director of West Point's celebrated Office of Institutional Research, which conducted the surveys. "What is the result if, after ten years, you find out there is still a large percentage of men or women who don't feel they've been accepted. Therefore the 'experiment' has failed? This is not an experiment. This is an operational reality. And we don't make operational decisions about whether to continue or to discontinue a practice on the basis of people's feelings."

More important to Toffler was the operational efficiency of the Army. "Is the sociological challenge of women's integration within the service a showstopper? Absolutely not. Unless we, of course, allow it to be," he says. "We know that there are some women who do not feel they have been fully accepted. And we know that there are some men who do not fully accept women. We *think* we know that the fundamental, underlying problem is the physiological difference and the male resentment that men get 100 points for doing 10 pull-ups and a woman does 3 and gets the same grade. But are the physiological differences a showstopper? In the case of women as a group, the answer is no."

The colonels dismissed one male complaint after another, including the academy's controversial doctrine of "comparable training," or "gender-norming," as Schlafly and Donnelly referred to it.

"I'm the guy who designed the program and I think I did it for good and valid reasons," says Colonel Anderson in his office at the Arvin Gym. "The men resent it, but they'll get over it. It's explained well enough to them so that if they want to understand, they will. If they don't have anything else to bring attention to themselves, then this can be their issue."

The persistent complaint that physical standards had been lowered at West Point, that training was softer, was as predictable to Anderson as it was laughable. "Old grads always think they had it tougher," chuckles the former Army Ranger and instructor who presided over the integration of women in 1976. "In my Founders' Day talk this year I'm going to tell them, 'Yup, the corps really has gotten softer. Can you imagine, at the end of the indoor obstacle course we put out a bucket for the cadets to vomit in. It used to be, when you upchucked, it was just all over the floor.' "

In contrast to the male cadets, the colonels welcomed women at West Point. "The academy is so much more a better place because women have come," says Colonel John Wattendorf, head of the Department of Behavioral Sciences and Leadership and chair of West Point's Human Resources Council. "There is so much for us to learn from what we have traditionally called feminine traits. Personally, I think those are human traits that women exhibit more frequently than men."

The enlightened colonels showcased the hundred plus female officers assigned to the academy, among them thirty-five graduates, as role models for both female and male cadets.[62] Women officers represented close to 10 percent of the academic faculty at West Point —forty-four of the 458 officers. Five of the academy's thirty-six company tactical officers were female, as was one of the four regimental executive officers, all of whom worked directly with the cadets on every aspect of their day-to-day life at West Point.

"I'm in charge of 1,076 cadets, one-fourth of the corps," says Lieutenant Colonel Peggy Bahnsen, the most senior female officer at West Point and the first to head a West Point regiment. "I'm responsible for their discipline, the billets they live in, what they eat in the mess hall, whatever they do here, day to day, including their off time."

The colonels were up to speed on "Chill in the Classroom," the recent breakthrough on gender barriers to learning. "We discovered

. . . we didn't just discover . . . we became more aware that a number of our problems stemmed from the faculty. It wasn't just cadets with cadets," says Colonel Wattendorf.

The academy had developed its own syllabus on "chill," including cadet videotapes which, according to Wattendorf, showed "caricatures of just about everything wrong." References to women's weight was a natural. Not only did fat jokes abound in the male culture, but one out of three female cadets was estimated to be suffering from bulimia or anorexia.[63] "One video starts out with three male cadets joking in class about three female cadets standing on the top of the barracks and wondering who's going to fall first. 'The barracks because of overweight.' The male cadets laugh at the punch line while the instructor just rolls his eyes and smirks without intervening," says Wattendorf. "Another starts with the instructor saying, 'Why, Miss Johnson. You look different. Have you lost weight?' "

The colonels were taking the same innovative aim at identifying and preventing "date rape." While feminists on both sides of the controversial issue were arguing publicly in 1992 as to whether date rape was epidemic on civilian college campuses or the figment of female guilt, West Point quietly launched its own probe of date rape in the corps of cadets. The result was a cadet endeavor to write and act out on stage a date rape scenario, modeled, according to Wattendorf, on the Cornell psychodrama and designed to educate the entire corps in West Point's "very aggressive, macho environment."

The colonels were finally becoming aware of the effect of the academy's combat culture on women. The very names given to the second summer sessions of Cadet Field Training—Armor Week, Infantry Week and Artillery Week—underscored the young male image of themselves as warriors and women as useless tagalongs who received the same combat training but could not serve in combat. "Some of the men felt women shouldn't participate because they couldn't be in infantry or armor," says Wattendorf.

That female cadets dropped out of West Point at twice the rate of men after the second summer suggested a correlation between the combat training and women's higher attrition rate. The training neither prepared them for the noncombat jobs open to them nor awarded any status to their support roles. "We were guilty of doing things that tended to suggest to women that 'you're not part of the fraternity' after plebe year," says Colonel H. Steven Hammond. "I think women began to realize that 'hey, this organization doesn't really want me.' "

The colonels' solution was not to advocate changing the Army policy against women in combat. Even after the Gulf war the idea was anathema to the colonels. Instead, the colonels chose to downplay the male exclusivity inherent in the combat training by changing the names of the weeks. With one stroke of the colonels' gender-sensitive pens in 1991, Armor Week became Maneuver Heavy Week, Infantry Week became Maneuver Light Week, and Artillery Week became Fire Support Week.[64]

The colonels were cautiously optimistic that the academy's new programs, combined with the fifty-three curriculum hours on social issues and social dynamics, would save West Point the embarrassment of the Naval Academy after the Dreyer handcuffing and the Air Force Academy after all thirty-two members of the 1992 "Wings of Blue" parachute team were disciplined and the Air Force captain in charge fired for allowing underage drinking, lewd rituals and the sexual harassment of two female cadets competing for team slots.[65]

"Nothing has happened here on the scale of what has happened out at Air Force or at Navy, but, I will quickly add, there but for the grace of God, go us," says Colonel Hammond. "I am not at all so naive as to believe that kind of thing couldn't happen here. But I really believe that we take much more seriously our responsibility to ensure that we provide an environment that minimizes the likelihood of that kind of thing happening."

West Point did seem to have a winning formula as evidenced in the charts and graphs of the academy's 1992 report to DACOWITS on women's integration and performance. Women were excelling academically; fully 68 and 64 percent of senior women in the classes of '90 and '91 made the dean's list, compared to 52 and 56 percent of the men.[66] Women were holding their own in physical education. Though proportionately more upperclass female cadets than males got final grades of D in the classes of '91, '92 and '93, a higher percentage of women than men in all three classes got As. Women were hard on men's heels in the academy's military program as well, achieving overall performance ratings of 3.21 to men's 3.23.[67]

The environment for women also seemed measurably improved since the turmoil of the 70s. Women's historically higher attrition rate seemed to be leveling off. For the first time since integration, a higher percentage of men (16.1 percent) in the class of '94 had dropped out by the middle of their second year than had women (15.6 percent). And though the academy's report admitted that "vestiges of resistance continue to persist," the colonels were equally quick to point out that 73 percent of female cadets in the class of '91, the same percentage as the males, reported that they would recommend West Point to high school seniors.[68] "In spite of the evidence for some level of gender bias in the Corps, women seem to value the West Point experience as positively as do men," the report concluded.

What the report to DACOWITS glossed over were the early results of the GAO's survey of sexual and gender harassment tacked on to the end of the 102-page report as Appendix B and expanded in the GAO's published survey of harassment in 1994.

The "vestiges of resistance" to women reported to DACOWITS by the colonels translated in the GAO surveys to over half the female cadets experiencing "mocking gestures," offensive posters or graffiti and "derogatory comments" at least once a month. One in six female cadets reported being repeated targets of "unwanted horseplay or hijinks" while one in seven reported "unwanted sexual advances."[69] "There is still a lot of resentment of women being here and a lot of harassment and sexual harassment cases that never get reported . . . ," a female cadet told the GAO.[70]

Officially, the colonels didn't know the half of it. While a substantial majority of both male and female cadets believed the academy's officers would investigate any reported incidents of discrimination or harassment and discipline the offenders, the perceived cost of reporting their peers was higher at West Point than it was at the Naval or Air Force Academies. Eighty-eight percent of the female cadets (and 83 percent of the male cadets) agreed with the GAO statement that they would be viewed by their fellow cadets as "crybabies."[71]

For all the colonels' efforts, the entrenched resistance to women hadn't budged an inch. "Women don't belong here!" one male student told the GAO. "The majority of women here expect special treatment because they are women. They enter a world that has been dominated for a long time by men and they expect us all to get along. It doesn't work!"[72]

Said another: "I wish I had been born with my parents' generation before females destroyed this place. The West Point I attend is nothing like that I read about that produced MEN like Lee, Eisenhower, and the many other brave SOLDIERS. What makes them want to become men? Even [though] I would never openly harass women, I hope they understand they are not welcome here."[73]

The academies would protest when the GAO's sexual harassment reports were published in 1994. The survey had covered the 1990–91 academic year, the Naval Academy complained, and was as outdated as it was inaccurate. "Since that time, many corrective actions, policy changes and new programs were initiated," read a statement released by the Naval Academy. "The results have already been marked and significant."

The GAO would return to the academies in 1993–94 to update the surveys of sexual harassment. The results, published in 1995, found that incidents of sexual harassment had gone up, not down, at all the academies.[74] The rise in harassment was most pronounced at the Air Force and Naval Academies.[75] But the cadets at West Point still led the pack.

The female tactical officers gathered in Lieutenant Colonel Peggy Bahnsen's office, a masculine mosaic of black leather, eagle-embossed curtains and heavy wood furniture leavened only slightly by West Point's most senior female officer with her own plants and a candy dish. In spite of the winter raw day, the junior officers, two majors and a captain, wore skirts. So did Lieutenant Colonel Bahnsen, a strikingly attractive woman who fit somewhere into the age range of forty-seven to fifty-one on the Army's physical training charts and twice a year aced the Army's required two-mile run a full three minutes faster than the 20 minutes and 36 seconds allotted her age group and gender.

Wearing their uniform skirts instead of long pants was neither incidental nor a fashion statement to the officers. Neither was their long hair, which they arranged the regulation inch over their collars in a single French braid or in the more formal French twist, nor their lipstick, eye shadow or faint suggestion of blush highlighting Lieutenant Colonel Bahnsen's cheekbones. The officers' studied feminine appearance was a gender manifesto for the female cadets in the numerically daunting community of hostile young men.

"That was one of the reasons I was brought in, to be a senior woman role model," says Bahnsen, the wife of a retired general. "The cadets can look at me every day and think, Number one, she wears skirts. Number two, she's not overweight. Number three, she's not a butch/dyke. And number four, she still does this job. By God, it can work and I can do that, too."

That the female cadets at West Point in the 90s felt as compelled as their 70s predecessors to adopt a mannish, short-haired, no makeup appearance in order to blend into the male majority underscored how little had changed at West Point. Though the gender camouflage so many women had adopted twenty years before to disguise their entry into male worlds should have been long gone, it wasn't.

"You see it here with the cadets," says Major Heidi Brown, her eyes accented by blue eye shadow. "They act like the men, they look like the men. They do their hair real short and start cussing like sailors, just to fit in. That's the good thing about having the role models here that we do, to show them you don't have to do that to fit in, to succeed. You can just be yourself."

West Point had forecast just such a scenario for women cadets as early as 1980. The futile warning then in the superintendent's report to "communicate to both cadets and officers alike that the physiological differences between the sexes do *not,* in and of themselves, restrict women's ability to serve in the Army, nor the propriety of their involvement"[76] mirrored the equally futile warning about the consequences of too few women among too many men.

"Women presently constitute eight to ten percent of the Corps, and it is unlikely that their proportions will increase significantly in the near future," the report had concluded with the graduation of the first class of women. "Thus women will continue to face the peculiar problems which result from being in a minority."[77] Over a decade later, the ratio of women to men was roughly the same.

The consequences of women's tokenism had been identified in 1977 by Yale sociology professor Rosabeth Moss Kanter, which included their high visibility, one-size-fits-all stereotyping, performance pressure and social isolation.[78] She had also identified the dynamic of "boundary heightening,"[79] in which the token presence of a few "outsiders" served to magnify the bonds and traits "insiders" didn't even know they shared. Such "peculiar problems" of tokenism were everyday realities for the 130 freshmen women among the 1,188 cadets entering West Point in 1992, and a major contributor to the high rate of harassment reported by all female cadets.

At the DACOWITS summit meeting with the academies in the spring of 1992, the members seemed startled to discover that women still made up only 12.6 percent of cadets in the class of '96 at the Air Force Academy, 11.4 percent at West Point and a more robust 13.7 percent at the Naval Academy, which had embarked on a flurry of female recruitment after the Dreyer handcuffing and bettered the ratio for women from one to ten to one to seven. In one of the sweeter ironies, female athletes had become the golden fleece to Naval Academy recruiters after the academy's post-Dreyer report identified athletes as the most successful women to navigate the academy's rough waters. Because only 9.5 percent of the female midshipmen who dropped out of the academy were varsity letter winners compared to the 46.3 percent who had never played on a varsity team,[80] the Naval Academy was actively recruiting women with the same athletic talents that had categorized them as lesbians just ten years before and the targets of Navy witch-hunts.

But the number of women at the academies seemed suspiciously low and their attrition rate too high to the members of DACOWITS, especially at the Air Force Academy, where between 32 and 37 percent of the female cadets in the last three graduating classes (of '90, '91 and '92) had left before graduation, compared to 24 to 27 percent of the males.[81] Still enraged by the revelation of treatment of women midshipmen at the Naval Academy, DACOWITS was not about to tolerate the same cultural hostility or indifference to women at the other academies.

"Do you know why there is a difference in male and female attrition rates?" DACOWITS member Thomas Stafford charged the Air Force officer presenting the academy's status report on female cadets.

There was a long pause. "No," the Air Force officer admitted

"Do you have any idea? What is your guess?" Stafford pressed.

"They leave for the same reasons as the men, sir," the officer replied casually. " 'I have a change in career plans.' 'I don't like the academics.' Some are flunking out."

The answer hardly satisfied the committee members who had seen much more positive change for women on civilian campuses than they were seeing at the military academies. "The climate has changed so dramatically for women in the past decade," persisted another DACOWITS member. "I thought the acceptance rate would be much higher and the attrition rate lower. But it doesn't seem to have any impact on the service academies. I wonder why."

"There is a finite limit to the proportion of the female population that is interested in the military," the Air Force officer responded, recycling the half-truth used by all the academies that it was women's disinclination to military service that limited their representation at the academies, not the academies' lack of effort to recruit women. But while it was true that the pool of qualified female applicants was small for all the academies, it was also true that the pool was big enough to satisfy the academies' enrollment goals for women. And neither the services nor their respective academies saw any advantage to actively recruiting more women.

"Do we, in the interest of 'equal opportunity,' sweeten the deal for women to bring more in when we're in a market where we bring in an adequate number of people to meet our needs?" the Air Force officer challenged the members of DACOWITS, this time infuriating them. That sixteen years after integration, the academy's spokesman was still invoking the political motivation of "equal opportunity" as the rationale for women at the academies and not their military value as future officers signaled to DACOWITS exactly why there were still so few women at the academies and why so many left.

"I would like you to consider the possibility that the way the military treats women may have a significant impact on the interest of women to join the military!" Stafford thundered at the Air Force officer. "Therefore, another way to look at that problem is to look at the way women are recruited and treated and assimilated into the services!"

It was confrontations like this one that endeared DACOWITS to servicewomen, including the female officers at West Point gathered in Lieutenant Colonel Bahnsen's office. But while the officers knew that no other civilian group had the clout or the access to challenge the military mind-set, the officers also knew that not even DACOWITS could alter the anti-female bias in the numerically skewed cadet culture. All the officers could do was wear skirts.

"It takes women with experience telling these young cadets right now that we know what you're going through and it's OK to be a woman. Don't apologize for it," says Captain Laurie Barone, class of '83. "I never had the role model who said to me, 'You're going to feel better about yourself if maybe you wear a little makeup to class.' Not that femininity has to be associated with makeup and nail polish, but I think it's a part of it while you're here when you're not sure who you are."

The plebe women settled nervously into the first few rows of a classroom in Grant Hall in March 1992. Still ten days short of Recognition Day when upperclassmen could call them by their first names and perhaps make friends, when the plebes could speak to each other outside the permissible zones of their bedrooms and the academic building, walk at their own pace instead of double time and actually look around them instead of straight ahead, the young women didn't know what rules existed for the interview, or whether they could talk anything but the required "company" pep talk.

"Right now, every time we go by an upperclassman, we have to say, 'Good morning, sir. Go Dragon!' or 'Go Zoo!' or 'Go Where Eagles Dare!' or 'Go Cock!' I hate that one," says one plebe. "My company used to be 'Go Naked,' but they made us change it."

The plebes were about to pass another milestone on Recognition Day. After nine months of the academy's gender-neutral indoctrination during which they had been treated exactly like male plebes right down to a short, regulation haircut, they would be allowed to start growing their hair and to wear skirts. But just as the female officers predicted, few of the cadets were going to exercise the option. Wearing skirts set them apart from the male majority and drew sexual taunts. But so did wearing uniform pants. "They call female cadets Gray Trou, and talk about us in real derogatory terms," says a plebe. In the catch-22 of token gender at West Point, the only "real" women to the young male cadets were their girlfriends pictured in frilly dresses or bathing suits in their rooms.

The reality of stereotyping had set in for the plebes during the initial six summer weeks of physical and military Cadet Basic Training at Camp Buckner before the academic year began. "One female stops and can't finish a road march and suddenly no females can finish a march and no female can do anything the guys can do," says a plebe. When women did well, the dynamic reversed. "The problem with small proportions is that if somebody within that small proportion does well, they are considered an exception to the rule," says Bill Beusse, who directed the GAO research on sexual harassment at the academies.

Senior women often exerted more performance pressure on the

plebes than did their male colleagues. Some female plebes responded by overexerting themselves, contributing to women's higher injury rates which, in 1984, accounted for twice as many stress fractures as among men.[82] But the injured female plebes received no praise, as the male plebes did, for motivation. "As a percentage, more girls hurt themselves than the guys in my company, but as a ratio it was like one guy for one girl," says a plebe. "But the guys never saw the guys. They always just saw the girl. The word was 'She's weak' and 'She's a quitter' and 'She's not good enough.' "

The social isolation began after the plebes marched the fourteen ritual miles back to the academy in August to join the upperclassmen. They learned quickly that the bonds of brotherhood did not extend to sisters. "All of a sudden the guys who had talked to you all summer are not speaking to you because they don't want to be seen talking to you," recalls Captain Kathleen Batton of the long march she had made back from Beast Barracks in 1977. "What was normal was suddenly abnormal because they'd been told women didn't belong at West Point. You get shunned. Oh, you definitely get shunned."

Women's perceived threat to young male cohesion was as powerful in the 90s. "I was in a great company this summer," says one plebe in the class of '95. "If we were on a hill I couldn't get up, the guys would pick up my ruck, but wouldn't cut on me about it, even behind my back. Now they're coming into my room all the time making sexual jokes referring to me." Adds another: "My best friend wanted to go to the Naval Academy, but he didn't get in so he came here with me. Incidentally, we don't talk to each other anymore."

With their gender an obvious disadvantage, the plebes fulfilled the prophecies of the female officers by entering a gender limbo, subverting their own feminine identities to adopt a more acceptable male identity. They had no alternative in West Point's cadet command structure, which dispersed all four classes of female cadets by twos among companies of around 120 cadets each. In the academy's barracks culture, the thirty-six cadet companies were West Point's leadership training, hierarchical and social units.

"Your roommate's a girl, but there are eight other guys in your squad, and you do everything with your squad from 5 a.m. to 11:30 p.m., when you go to bed," says a senior. "They tell you their jokes and call you by your last name and you begin to look at the world through male eyes because that's who most of your friends are. As long as you recognize it, it's not bad. So long as you know when you're doing it."

By adopting the posture of a third sex, neither male nor female, the female cadets tried to blend in with the male group, to belong without being noticed. In their eagerness to "bond," the female cadets learned to be passive participants in male traditions. "I'll be the only girl in a room and they'll be talking about girls and what they did with them over the weekend and I go, 'I'm going to be quiet because if I tell them to stop talking that way, they'll never talk to me again,' " says a sophomore. "So I just put up with it."

So valued was the male stamp of approval that the token female cadets embraced their sometimes puzzling status as a third sex. "The guys call civilian girls 'regular' girls. I take that as a compliment in a way," says a junior. "We do a lot of the same stuff the guys do and they classify us on a different level than civilian girls. They call them chicks. Now I find myself calling civilian girls chicks. It's weird. We end up disparaging our own sex."

The gender puzzle at West Point became more puzzling when the female cadets occasionally dropped their male disguises and reverted to their identity as women. "Sometimes you want the guys to think of you as a girl and not as a cadet and other times you want them to think of you as a cadet and not as a girl," says a plebe. "You get confused here a lot."

The simpler course for the female cadets was to remain neuter and define their relationships with male cadets as "sister-brother." When the sibling relationships went sour, the female cadets felt betrayed. One West Point sophomore almost left the academy after coming close to becoming a sex exercise for a group of drunken cadets just before final exams in December. An upperclassman in her company chanced on the scene and broke it up.

The barracks incident shattered whatever male bonds the female cadet thought she had achieved in the teamwork environment at West Point. "I nearly started crying in formation," she says. "These guys and I had gone through all this stuff together and I should be able to trust them. But no."

The cadet's story opened a Pandora's box among plebes and other second-year cadets of their own near misses, including the male cadets who entered their rooms at night. In profiles close to those of battered women who forgive, the female cadets blamed extenuating circumstances for the incidents, not the male cadets. It was alcohol, the female cadets argued, that had made 20 percent of them, one out of five, subject to the uninvited night gropers.[83]

The female cadets dismissed the academy's solution to barracks' predators of installing locks on the bedroom doors. "We never use the locks," says one plebe proudly. "That's like saying you don't trust your own classmates." Moreover, the plebes said, the male cadets had broken most of the locks by horsing around in the halls and "accidentally" falling against the doors.

It was just this tolerance of male misbehavior by female cadets that West Point's female officers were trying, unsuccessfully, to over-come. From the sophomoric male tradition of channeling a slit in the top of the peanut butter jars found on every table in the cadet mess, raising one end to mimic a clitoris, then filling the cavity with jelly and passing it to the female cadets—"They *still* do that?" says one officer—to the more serious sexual advantage upperclassmen continued to take of female plebes, the young male culture marched on, unchanged.

"If we catch them, they're out," says Captain Barone. "But the plebes won't identify the upperclassmen who hit on them because they don't want to get anyone in trouble. After all this time, it still happens."

The female cadets who did report infractions risked double jeop-ardy. In the spring of 1992, the entire male corps had dedicated itself to driving out one sophomore who had named the male cadets who had injured her as a plebe in an illegal physical hazing exercise. "They made her jump over a broomstick at the top of the stairs," says a classmate. When the plebe returned to the academy, she faced round-the-clock intimidation from the classes of '91, '92 and '93. "They thought they'd gotten rid of her, but she was determined," says the classmate. "She almost left at the end of last year. 'I'm sorry. I've tried my hardest but they're getting me again,' she wrote us on e-mail. But she made it through and I'm glad she did. She's a year-ling [sophomore] now."

The tradition of targeted hazing continued to escape every effort the colonels made to eradicate it. "If they're determined to get you out, they won't stop until they succeed," says a sophomore. "With someone watching you all the time, you're bound to screw up on something. If they can't get you out on a military grade or something like that, they'll invent something for honors, whether you're male or female." Women remained the preferred target, however. The

GAO's 1994 study of gender and racial disparities at West Point found that a higher ratio of female cadets were charged with Honor Code violations than were male cadets and received lower military grades in four of the five classes reviewed.[84]

It was far more beneficial to the subculture of women at West Point to prove their loyalty to the male group by passing their tests. So they jumped over broomsticks, badmouthed their own gender and learned quickly to laugh off the ritualistic male taunts and dirty jokes to assure the men they shared their cultural attitudes.

Less easy to laugh off were the fat jokes and innuendo, a particularly effective and sometimes dangerous weapon to use against young women in the pressure-cooker environment at the academies. "The level of anorexia and bulimia at West Point is terrible," says Judy de Bock, '94. "Every time you turn around someone is telling you you're fat, your clothes don't fit right. It drives girls not to eat at all or to eat too much and throw up because you can't deal with the pressure. Girls come here looking fine, and after a while their bodies get so messed up from not eating or overeating or not knowing what to eat."

The female officers at West Point acknowledged the gender issue of eating disorders, which were prevalent as well at the other academies. A 1988 Air Force Academy study had determined that the female cadets there had a significantly higher level of bulimia (12 percent) than was typically found among women at civilian colleges. But the West Point officers were thwarted by the secrecy inherent in the disease and in the cadet culture itself. "I know it's a serious problem, but we can't get a handle on it because the gals will not talk about it," says Lieutenant Colonel Bahnsen. "Can I point out the gals who are anorexic or bulimic? No, I can't."

The time warp of tokenism at West Point perpetuated another phenomenon unique to the academies. Instead of women's harassment diminishing during their last two years at the academies, it *increased.*

Colonel Hammond tried to put a positive spin on the conundrum to the DACOWITS committee in 1992 by linking the increased harassment at West Point to the rise in women's academic scores. "Women don't do as well in the first two years, mostly because of the physical demands," he suggested. "They gain on men academically in the last two years, which might play into attitudinal problems." A DACOWITS member accepted the upbeat rationale, noting the exact same ratio of increased harassment to increased academic achievement at the Air Force Academy. "Women start to achieve in the fall of their junior year and keep going," said Dr. Carole Garrison. "The women are catching up and I think the men are pissed about it."

But the more plausible explanation lay less in women's academic success, about which the male cadets cared little, than in the reality that the female cadets were actually going to become officers. West Point cadets could resign without penalty from the tuition-free academies during their first two years but lost that option at the stroke of noon on the first day of formal classes in their junior year. The apocryphal moment simultaneously marked the commitment of the cadets to at least six years of active-duty military service and the redoubled efforts of the males to drive women out.

The escalation of harassment was just as pronounced at the Coast Guard Academy, where the difference between men's and women's attrition rate was statistically higher than at any other service academy. "You look left and right and one female cadet won't be there when you graduate," says a junior grade lieutenant graduate just off the icebreaker *Penobscot Bay.* "The Coast Guard Academy is the biggest white male club of all. Not one black male or female graduated with my class." The source of the increased harassment, a Coast Guard Academy spokesman suggested to DACOWITS, was male elitism. The longer the male cadets stayed at the Coast Guard Academy, the more they assumed male officer stereotypes and therefore more negative attitudes toward their female classmates who dared think they, too, could become Coast Guard officers.

What none of the academy studies or officers pointed out was that women, too, adopted male officer stereotypes in their junior year. Whether the committed female cadets at West Point became more "masculine" to avoid the increased harassment or whether their increased harassment led them to deeper disguises as "men," the female cadets nonetheless redoubled their efforts in their last two years to join the brotherhood of male cadets. "It's almost as if you live your life for that, especially after yearling year," says a senior. "Women change their minds about how they feel about virtually everything, including their female friends, just to be accepted more."

Junior and senior cadets competed for hotly contested leadership positions, but with different results. The selection of male cadets won universal acclaim; women's selection was laid to political correctness. In keeping with an academy report in the 70s which attributed women's token status to male charges of institutional "favoritism . . . in the selection of women for leadership positions," male cadets in the 90s remained just as convinced that the academy disproportionately selected women for cadet honors when the opposite was true. The GAO's 1994 report on gender and racial disparities at West Point found that senior cadet women were consistently selected at *lower* rates for top positions than were men. It was women's high visibility as tokens that translated into a female takeover of the academy's coveted leadership roles.[85]

"If there's a female CO in front of her company in parades and they announce her, everybody goes, 'Oh, there's a woman' and everyone applauds, but the guys don't stick out because they're so many of them," says a senior. "We came to the conclusion that they think there are more women in leadership positions because we're more noticeable."

So hassled were the female cadets who were awarded leadership positions that they half believed the male charges of institutional favoritism. "We're told there are no quotas, but realistically they probably feel they have to have a woman on staff," says a senior. "I was told that flat out for a march-on last year when we were going to be on national TV and it turned out the entire company staff was male. They quickly stuck in a girl because it was supposed to be politically correct."

The possibility of gender manipulation caused the female cadets to doubt their academy achievements, a doubt the male cadets never had to consider. "The march-on really bothered me because sometimes it makes you wonder," says the senior. "I've got a pretty decent position, but did I earn this position or am I just on a quota? It bothers me and I know it bothers others."

The female cadets took heart from West Point's female officers, especially the graduates who had obviously survived their own experience at the academy. The older cadets scrutinized the leadership styles of the officers and talked to them about the particular circumstances they would face out in the Army. "I went on a ski trip with Major Haas, and she told me how she can't have children right away if she wants to be promoted, all these different things that people don't think about," says a junior.

It was for these cadets that the female officers continued to do battle at West Point, to spearhead the change that remained so elusive. "You get worn down by it if you allow yourself to be," says Lieutenant Colonel Bahnsen. "You get tired sometimes of always walking point, of being the person who walks a considerable distance ahead of the main group. That's the person who gets shot."

The payoff for Lieutenant Colonel Bahnsen came from the senior cadets who had taken note of her studied femininity over their four years at West Point and were about to emerge from their protective male shells. "The more mature ones come up to me around graduation time, but never before, and say, 'Thanks. I know it's all right to wear makeup, have long hair, wear skirts and be feminine,'" says Bahnsen.

Among Bahnsen's more "mature" cadets in 1992 was graduating cadet Judy DeBock, who was sporting a fresh coat of clear polish on her fingernails, and Karen Roe, who was withdrawing from the bull sessions in the barracks. "I've been male bonding with these guys for three years, listening to their weekend sexual conquests and going, 'Yeah, great,'" says Roe. "I don't need to do that anymore."

The unique pressures on the token young women in the combat culture at West Point were only really understood by the long, thin line of women who had preceded them. "Are things easy for them? No. Do they feel integrated? No. Yet cadet women are achieving well militarily, academically and physically in spite of all the machismo and not feeling accepted," says Captain Mimi Finch, a former officer at the academy. "In a nonnurturing environment, they are kicking ass. And that is the bottom line."

In the complexities of the academy culture, it is little wonder that only 15 percent of graduating female cadets surveyed by West Point in 1991 reported feeling "totally accepted" by their classmates, a far lower percentage than graduating Asians or Hispanics and substantially lower than African-Americans (37 percent).[86] Almost twenty years after the first class of women entered West Point, gender continued to override the liabilities faced by every other minority in the white male culture. "About 90% of the women perceived that the harassment they experienced was based on their gender, as opposed to race, religion, or ethnic origin," the GAO would report in 1994.[87]

Black male cadets, slightly less than half of whom in the class of '91 felt that the integration of minorities had been a success at West Point, were, in fact, the only young men who had actually welcomed women to the academy. "Black cadets have told me that one of the benefits of having women come here is that they weren't being picked on anymore," says Stephen Grove, West Point's historian. "Black cadets were now one of the 'good guys.' 'You belong in the corps,' the white cadets said. 'It's the women we don't want.' "

The male cadets were sitting in neat rows in the Thayer Award Room, a Military Gothic stone reception hall donated by the Class of '31 for its fiftieth reunion. Broad-shouldered, athletically slim, their gray uniforms blending seamlessly into the floor-to-ceiling stone, the cadets seemed sculpted out of West Point's timeless granite. The only spots of color in the otherwise humorless, vaulted stone expanse were West Point's regimental flags and the startling cheerfulness of the spotlit American flag.

The male cadets were the very model of enlightenment advanced by the colonels. They seemed to have overcome the culture's "warrior" mentality. "West Point's mission is to provide leaders of character not only in the military, but industry, politics and everywhere leadership is needed in the nation," intones one cadet.

They supported women at West Point. "I think the Army has to reflect changes in our society," says one of the eight cadets—five seniors, two juniors and one sophomore. "Women are becoming more important and more visible in the workplace. If the Army doesn't reflect that, it doesn't reflect the nation."

The male cadets insisted that women did not experience sexual harassment at West Point. "We have a real tight-knit society in the Army and we can say things in front of the girls that people on the outside might find offensive," says a male cadet. "But I think that's good training for when they get out in the Regular Army."

Women were definitely sexually safer at West Point than they were at other colleges. Though almost every one of them went on to identify a sexual incident—a female cadet "nearly raped" by a cadet processing out of the academy, the sexual assaults "of several girls I know," male cadets walking through the women's bathrooms and prowling women's rooms, taking their "panties"—the cadets insisted women at West Point "have less exposure to sexual assault than other schools." "There are isolated incidents," says a cadet company commander.

There were problems, however, especially with the idea of

women in combat. "Anyone's fibbing you if they tell you it's not the girls who're falling out of the road marches at Camp Buckner," says one cadet. "We stick all the girls right up front so everyone else pushes them up the hill."

The heretical suggestion from a lone male cadet that some women did have the strength to serve in the infantry—"I was huffing and puffing along at Camp Buckner and there were girls just tracking along, sometimes carrying rifles for the guys who fell back. If there are some females who can keep up, why slam the door on all females?"—brought the other cadets to their feet.

"We're a country of the majority and we can't look at the minority and isolated events, especially coming out of here," shouts one cadet.

"Is our nation ready for female kills and POWs?" charges another.

"Is it worth the experiment?" says another.

"How many people here have carried either a woman's body or some of their gear during a road march?" shouts a cadet. Every arm in the room went up, some ending in clenched fists.

Having finished off women in the infantry, the cadets turned to tanks.

"The rounds are fifty to seventy-five pounds," says one. "You have to pull them out above your head and shove them up in the breech and do it fast over and over again for two hours."

"There's no latrine in a tank. If a woman is going through her menstrual cycle there's no opportunity for her to take care of herself," says another.

"You stop once and everybody gets out!"

"There are other tanks behind you and she'd hold up the entire column!"

"Being a tanker isn't just firing a round downrange or picking it up. There's a lot of heavy maintenance work. We have to carry our water, fuel, tools for the tracks."

The physical strength required to wield a sixty-eight-pound track wrench was a familiar argument against women in tanks. "Have you ever used the wrench to fix the tracks?" I ask. "No," they answered.

It fell to a prior-enlisted cadet who had served in the infantry before coming to West Point to deliver the coup de grâce. "If you're out in the field, you have to dig separate trenches to go to the bathroom, and if you have females, that's an extra trench to dig," he says. "The women didn't have their trench done on time, so the males had to dig the female trench, too. After that, the males were so mad at the females they didn't work together the rest of the time out in the field. It doesn't work!"

Colonel Wattendorf was furious when he heard about the male cadets. The countless hours and years of explanation about the equivalent physical effort made by female cadets given their physiological differences, the downplaying of combat training at Camp Buckner by renaming the weeks of field instruction, the colonels' steadfast support of women at West Point, hadn't made a dent in the young male culture. "Damn," he said, slamming his fist into the palm of his hand.

Lieutenant Colonel Bahnsen was not surprised in the least. The cadets in the Thayer Award Room had simply recycled the young male attitudes at West Point that had stereotyped women as failures for almost twenty years and dismissed their strengths. "The women who have come through West Point have my admiration because they have survived this place," says Bahnsen. "And to a great extent, it's still survival for the women."

Captain Barone merely shrugged. "The institution thinks it's making great strides and on the surface it is," she says. "But when you dig down, the culture really hasn't changed at all."

8

GROUND ZERO

The Siege of the Combat Exclusion Laws

THE BEGINNING of the end to forty-three years of gender discrimination in the military came so abruptly that even its strategists were stunned. On May 8, 1991, Congresswoman Pat Schroeder entered the House Armed Services Committee room with the other committee members to mark up the 1992 defense authorization bill. When she emerged, she had pulled off a stunning political coup. With no advance notice of her proposal, no formal debate, no input from the services or any pressure from grassroots groups, Schroeder had succeeded in attaching the repeal of the combat exclusion law against female pilots to the Defense Department bill. In what a congressional news release would herald as a "landmark action" and conservative organizations would condemn as a "voice vote . . . taken late in the evening behind closed doors,"[1] the committee had voted unanimously to relinquish congressional control over military gender and allow the services to assign women to combat aircraft.

Professional committee staffers inside the congressional meeting room burst into cheers while outside in the hallway the two architects of the Schroeder initiative literally danced for joy. Lisa Moreno, Schroeder's legislative assistant, and Tanya Domi, a defense legislative staffer for Congressman Frank McCloskey of Indiana and former Army officer who had been hounded out of the service by sexual harassment, knew that the proposal's unexpected attachment to the defense authorization bill virtually guaranteed its passage by the House of Representatives. Removing any committee-sponsored amendment was so difficult and took such tremendous political clout that the repeal of the 1948 law by the full House was as good as done.

The victory was all the sweeter to the Schroeder camp because of its serendipity. The proposal Schroeder had put to the committee had been intended as a probe to determine what support, if any, the aviation repeal might have after the Persian Gulf war. Nobody expected it to pass. "It was a test case," says Moreno.

Schroeder and her young collaborators had picked the specific 1948 statute which kept Air Force women out of "aircraft engaged in combat missions"[2] for their test. The statute relegated even the most accomplished women graduating from pilot training at the top of their classes to flying "heavy" transports and tankers or "VIPs" while allowing less accomplished male graduates to fly high-performance fighter jets. The closest women could come to similar jets was as instructors.

The Schroeder camp had decided not to include Navy pilots, though unlike Air Force women, Navy women had been flying combat jets since 1975. The addition of one word in the Navy's combat exclusion law—"Women may not be assigned to duty on vessels or in aircraft that *are* [emphasis added] engaged in combat missions"[3] —allowed Navy women to fly combat jets, but not in combat squadrons. The semantic loophole found the Navy's female pilots qualifying as "Tailhookers" by trapping onto aircraft carriers but not being allowed to join carrier squadrons, flying combat helicopters but only off noncombat ships, and being trained to fly air-to-air gunnery and air combat maneuvering, but not against an enemy.

Broadening the legislative test to include Navy pilots would have been complicated by the restrictions against women on Navy ships. "Mrs. Schroeder felt the Air Force repeal would have been the easiest thing to get through because you wouldn't have to deal with combatant vessels," says Domi.

The law governing women in the Air Force seemed an easier test case as well because it involved so few women; only 3 percent of Air Force jobs were still legally closed to women in 1991, compared to 41 percent in the Navy.[4] And the Air Force itself seemed ready for change. At the post-Panama hearing on Army women in combat the year before, the Air Force deputy chief of staff had all but invited Congress to repeal the law governing its female pilots. "They can fly fighters, they can pull Gs," testified Lieutenant General Thomas Hickey. "They are physically capable and, I think, emotionally capa-

ble. . . . If you want us to put them there [in combat], just remove
the law and the Air Force will do that."[5]

What neither Schroeder nor her young cabal of women on the
Hill had anticipated was the insider momentum their test case would
gain among the House Armed Services Committee. The first chip
had fallen into place when Schroeder persuaded Les Aspin, the committee chair, to let her introduce her Air Force amendment at the
full committee vote on the defense authorization bill, not in subcommittee. The second chip had fallen when women staffers on the Hill
successfully lobbied Aspin to support the proposal himself. "Some of
the staffers, especially Aspin's staffer Debby Lee (who would go on
to be assistant secretary of defense for reserve affairs in the Clinton
administration), really lobbied Aspin hard on it and he indicated
he'd support it," says Domi.

The third chip had fallen into place when the combined support
of Schroeder and Aspin unexpectedly converted subcommittee chair
Beverly Byron, and dramatically upped the ante. Byron, who just the
year before had testified of her "misgivings about any change in the
current combat exclusion law,"[6] stunned the Schroeder camp by
abruptly changing course when she heard about Schroeder's Air
Force repeal and proposed extending it to Navy pilots. "The way we
saw it was that Byron was getting on a moving train that was going
to leave the station without her," says Moreno. "And being the
chairwoman of personnel and compensation, she wanted to have
her stamp on the amendment, which was fine by us."

With the powerful troika of committee heavies lined up, Domi
and Moreno started testing the full committee. "We faxed the
Schroeder/Byron language to the committee members and told everybody that Aspin supported it and that Byron had jumped on,"
says Domi. "Staffers were saying, 'God, we didn't know anything
about this. I don't know. We're going to have to get back to you.' So
going into the committee vote, we didn't know if we had the votes
or not. We didn't even know if Mrs. Schroeder was actually going to
introduce it."

Moreno and Domi were still calling staffers and whipping votes
on May 8 as the members of the House Armed Services Committee
entered the committee room to mark up the defense authorization
bill. Inside the committee room, Schroeder and Byron were doing
their part by lobbying the members. "They were putting the arm

on people while they were standing around," says Domi. And the impossible happened.

The repeal for female pilots in the Air Force and Navy met no resistance at all from the full committee, not even from Congressman Robert Dornan, a former Air Force pilot and arch conservative from California. "He said something like, 'Women will fight ferociously to protect their young and so will the women flying these aircraft to protect their country,' " reported a staffer who had been in the room. The insiders' victory was complete two weeks later when the full House passed the defense authorization bill 268 to 161.[7] There were some last-minute protests on the floor, especially from Congressman Dornan, who had undergone a quick attitude adjustment by his conservative cohorts. But Dornan's recycled and unsubstantiated claim that 1,200 pregnant women had to be evacuated from the Gulf did not start a political stampede. As the young staffers had forecast, there was no organized resistance to the repeal amendment. "It was a straight up and down vote," says Domi.

Servicewomen's advocates were exultant. "I'm thrilled, I'm surprised, I'm optimistic," marveled DACOWITS chair Becky Costantino, who had marshaled the DACOWITS resolution for repeal just three weeks before the House vote. After all the years of frustration everything seemed to be going their way. With the Gulf war ending in February, just two months before the 1992 defense authorization bill was due in the House, the images of women in uniform were still seared in the public consciousness. "If Desert Storm had ended in August, I don't think it would have happened," says military policy analyst Carolyn Becraft, who would become deputy assistant secretary of defense for personnel support, families and education in the Clinton administration.

Conservatives like Elaine Donnelly were furious. Schroeder's surprise maneuver had preempted any opposition from Donnelly and her Coalition for Military Readiness. "I was afraid something like that was going to happen because of the DACOWITS motion for repeal," said Donnelly at the time. "I was on the lookout for something to happen, though I didn't know quite what or when or where."

The conservative bloc was particularly angry at Schroeder's stealthy tactics on the House Armed Services Committee. Though the committee's secret markup was standard procedure under the chairmanship of Les Aspin, the process would become as big an issue as the substance in the political fight to come. "Schroeder railroaded the amendment through the House Armed Services Committee in the middle of the night," Donnelly complained. "People who should have known better, including Congressman Dornan, didn't catch it and didn't oppose. They should have had a little fight on the repeal right then and there and that would have ended it. But it got out."

Schroeder's amendment drew early and critical support as it headed to the Senate in the defense authorization bill. The Defense Department "welcomes the legislation," spokesman Pete Williams told a press conference the day after the House vote.[8] Two of the Senate Armed Services Committee's most influential Republican members, Senators John Warner and former Vietnam pilot and POW John McCain, expressed their support for repeal. "McCain was quoted at a public dinner on the eve of Schroeder's move that women did so well in Desert Storm, maybe we ought to put them in combat," says Donnelly.

Republican Senator William Roth of Delaware added his support in mid-May by introducing his own legislation for repeal in the Senate. Major Marie Rossi's "vital role" in Operation Desert Storm, coupled with other women's "outstanding performance," Roth announced in a statement, was reason enough for Congress "to remove restrictions that preclude women from competing for combat pilot positions."

All the evidence indicated that the Senate Armed Services Committee was set to follow the House. "Republican staffers were telling me that repeal was on a freight train, there was no way you can stop it," says Donnelly. "I persuaded them to have a hearing."

On June 18, 1991, C-Span recorded the first hearing that Sam Nunn, chair of the Senate Armed Services Committee, and John Glenn, chair of the subcommittee on manpower and personnel, had ever held on women in the military, let alone in combat. Expectations were high among the observers in the Senate hearing room. Retired Air Force Major General Jeanne Holm was there for the historic moment, as was retired Army General Evelyn "Pat" Foote. DACOWITS chair Becky Costantino was there, having canceled her trip to a NATO conference on women in Brussels even before she was asked to testify. Female pilots past and present were there from Women Military Aviators (WMA), a multi-service organization formed around the repeal of the combat exclusion laws. Of all the women in the military, female pilots had been the least recognized for their service.

Members of the unsung WASP (Women Airforce Service Pilots) who had flown for the Army Air Forces as civilian volunteers during World War II were particularly eager for the congressional support of their younger sister pilots. The WASP had had little themselves, though they had logged 60 million miles between 1942 and 1944 ferrying virgin fighters off factory assembly lines on the West Coast to embarkation centers on the East Coast, flight-testing damaged aircraft and towing training targets through barrages of ground artillery fire, all at their own risk.

Because they were civilians, the WASP had flown every plane in the Army Air Forces inventory (including the first primitive jet) with no military insurance or benefits for accidents, hospitalization or death. The thirty-eight WASP killed[9] had not been entitled to military burials nor their families to any government compensation. "When the girls died, either the families had to pay to bring their daughters home or the group got together and we paid," recalls former WASP pursuit pilot Bea Haydu, seventy-one, whose best friend died in a training crash in Texas. "There was no military payment."

It had taken the WASP thirty-three years for their service to be officially recognized as military by Congress.[10] "We had to prove that we lived a military life, that we were subject to court-martial, that we were given military orders to fly the airplanes," says Haydu. "The American Legion testified against us. So did the head of the Veterans Administration, who didn't think we were veterans or that we deserved veteran status."

The World War II pilots' struggle for recognition had been won finally in 1977 by a single piece of paper out of the thousands the WASP had squirreled away in their individual scrapbooks. The yellowed discharge paper certifying that WASP Helen Porter had "honorably served in the active Federal Service in the Army of the United States"[11] was identical to every discharge paper granted to every male Army veteran in Congress. Two years later the women in their fifties and sixties were officially presented honorable discharges.[12]

The civilian women selected for astronaut training in 1961 had had no recognition at all. The Mercury 13, as the female pilots came to be known, had eagerly accepted the invitation of NASA officials to join the race for space against the Russians. They had gone through the same battery of punishing medical and psychological tests as the Mercury 7 men immortalized by Tom Wolfe in *The Right Stuff*. Jerrie Cobb, a professional pilot who had logged 7,000 hours in the air, had aced the tests, including having ice water injected into her ears to induce vertigo and floating for 9 hours and 40 minutes in a pitch-dark isolation tank before hallucinating; prior test subjects had lasted only 4 hours and 30 minutes.[13] Mary Wallace Funk, who held several world records in flying, had beaten John Glenn on the stress tests, bicycle analysis tests and lung power tests and Wally Schirra on vertigo while setting a record in the bicycle endurance and isolation tests; she lasted 10 hours and 30 minutes before hallucinating. "I was sure I was going to make it," said Funk, then twenty-eight. "I just knew it."[14] And then, without explanation, the Navy canceled the women's tests.

The male astronauts rocketed into the history books in 1961 while the women faded into obscurity. It would be 1978 before NASA accepted women into the space program, 1995 before the first woman pilot flew the shuttle. Air Force Lieutenant Colonel Eileen Collins would invite the Mercury 13 women, as well as members of the WASP, to her historic liftoff from the Kennedy Space Center on February 3, 1995. Among the artifacts Collins would carry with her into space were memorabilia from the Mercury 13 and the hard-won wings of the WASP.

The different generations of military pilots had joined ranks in 1981 to form the WMA. The organization allowed them to network and to muster whatever collective influence their small numbers afforded them. Two hundred members of the WASP were listed as members of the WMA in 1991, but only 330 pilots on active duty. The low number of active duty pilots reflected the low number of female pilots in all the services. In the Navy, women represented only 1.5 percent of aviators, 173 pilots and 80 navigators.[15] In the Air Force, the rate rose slightly to 2 percent of the pilots, 230 women. The 350 women helicopter pilots in the Army represented only 1.2 percent of aviators.[16]

Women's hesitation to go into military aviation partially accounted for the low number of pilots. But so did the gender quotas imposed by the combat exclusion laws. In 1987, the year Air Force Captain Linda Tobin entered flight training after four years of ROTC at Sacramento State College, only twelve ROTC flying slots were open to women nationwide in contrast to 1,500 slots open to men.

In 1989, the year Lieutenant Beth Martin got her wings, the Air Force allotted only thirty-five pilot slots to all the women graduating that year from ROTC, Officer Candidate Schools and the Air Force Academy combined. Martin had to wait to enter flight training while her less proficient male colleagues in ROTC shot by her.

"They put your SAT scores and GPA, everything, in a computer and it spits out a number," says Martin, a T-38 instructor pilot. "There were guys whose numbers were half my number but they got the pilot slots before me." Of the Air Force's inventory of thirty-three aircraft in 1989, only sixteen were deemed noncombat by the Air Force and open to women.

The restrictive laws were driving the women pilots out of the services. Navy Commander Lucy Young, who taught air combat to the hot-shot male pilots at the Navy's TopGun school and regularly shot them down in mock exercises, left active duty service because she was tired of playing support roles.[17] Stephanie Wells, NASA's only female instructor pilot, left the active-duty Air Force after ten years because there were no planes left for her to fly. The C-130s she had flown through the eye walls of typhoons during her assignment to a weather squadron in Guam were off bounds to her throughout the rest of the Air Force. "Almost all C-130s were combat-coded and women couldn't fly them," says Wells.

The Air Force was so determined to keep women out of its prized aircraft that it was courting legal action from a Navy pilot in 1991. The Navy wanted Lieutenant Commander Trish Beckman, a navigator and F-18 test pilot, to have the same cross-training as her male colleagues in the Air Force's F-15E, a combat jet. Three days before she was due to report to the F-15E school, the Air Force denied the Navy's request. "The Air Force said, 'No. She can't go. She's a girl,' " says Captain Anne McGee, an Air Force tanker pilot.

The combat exclusion laws brought the aviators to the boiling point after the Gulf war. Air Force Captain Bernadette Kucharczuk, a tanker navigator, had flown some thirty-one refueling missions during the air war, delivering one million gallons of gas in midair to Navy and Air Force fighters stacked over the desert. Geographically, Captain Kucharczuk was in what the Air Force calls "the threat envelope" and therefore on a combat mission. Legally, however, Kucharczuk could not be in combat, leaving the designation of what she and her tanker crew were doing in the Gulf in gender limbo. But that was nothing new.

The combat exclusion laws had clouded mixed-gender crews in every military operation since Air Force women first got their wings. "Grenada. Libya. Panama. Operation Desert Shield/Storm. Every time the question has arisen as to whether or not the tanker crews and the transport crews can log combat time," says Air Force Lieutenant Colonel Kelly Hamilton, who was in charge of flight records in the Gulf.

The laws had become increasingly impractical as women achieved more senior positions. In 1983 astronaut Eileen Collins, then a C-141 transport pilot, had been returning home to Travis Air Force Base in California from a mission in Europe when she and her crew were "short-notice" diverted to Polk Air Force Base in Louisiana to pick up combat troops. American medical students on the tiny spice island of Grenada were supposedly in danger after a military coup and the Air Force had been ordered to deliver ground troops to the island.

"It was so critical that we get people down there that the Air Force did not have time to go in and say, 'OK, which crews have women on them—they're not going,' says Collins, who flew combat troops into Grenada and thirty-six of the medical students and their families out. "The Air Force just sent down the crews that were available."

The combat exclusion law had kicked in on the second day in Grenada. "Someone took notice that there were female crew members—pilots, engineers and loadmasters on different crews partaking in the operations," says former Air Force Captain Terry VandenDolder, who left the service to fly for American Airlines. "They looked at the flight orders, figured out which crews had females on them, separated them out and sent those crews home. They said, 'Now, wait a minute. This could actually be construed as a combat area. Therefore, just to err on the safe side, we'd better take the women out of it.' There was a lot of bitterness among those crews."

There was even more bitterness among the aircrews sent hastily from California to England in 1986 to support U.S. air strikes against Libya. Not only did General Gabriel, then the four-star chair of the Joint Chiefs of Staff, try to get the women off the aircrews the night before the combat mission and replaced with men, the crews also got no recognition when they returned to the United States.

Instead of the tanker crews being issued combat medals, they

were awarded expeditionary medals, the lowest honor in importance. "In Korea, guys got it for flying in a parallel that was near the
DMZ or over a certain border in Vietnam," says one of the tanker
pilots who has been advised not to use her name because of threatened Libyan retaliation. "It didn't even give the enlisted any points
toward their promotion. The guys were furious that they didn't get
medals because of us. But there was nothing they could do. The slap
in the face went across the board. None of the tanker crews got
medals."

The pilots gathered in the Senate hearing room in June 1991
were convinced that the disruptive and inequitable laws would finally be repealed. They had gone through the exact same selection
process to become military pilots as their male counterparts, including passing a male-oriented psychological test. "In Navy ROTC, you
had to check yes or no to the following things you have done or
experienced before the age of sixteen: Changed the oil in a car.
Constructed or fixed anything around the house. Driven a car at a
hundred miles per hour. Skinned a small animal," recalls former
Navy Lieutenant Paula Coughlin, a helicopter pilot. "What they
should ask is: 'Have you made anything out of a cookbook and
followed step-by-step instructions' because that's how every emergency procedure is outlined. But they don't ask if you've ever baked
a cake."

The women had also made it through the twelve pressure cooker
months of flight school, where the attrition rate is as high as 50
percent. The stress was high on all the students, but higher on the
women, who were often the only females in their classes. "One
instructor pilot yelled and screamed at me the whole time, which is
not so unusual, but I didn't have another woman to say, 'Hey, that's
just part of the game,' " says Air Force Captain Linda Tobin. Another
pilot whose instructor, too, was a "screamer" and pounded on the
dashboard during every flight while shouting obscenities at her got
physically ill before she went flying with him every morning. But at
least he flew with her. "There were some instructors who wouldn't
fly with me because I was a woman," says Lieutenant Martin. "They
would sit around telling war stories with the male students, avoid
eye contact with me and pretend not to hear my questions."

The female pilots had "male-bonded" with their colleagues by
ignoring their ritualist dirty jokes and sexual slurs, hitched themselves onto urinals during the six years it took the Air Force to put

portable toilets on board tankers, endured the persistent incredulity of male students at having female instructors. "Do they think I got my wings out of a Cracker Jack box?" says T-38 instructor pilot Jennifer Rohrer.

But the combat exclusion laws were simply unacceptable to senior officers like Lieutenant Commander Beckman, whose aviation test scores in 1980 would have qualified her to fly any airplane in the Navy had she been male. They were just as unacceptable in 1992 to the most junior officers like Second Lieutenant Jeannie Flynn, who defiantly picked the Air Force's forbidden F-15E to fly after graduating at the top of her class at Laughlin Air Force Base in Texas, but had to settle instead for a "heavy" KC-10A refueling tanker.[18] "I would probably have a better chance of becoming a colonel or a general as a shoe clerk," says Captain Kucharczuk. "Flying is not the best thing for a woman to be doing in the Air Force."

Elaine Donnelly and her coalition members had more than made up for lost time in the three weeks since the House vote. While Schroeder's office was being flooded with ugly mail from male retirees, Senate offices were being deluged with anti-repeal warnings from conservative organizations about the negatives of military pregnancy and military motherhood, and the nonissue of dual physical standards for pilots. "The lives of both men and women, not to mention expensive aircraft, may be at risk," Donnelly warned the Senate in writing.[19]

Phyllis Schlafly reemerged from her fight against the ERA in the 70s to rekindle the same argument against repeal: the draft. Schlafly's written statement was among many to remind the Senate that the Supreme Court (*Goldberg* v. *Rostker,* June 25, 1981)[20] had upheld women's ineligibility for draft registration because of their legal exclusion from combat.[21] Though the draft had been politically dead for almost twenty years and pilots had always been volunteers, the concept of women's involuntary service had been a proven showstopper.

Short of the draft, the naysayers warned the senators that a repeal for pilots would inevitably lead to the repeal of the law against women on Navy combatant ships and, from there, to the Army policy against putting women on the front lines. At the end of the domino theory were the enlisted women who would be involuntarily sacrificed to "the narrow interests of a small group of ambitious female officers," as Donnelly described the pilots, "some of whom feel they have an inherent right to be members of the Joint Chiefs of Staff." [22]

Donnelly played the "foxhole" card over and over, as did Schlafly and Brian Mitchell, her conservative colleagues. Diverting the specific repeal for pilots to the emotional images of women in hand-to-hand combat in enemy trenches was proving very effective in the growing public debate known generically as "women in combat." That the combat exclusion laws specifically covered women on ships and in the air but not on the ground, and that the Army and the Marine Corps, not Congress, set their own policies on ground troops, was of little consequence to the conservative campaign. If the senators overturned the protective laws, Donnelly warned the lawmakers, there would be no legal basis to exempt women from "close combat positions" in "foxholes, tanks and amphibious landing craft." [23]

The strategy worked. Sam Nunn and John Glenn, the Senate subcommittee chair holding the hearing, broadened its scope from the specific repeal for pilots to the nonissue of combat for all women in the military. That Sam Nunn was the great-nephew of Congressman Carl Vinson, the author of the 1948 combat exclusion laws, may or may not have been a coincidence. But the Senate hearing on June 18 was an orchestrated rout for pilots from the beginning.

The Joint Chiefs of Staff testified as one against repealing the combat exclusion laws, mirroring the same display of military male cohesion that had marked the collective opposition of their predecessors seventeen years before to integrating the military academies. "I do not want you to change the law, nor do I want Congress to direct us to make any policy changes that would inhibit the policy that we have now," Army Chief of Staff General Carl Vuono told Sam Nunn. [24] The commandant of the Marine Corps, who was never questioned as to why the Marine Corps didn't allow any female pilots at all, stood just as firm. "I see no need to change the law or the exclusion policy at this time," said General Alfred M. Gray Jr. [25]

The chief of naval operations, Admiral Frank B. Kelso II, at least admitted his "great sympathy" for the "excellent aviators" who happened to be women. But he, too, toed the collective male line. "It is my personal view that the law should remain as it stands," said Kelso just three months before the seminal Tailhook convention would change his mind. [26] It was Air Force chief General Merrill A. McPeak, however, who exposed the sentiment underlying the male lineup against women in combat and drew gasps from the women spectators. Asked by Senator William Cohen if he had to choose between a qualified woman and a less qualified man to fill a combat role, McPeak responded he would go with the man. "You would have a militarily less effective situation because of a personal view?" Senator Cohen asked McPeak. "I admit it does not make much sense, but that is the way I feel about it," McPeak responded.[27]

The senators resolutely followed Donnelly's outline, asking the joint chiefs about pregnancy as a readiness issue, dual physical standards, the draft. Though the courts had historically deferred to Congress on military personnel matters and Congress had historically deferred to the services, the specter of a court battle over the registration of women for the draft loomed in the Senate. "I think that issue would clearly be revisited in the courts if the combat exclusion were lifted," Senator McCain said to General Vuono. "I think absolutely it would have to be revisited," agreed the Army chief of staff.[28]

The final blow fell for the pilots when the service members picked to testify arrived in Room 216 of the Hart Senate Office Building. Only two were pilots. The other six, with the exception of a Navy submariner, were ground troops. "Only an uninformed spectator could not have realized that this was a deliberate ploy by those who orchestrated the hearing," retired Air Force Major General Jeanne Holm would write later. "Why else was the witness list so heavily weighted with Army and Marine Corps ground soldiers? And why else was the testimony elicited by the senators almost devoid of any meaningful discussion of the pros and cons of women flying combat missions?"[29]

The pilots, both women, unwittingly played into the Donnelly/Schlafly profile of the "small group of ambitious female officers" motivated only by self-interest. One, a Navy combat support helicopter pilot just off a two-month deployment in the Red Sea, testified that it was "very selfish" of her to support repeal "just because that would afford me more opportunities."[30] Opportunity drove the other pilot as well, a senior pilot in the Air Force with fourteen years' flying experience. Though she had been fighter qualified in pilot training, Major Christine Prewitt testified, she could only be an instructor pilot. "It seems to me, if you have made that cut, you should be able to go on and fly those kinds of airplanes," she said.[31]

The enlisted women on the witness panel completed the negative profile of the aviation officers. Though neither the Marine gun-nery sergeant nor the Army staff sergeant in the 82nd Airborne motor pool had anything do with aviation, their aversion to ground combat in their respective services cemented the selfishness of the female officers. "We do not wish to carry a rifle and lug a pack around and live like the grunts do," testified the Marine sergeant.[32] The Army staff sergeant cited the space her "female hygiene" sup-plies took up in her footlocker in the Gulf and her conjecture that women would not be able to physically keep up with the men in the infantry. "I think the policies and laws should stay the way they are right now," she testified.[33]

Though the missions of pilots in the Navy and Air Force bore no relation to the enlisted ground troops in the Marines and the Army, they blended into a conveniently seamless package in the Senate hearing room. "There seems to be a significant difference in views between enlisted and officer on this issue," said Senator McCain.[34]

McCain backed off his initial support for repeal after the hear-ing. So did John Warner. When the full Senate Armed Services Com-mittee emerged from their markup of the 1992 defense authorization bill on July 9, the proposal for pilot repeal had vanished without a trace. In its stead was a proposal for the establishment of a presiden-tial commission to "study" the roles of women in the military.

The ploy was a familiar one. By clouding the central issue of the pilot repeal with peripheral issues, Nunn and Glenn had justified the political cover of a commission and avoided a politically dangerous vote either for or against women. "With the commission, they could stop the train," says Carolyn Becraft.

There hadn't been a more pivotal moment for women in the military since the furor in Congress over the Women's Armed Ser-vices Integration Act of 1948. It had been General Eisenhower then who had faced down Sam Nunn's great-uncle Carl Vinson and his dismissal of women's permanent value to the armed forces. "In all the war, I never had a woman ask of me a favor except the one of service to the front," Eisenhower confronted the House Armed Ser-vices chair. "I had men say they would be better fitted back home as instructors. I never had a woman say that to me."[35]

Forty-three years later, great-nephew Nunn would face his mili-tary gender crusader in the surprise challenger from Delaware, Sena-tor William Roth. Joined by Senator Edward Kennedy, who had supported the aviation repeal from the beginning, the legislators decided to risk bypassing Nunn's Armed Services Committee to take the vote for repeal directly to the Senate floor.

The political odds were formidable; Nunn had lost only one vote in his long stewardship of the Senate Armed Services Committee. But Nunn's challengers would turn out to be equally formidable. In the countdown to the Senate vote, a phalanx of women would materialize in support of the female pilots, including the pilots themselves.

Dr. Heather Wilson was worried. A former Air Force captain, graduate of the Air Force Academy, Rhodes scholar and now National Security Council staff member and new appointee to DACOWITS, she was reading the latest salvo in the *Washington Times* against women pilots over the phone to Lieutenant Commander Trish Beckman in St. Louis. It was July 19, ten days after the Senate Armed Services Committee "disappeared" the repeal for aviators and barely a week before Kennedy and Roth were due to publicly reactivate the aviator repeal in the Senate as an amendment to the 1992 defense authorization bill. The senators and their staffs were worried, Wilson told Lieutenant Commander Beckman. If the pilots didn't help counteract the efforts of their opponents, the Kennedy-Roth bill would fail.

Strategist Carolyn Becraft at the Women's Research and Education Institute in Washington was doing all she could. Right after the House passed the Schroeder amendment, Becraft had activated the civilian groups she had been briefing on military women's issues throughout the Gulf war. Shirley Sagawa, senior counsel at the National Women's Law Center, had testified for repeal at the Senate hearing. The Virginia Federation of Business and Professional Women's Clubs (BPW) had entered a statement for the record. NOW had issued a press release calling for the end of "government-sponsored job segregation" against women.[36]

Becraft had been working the press as well. WREI had hired a public relations firm to send out media alerts after the Senate hearing, along with a list of spokespeople for repeal. "We had to recapture the dialogue and take it away from the joint chiefs," says Becraft. Members of Senator Roth's staff were using their contacts on the television talk show circuit to book Commander Rosemary Mariner and other advocates for repeal like retired General Pat Foote.

But they seemed to be fighting a losing battle with the emotional arguments from the well-funded conservative opposition. "The military women who appear on panels and on television to argue that pregnancy is not a problem are usually career women with no children and well over childbearing age," charged Phyllis Schlafly. "The women eligible for combat assignment are in their prime childbearing years: 18 to 26 years old." [37] Elaine Donnelly was beating the same drum in the corridors of the Senate, distributing a nineteen-page booklet of excerpts from the Senate testimony against repeal with such hot-button index headings as "Registration of Women for the Draft" and "Concerns About Child Care, Single and Dual-Service Parents, and Pregnancies." [38]

The campaign against repeal was in full swing inside the military as well. Male pilots in the Air Force had taken their case to the *Air Force Times*. In a signed statement, ten male pilots had publicly questioned women's physical abilities to withstand 9 Gs, their mental abilities to "come up with the split second plan that will make the difference between life and death," the wasted fighter pilot training cost of $6 million which would inevitably be sacrificed to pregnancy. "Is this equal opportunity enough reason to allow a fighter pilot to be unable to work for approximately a year in order to bring a pregnancy to a successful end?" the male pilots had written.

Air Force chief Merrill McPeak had redoubled his crusade to keep the best jobs in the Air Force for men. Not only had he read the male pilots' statement verbatim to the senators at the hearing and entered it into the *Congressional Record,* [39] he had also invited conservative columnist Suzanne Fields to fly in the same F-15 he had denied to Navy test pilot Trish Beckman. It was Fields's predictable response in the *Washington Times* querying women's capacity to hack the physical demands of combat flying or withstand the G-forces at nine times the weight of gravity that had sent Wilson to the phone on July 19 to call Lieutenant Commander Beckman.

The pregnancy issue was a red herring to the female pilots. Senior women in their thirties like Navy Lieutenant Commander Beckman, Commander Mariner and astronaut Eileen Collins were still waiting for the right moment to start a family. The younger women in their twenties were well aware of the added pressure of combat status. "You certainly could not get pregnant," said Lieutenant Jennifer Rohrer at the time. "There's no way because we'd have to deploy with everybody."

The insinuation that women couldn't hack the physical demands of combat flying or take the G-forces was false. Women had been successfully counteracting G-forces since 1942, when the WASP flew dive-bombing runs to test the reaction of anti-aircraft gunners on the ground.

Indeed, there was a solid body of evidence that women's physiology made them more tolerant of G-forces than men. A 1991 Air Force study of 102 women and 139 men reported that height, not strength or gender, was the most negative factor in a pilot's ability to tolerate "G stress."[40] Because women were smaller on average than men, the shorter distance between their hearts and their brains made it easier for their hearts to counteract the G-forces trying to draw the blood out of the brain and keep the brain supplied with blood. The magic figure of G-forces at nine times the pull of gravity was a safe one for the male pilots and columnist Suzanne Fields to bandy about because women hadn't been scientifically tested at G-forces in excess of 7.

"The saying is that the best fighter pilot is the short stocky guy with high blood pressure," says Lieutenant Commander Beckman, who regularly tolerated G-forces in excess of 7.5 as an F-18 test pilot. "But women can usually tolerate the Gs better than the average man."

The pilots had one week to mount a counter campaign. Senators Roth and Kennedy had set July 25 to publicly announce their joint bill attaching the aviator repeal to the 1992 defense authorization bill. The vote on the Senate floor would follow.

Carolyn Becraft faxed the phone numbers and addresses of the members of both houses of Congress to the president and vice president of the WMA stationed on the West Coast. They, in turn, faxed the information to the entire WMA membership of five hundred with the most important senators starred and the legislative districts broken down.

Faxes, letters and phone calls poured into Senate offices from the WASP, the active duty members of the WMA and their families, friends and supporters. "I passed out the phone numbers and the addresses of all the senators and congressmen to everyone I knew," says Lieutenant Commander Beckman. Navy Lieutenant Kara Hultgreen's mother took up the cause from San Antonio. So did Lieutenant Paula Coughlin's mother from Virginia Beach. Washington was buried. "I've never seen more faxes and mail over a single issue in my entire career," Tony Cordesman, John McCain's military aide and Gulf war consultant for ABC News, told a friend.

Becky Costantino flew in from Wyoming to join Heather Wilson and other DACOWITS members to lobby for repeal on the Hill. They were joined by members of NOW, the BPW, the American Nurses' Association and the ACLU. Members of the WASP came to Washington along with retired Army General Pat Foote and retired Air Force General Jeanne Holm.

Men came to support the women, all from the Navy. There were F-18 combat pilots on the Hill, enlisted men and retired Navy brass. Retired Admiral Elmo Zumwalt Jr., who had opened Navy aviation to women in 1973, came to continue his stewardship. So did retired Vice Admiral William Lawrence, president of the Association of Naval Aviation and proud father of Lieutenant Commander Wendy Lawrence, who was about to be selected as an astronaut.

The pilots came to support themselves. Navy pilots flew in from Florida, California, Virginia and Missouri. Reservists flew in from their jobs with American Airlines and United Airlines. One Navy pilot flew to Washington for an hour. An Army pilot came for a week.

The pilots were in a tricky situation. Under Defense Department policy, members of the armed services were not allowed to lobby Congress. They were also not allowed on Capitol Hill in uniform unless they were appearing at a specific hearing. "The idea was that the congressmen and staffers would see too many uniforms and wonder who was really running the show," says a Navy pilot. "We really don't want the Senate and Congress to know how many people we have working on the Hill."

Lieutenant Colonel Kelly Hamilton, president of the WMA and the most senior woman in Air Force aviation, and Commander Rosemary Mariner, vice president of the WMA and one of the Navy's first women aviators, laid out a strict protocol to protect the pilots.

They were advised to get permission to come to Washington from their reporting seniors to prevent retaliation and damage to their careers. Navy officers, ironically, had been the most supportive of the pilots; Air Force officers, the least. "Some Air Force women were warned that it would not be in their best interests if they came to Washington to help us," Lieutenant Commander Beckman would write in the WMA newsletter. "Some were even harassed because they received faxes about the subject."[41]

To distance the pilots from officially representing their services, they were told to take personal leave and come to Washington on their own time. "You can do anything on leave that you want to as long as it's morally proper," explains one pilot already stationed in Washington who nonetheless took leave to go across town to Capitol Hill. "We made sure we were not on the government clock."

Navy pilots were to wear their "leave and liberty" uniform on Capitol Hill, Army pilots their Class A uniform. The formal uniforms were considered a personal expense by the IRS and disallowed as a deduction. "You can't take your Class A uniform off on your taxes," says an Army pilot.

The pilots were enjoined to preface any remarks to the senators and their staffs with the disclaimer that their opinions were their own and did not represent official service or Defense Department policy. "I could say I personally disagreed with the combat exclusion laws, but I could not give the Army's position on women in combat," says Major Diana Davis, who double-checked with the Army's congressional liaison to keep her out of trouble. "If someone asked what the Army thought of women in combat, all I could say was, 'Women are not allowed in combat aircraft in the Army.' "

The forty or so advocates of repeal fanned out from the central command post in Senator Roth's office, armed with fact sheets about the combat exclusion laws and women's historical contributions to the military. Sightings of the uniformed pilots and the civilian lobbyists rippled up and down the Senate corridors. " 'God, they're coming to Senator Stevens's office now,' " recalls Becraft of the Senate stir.

The coalition for repeal found converts in some Senate offices. "We turned around Senator Connie Mack," says one pilot. "It turned out his aide was dating a helicopter pilot." The Senate aides, mostly young, Ivy League graduates with few military contacts, were particularly receptive. "The young staffers, almost to a person, said, 'This is really dumb. What do you mean you can't fly off a ship or fly a bomber? You're pilots,' " says Becraft.

The pilots' corridor campaign met resistance in other Senate offices, especially Senator McCain's, and so infuriated Captain Bud Orr, a former fighter pilot in the Navy's Office of Legislative Affairs, that he called his boss in the Pentagon and persuaded him to punish them. "They weren't supposed to be lobbying in uniform, so I sent a lieutenant to round them up and get their butts over to my office," says Orr.

The intimidation campaign was brief. Alerted to the pending reprimand, Senator Roth called the Pentagon. "You got a problem, you call me," a pilot recalls Roth saying to the two-star admiral. But the admiral had already been called off by the secretary of the Navy. "Regrettably, my boss called Larry Garrett and Garrett told him, 'Let them go. It's too hot,' " recalls Orr. "Because of the women's rights movement, these women were allowed to continue their formal lobbying in uniform and represent views that were not necessarily aligned with the best interest of the Navy." And the blitzkrieg continued on the Hill.

On July 25, only six days after the first call went out to the WMA, Senators Kennedy and Roth announced their joint legislation at a press conference. They were flanked by the pilots whose rationale for repeal was just what the senators needed. "For the last 15 years, Navy women aviators have instructed air-to-air and air-to-ground tactics in high performance jets, Air Force women aviators have, through their instructor skills, produced many of today's F-15 and F-16 fighter pilots and Army women pilots have flown unarmed helicopters into areas of hostile fire," WMA president, Lieutenant Colonel Hamilton, was quoted in the press.[42]

Four days after the press conference and two days before the Senate vote, the *Washington Post* graced every Senate desk with a front-page story of Navy women at the Navy's elite Test Pilot School in Patuxent, Maryland.[43] Every woman pilot interviewed for the article described how she was blocked by the combat exclusion laws. "Front page. Above the fold. It doesn't get much better than that," exclaimed a triumphant Becraft.

The vote on the 1992 defense authorization bill went to the Senate floor on July 31. The role Lisa Moreno and Tanya Domi had played whipping votes in the House just three months before was performed by Kennedy aide Bill Lynn and DACOWITS chair Becky Costantino. "We figured we probably had the vote, but we didn't know," says Becraft. "It was a great gamble."

Senators Kennedy and Roth took on the old guard military senators: McCain the ex-POW; Warner the former Navy secretary; Glenn the ex–Mercury 7 astronaut; and Nunn, Vinson's great-nephew. And both sides won.

The Senate approved the Kennedy-Roth bill overturning the legal statute against women pilots by voice vote. But the Senate also voted 96 to 3 for the presidential commission advanced by the Senate

Armed Services Committee. The contradictory legislation swept away one barrier to women pilots while setting up a new one. There would be no assignment of women to combat aircraft, Defense Secretary Dick Cheney announced, until the presidential commission completed its study and made its recommendations to Congress in November 1992. The men in the military and the lawmakers who protected them had bought another seventeen months of political cover—and maybe more.

When the members of the presidential commission were announced by the Bush White House in early 1992, a shudder ran through the WMA. It read like an enemies' list. Elaine Donnelly was on the commission. So were a vice president of the conservative Heritage Foundation, a member of Concerned Women for America, the religious right husband of dissenting DACOWITS member Eunice Van Winkle Ray and the retired Army general who had created the combat coding system that had closed so many Army jobs to women. The commission's executive director was the Navy's congressional liaison, Bud Orr.

The presidential commission would receive scant public attention. Six weeks after the Senate vote, Navy Lieutenant Paula Coughlin went to the Tailhook convention with her boss, Rear Admiral John W. Snyder Jr. Coughlin anticipated the good news from the admirals gathered at Tailhook that the Navy was going to implement the repeal for which she, with her fellow members of the WMA, had taken leave and risked reprimand. Instead, she was sexually assaulted in the now infamous gauntlet of Navy and Marine fighter pilots on the third floor of the Las Vegas Hilton.

The repeal had landed the female pilots in the center of ground zero. And Paula Coughlin was in the crosshairs. "The pilots knew she was an admiral's aide, an aviator and an extreme feminist. They didn't like her," says Bud Orr. "It was intolerable to them that all the things they think are worth dying for were suddenly going to be done by women. They had her out of anger."

9

THE UNWINNABLE WAR

Successful Women, Threatened Men

THE DAY was hot and sultry at Patrick Air Force Base near Cocoa Beach, Florida, in July 1992. While the occasional jet thundered on and off the runways, seventy students at the Defense Equality Opportunity Management Institute (DEOMI), all senior members of the enlisted ranks, were studying a videotape of Navy Lieutenant Paula Coughlin's public debut on ABC News recounting to Peter Jennings the story of her assault at Tailhook nine months before.

The DEOMI instructor was not interested in Coughlin's first public description of the pilots who had grabbed her buttocks and thrust their hands down her tank top and under her skirt. Nor was he interested in her shock at being assaulted by the pilots she had thought of as professional colleagues. What the instructor was interested in were the Navy admirals and Pentagon civilians expressing their collective shock at the pilots' behavior. "Notice each one used the term 'we,' " the instructor pointed out to his students. "They did not take any personal responsibility for Tailhook. It was 'nothing I did.' Write down your comments on how you feel about what you just saw. Don't rationalize. Give us your straight feelings."

DEOMI was a little-known and underfunded Defense Department school housed, prophetically, in four condemned buildings. Ambitious in scope but low on institutional priority, the school trained some seven hundred enlisted personnel a year to "advise" their commanders on equal opportunity issues, including sex discrimination and harassment. Established by Defense Secretary Melvin Laird in 1971 to defuse the violent racial confrontations flaring in the services, the one-of-a-kind institute had since expanded its diversity training to cover every military subgroup which was not white, male and Christian.

Twelve and a half curriculum hours were devoted to women under such headings as "Concepts and Manifestations of Sexism," "Sexual Harassment" and "Feminism & Male/Female Roles." Other "outsiders" in the dominant white male culture were grouped under courses titled the "Black-American Experience," the "Jewish-American Experience," the "Native-American Experience," the "Hispanic-American Experience" and the "Asian-American Experience."

Very little time was dedicated to the "insider" military culture of white male Christians. While Jewish-Americans were awarded seven hours, the "White-American Experience" drew only two hours and forty-five minutes. White men drew even less. The ultimate "insiders" were confined to a two-and-a-half-hour time block titled "The White Male Club."[1] "What is the membership requirement? To be born white and male in America," says a DEOMI instructor, holding up the current *Army Times* with a full page of white men promoted to general. "If we have a white male value system, a white male power structure, white male policy and white male resources, what we have is a white male club. It's really kind of simple."

The heretical message at DEOMI was diversity. The concentration of power among white males in the military, where one out of five members was black and one out of nine was a woman, was counterproductive to military cohesion and perpetuated the marginalization of minorities. "If a woman challenges the white male system to effect change, she's dismissed as having 'the wrong time of the month' or 'bitching just like always,'" says the instructor. "When blacks say, 'We need change right now,' the reaction is, 'We expect minorities to say that.' But when a white male says, 'Hey, folks, we've got some difficulty here,' he's got their attention."

To the progressive staff at DEOMI, white men had written and enforced the combat exclusion laws to preserve the same exclusivity that kept blacks out of golf clubs. "The laws were based on old stereotypes and traditions held by the white male club which didn't want anybody else to play in the game," says Air Force Lieutenant Colonel Mickey Collins, Director of Academics at DEOMI. The paternalistic attitudes which held that women weren't "going to be strong enough and we're going to have to protect them and we're going to have a whole bunch of dykes and husband hunters running around" were just smoke screens for selfishness. "We should have let women in before," he says.

The women students loved the validation of their military experience at DEOMI. So did the black males. The unspoken verities that governed every day of their lives in the military were common grist for the classroom. "You have a bit of an identity crisis," the instructor tells the students. "The black male is treated equally for gender but not for race. The white female is treated equally for race but not for gender. Only the minority female and the white male do not have identity problems. She's on the bottom. He's on the top."

The white males took great umbrage at the power they supposedly held but didn't feel. Senior members of the enlisted ranks, they did not feel party to the white male privilege being assigned them. But their resentment was DEOMI's reward. "You may have had to encounter 4,283 things to get to where you are today. Poverty. Parents who beat you," the instructor tells the increasingly angry white men. "But if you weren't black, you also didn't have to encounter 4,284. And if you weren't, in addition to that, female, you didn't have to do 4,285."

DEOMI illustrated women's powerlessness within the white male culture with the curious, 1988 award-winning film *Ray's Male Heterosexual Dance Hall*. The visual expressions of white male exclusivity were white men in suits dancing with other white men in suits in the center of the floor. The few minority men allowed into Ray's Place, where white businessmen gathered to drink martinis and swap influence, were relegated to the far edges of the dance floor and danced only with each other. No women were allowed in the dance hall at all, let alone on the dance floor.

In discussions after the film, the black male students knew just where Ray's Place was for white males in the military. "The golf course," says one. "If the general play golf, then everybody play golf. If he dance, they dance. He golf, they golf."

Few female students knew where Ray's Place was; those who did didn't know how to get in. "We can see the game and see others play it. How do we get to play?" asks an Air Force sergeant.

In contrast to the academies, DEOMI lectured the students on the history of women in the military and in combat. "Women Warriors Around the World" was the title of one DEOMI text which chronicled such female combatants as the Danish female unit that fought against the Spanish Army in the sixteenth century; the Englishwomen who fought and died at the Battle of Waterloo; the tens of thousands of European and Russian women who fought the Nazis in World War II as snipers, spies, resistance leaders, infantrymen and pilots; the South Vietnamese women who ambushed and killed twenty-two Viet Cong soldiers in 1962, "picking them off as they ran and clubbing to death those who fell wounded."[2]

DEOMI did not shy away from women's reproductive organs, but featured them in another DEOMI text. Written for male military supervisors, the handbook attempted to defuse the male contempt for such natural female conditions as menstruation, premenstrual syndrome, menopause and pregnancy. "Historically, men have reacted to menstruation with a mixture of awe, pity, disgust and fear," the handbook advised. ". . . It should be emphasized that menstruation and pregnancy are not 'sicknesses'; they are normal physiological functions."[3]

DEOMI subjected male students to sexual harassment in a role-reversal exercise called Meat Market. " 'Bend over. Touch your ankles. Hmmm, good pair of buns,' " female students murmured about a male student in one classroom. In another, a woman ordered a male student to lie down on his back and hold his legs open in the ongoing tradition of the "leg-spreader."

"We want the males to feel truly uncomfortable," says one of the trainers watching the exercise approvingly from a central, one-way glass control booth. "The males have heard about sexual harassment in the auditorium and seen it in the movie, but if they still don't feel it, then maybe they'll feel it now."

At DEOMI the simple answer to gender discrimination was the elimination of the combat exclusionary laws. The complex answer lay in the purging of the biases and stereotypes ingrained in the white male Christian heterosexual culture. That role at DEOMI fell to Ted Paynther, a Defense Department consultant and former associate professor at Kent State University in Ohio who had worked on diversity issues with DEOMI for twenty years. Paynther, who performed under the name John Gray, was himself both the target and purveyor of prejudice. Paynther's parents were black, but he appeared to be white, a racial contradiction he didn't reveal to his audiences until the follow-up to his provocative psychodrama. Being a white male was part of his performance dynamic. "The group I stereotype more than any other are white males," says Paynther. "To the audience, what they see fits what they're hearing."

Paynther played the role of the quintessential white male bigot so convincingly that some minority students in the DEOMI auditorium rose out of their seats in fury. "What you black people, you Hispanic people have done as the result of the Los Angeles riots is to move the majority of people away from you who were trying to help," says Paynther angrily about the violence following the 1992 acquittal of four white policemen in the beating of Rodney King. "Well, I've had it. My children are fearful of coming into your communities to help, to work. I don't think there is any excuse for that violence in America."

Having stereotyped the enraged black students, Paynther turned to male attitudes toward women. "If any of you have been in combat, you know there is no way you or I would go into combat with a female," he says. "I was raised as a male, and if I'm in combat, my concentration isn't going to be on the enemy but on protecting the women. Women should do the computer sciences and the paperwork and let the men out of the offices."

While the women in the audience shot murderous looks at Paynther, he declared them lesbians. "Remember that Army Colonel Cammermeyer, who admitted to being a lesbian, wasn't a lesbian when she joined the service. She was married and she had children, which says to me that becoming a lesbian is learned behavior," warns Paynther. "What most gays have, what most homosexuals and lesbians have, they've got HIV virus. And that's what I'm concerned about as an American."

A white male student finally confronted Paynther. " 'American.' 'Un-American.' What do those terms mean?" the Army sergeant asked.

"To me, an American follows the laws in this country," Paynther shot back. "To me, an American is a good Christian who practices the Christian religion, not like these Catholics who go around worshipping false idols or the Jews in this country who don't accept Jesus Christ as being the son of God."

A black male spoke up. "I'm offended by your opinions."

"That's your problem," Paynther snapped.

The student stood his ground. "I don't believe a word you're saying," he said.

"That's because when you're confronted with the truth, you find it very difficult to deal with," says Paynther. "You can learn a lot from the women here. At least they know how to stay in their place, to sit here and listen." The DEOMI trainers quickly moved to the front of the room as the students roared with disapproval and Paynther, on cue, stormed out of the room.

The counterforce to diversity was playing out with equal drama at the presidential commission. The panel of nine white men and six women, one of whom was black, had held thirty public hearings on women in combat over a nine-month period beginning in March 1992. Sociologists, theologians and right-wing activists, including a converted 60s radical who called feminists "communists" and a Protestant minister to whom challengers to white male Christian tradition were witches, had testified before the commission. "Radical feminism is a type of neo-paganism, involved extensively in the Wicken faith, which is the worship of the earth as goddess and essentially what we know as witchcraft," the Reverend John Stewart told the commission at the Century Plaza Hotel in Los Angeles.[4]

The commissioners had made fact-finding trips to military installations all over the country and dispatched staffers abroad to Israel, Denmark, Holland and Canada and to Harvard to interview senior Soviet officers studying at the John F. Kennedy School of Government. The $4 million allotted to the commission had turned up little new information.

A staff trip to the Defense Civil Institute of Environmental Medicine in Toronto returned with the surgeon general's conclusion that "the only real differences between men and women in the Canadian Forces were in the areas of size and physical strength." The only myth-shattering revelation at home was that the cost of recruiting women for the Army was 50 percent higher than the cost of recruiting men.[5] Because women were three times less likely than men to consider military service, recruiters had to spend more time contracting them. "You make a lot more phone calls [to females] to get appointments," Sergeant Carlos DeJesus, an Army recruiter, told the commission in Chicago.[6] "Women ask more questions," said an Army colonel in Washington.

Nonetheless, the commission had tackled the gender issues that had divided the services since the 70s. With women poised to enter the last male club of combat, the commission would be the first and last forum to gather the disparate information on women's military performance and pass judgment on women's future. The advocates of women in combat would recycle their arguments that an individual's qualifications, not gender, should be the deciding factor. The advocates of the male status quo would recycle their arguments that women's gender was, in itself, a combat disqualifier. Any "difference" from men's "sameness" would be cast as a risk to national security. But was it?

Women's purported threat to male cohesion laced the arguments against women in combat, though there was no empirical evidence that gender played a negative role or any role in cohesion. Since World War II, when brotherly love had first been identified as a bigger combat motivator than the flag, Mom or apple pie, all the combat psychology studies the Army had conducted had been confined to combat units, and, therefore, to men.

Commonality of experience, equitable treatment and mutual confidence had been identified by cohesion experts as critical elements for unit cohesion among men.[7] "Trust, respect for tactical skill and, above all, a metaphor of familialism—the good unit speaks and acts as if they were members of a family—the better the unit performs," Dr. David Marlowe, the director of military psychiatry at the Walter Reed Army Research Institute for the Behavioral and Social Sciences, had testified to the commission.[8]

While the U.S. Army had studied only the combat family of men, there was evidence in foreign militaries that mixed-gender units performed more effectively than single-gender ones. The cohesion in North Vietnamese forces had been higher than that in U.S. units, and unit effectiveness was hardly diminished by women. The "deadliest, most vicious and cunning fighters I have ever faced were the Viet Cong women," said Admiral Elmo Zumwalt Jr. in congressional testimony.[9] The effectiveness of FMLN guerrilla units in El Salvador had been enhanced by male and female comrades in arms. "When a man was retreating from the front lines and saw a woman holding her position, he would think if she is going ahead, then I have to," a former female FMLN combatant told an interviewer. "It happened all the time."[10]

American commanders of mixed-gender units had noted the same positive dynamic; the women worked harder to gain male approval and the men worked harder not to be outdone by the women, thereby increasing unit effectiveness.[11] Familial bonds had formed in mixed-gender units in the Gulf. Tensions had come from outside the primary work group, not from within. "The distinction

between men in one's own unit and 'outsiders' was important,"
researchers from the U.S. Army Research Institute had noted, a distinction that would have earned the term "unit cohesion" in all-male
units, but was deemed "successful adaptation"[12] among mixed-
gender units.

Combat itself was the greatest formula of all for cohesiveness.
Group survival depended on teamwork, a reality that had overridden
racial prejudice in Vietnam. "Race was much more of a problem if
you were in Saigon in a support unit, or when you came back and
went to the PX or for a swim," Colonel Ronald Joe had said at
DEOMI. "Race was no problem if you were out in the jungle or in
the weeds fighting an attack." The cohesion argument against
women was a by-product of peace. "I guess I'm old-fashioned in my
values, but I cannot see myself running around in my flight of four,
doing the town in Song Tong City, if one of them was a girl," Air
Force pilot Captain Dave Freaney testified against women pilots. "I
think it would affect the effectiveness of my flight squadron."[13]

The strength factor was more quantifiable in the unit cohesion
arguments. Navy women's upper-body strength ranged between 46
and 58 percent that of men's, one study had found.[14] Air Force
women could lift the forty pounds required to enter the service, but
only 30 percent of women compared to 100 percent of men could lift
seventy pounds.[15] Women's smaller hearts and lungs reduced their
stamina and load-bearing capability in the Army. Treadmill tests of
male and female cadets at West Point had identified a sharp dropoff
over distance in women's capacity to carry packs weighing over
forty-four pounds.[16] "Women reach maximum oxygen uptake much
faster than men," Colonel James L. Anderson had said at West Point.
"The women just drop."

The presumption that all men are stronger than all women is
not true. Thirty-two percent of women (202 out of 623) had met or
exceeded the minimum male test scores on an Army Physical Fitness
Test.[17] With specialized training, women's strength and stamina
could be heightened dramatically. A 1996 Army study of forty-one
women would find that 78 percent qualified for "very heavy" military jobs after six months of weight lifting, jogging with 75-pound
backpacks and performing squats with 100-pound barrels on their
shoulders.[18] It was their gender, not their strength, that disqualified
them from competing for the same jobs for which men were automatically eligible. "I had a radio/telephone operator who couldn't

carry it and keep up with me. He shouldn't be in that job, but automatically, because he had a penis, he was qualified," says an Army captain. "It's just amazing how that appendage qualifies you for something."

The Canadian Forces had opened all combat positions to women, save for submarines, in 1987. While only one woman, a lumberjack, had made it through infantry training and her service obligation during the first three-year trial, four other Canadian women had partially completed infantry officers' training by 1992 and one was at the top of her class.[19] Canadian women were also serving as field artillery officers and tank crews, one sharp-eyed gunner having earned the title "Deadeye Dickless."[20]

The number of women qualifying for ground combat positions was understandably low. Only a few exceptional women had the motivation and strength, but they promised to make exceptional leaders. One Canadian officer had beaten out all her male and female peers in parachute training, an accomplishment traditionally recognized by the U.S. Army with an invitation to train on the Airborne Ranger course. The American invitation had not been extended to her because she is female.[21]

It was the disruption to the male order that dictated the resistance to women qualifying for combat. "Where are their bathrooms going to be?" asked a Marine infantry sergeant. "Where are their tents going to be?"[22] Military supervisors up and down the chain of command cited the "distractions" they would have to cope with among men, including the new distraction of sexual jealousies.

The 60s notion of soldiers and sailors making love, not war, had fast-forwarded to uniformed personnel making love and war in the All-Volunteer Force of the 90s. Almost three-quarters of the Army and Marine personnel polled by the Roper Organization for the commission reported sexual activity in their units in the Gulf, as did 64 percent of Air Force personnel and 41 percent of Navy sailors.[23] The numbers were roughly the same for sexual liaisons between members of different units. The poll didn't determine whether the same sexual incidents were being reported over and over again by different personnel, adding up to the high percentages of reported sexual activity. Nonetheless, the reality remained.

"There was sexual activity in Saudi Arabia," says a female captain in a Military Police reserve company. "A couple of women were viewed as being promiscuous, but maybe one compared to twenty

men. Relationships were more monogamous, one on one, not sleeping with everybody. People coupled up. It was the married men who
were apt to be the harassers and abusers. The single men found one
woman and that was fine."

With sex a documented inevitability between young service
members, the bigger issue was what effect that sexual activity had
on the morale and readiness of the military units in the Gulf. And
the answer was not much. Seventy-seven percent and 61 percent,
respectively, of Gulf veterans polled said sexual activity had little or
no effect on readiness and morale.[24]

Morale problems involved male officers using rank to hit on
young privates and getting away with it. "The major would slap
them on the hand and say, 'Dammit, lieutenant, what the hell are
you doing? I'm going to have to move you now because people have
heard and there's that degree of suspicion,' " says an Army supply
sergeant. "They did a lot of shuffling around to cover up for the
officers. Ultimately, they'll always cover up for the officers. It caused
a lot of hard feelings and problems with unit cohesion."

Nonetheless, sex was used as an argument against women in
combat. Although sex was a complicator in mixed-gender units,
there was no recognition that it was all-male combat companies that
had committed sex crimes in Vietnam, Okinawa, Norfolk, and Las
Vegas. "Our activities have probably not been quite as bad as Tailhook, but on the same mind-set," an infantry sergeant at Fort Ord,
California, told me. "They keep us separate from everybody else. I
imagine there's a method to their madness."

Pregnancy, single mothers and dual-service parents were recycled as arguments against women in combat before the presidential
commission. The public discomfort toward military mothers during
the Gulf war had validated the separate gender roles sought by many
men in the conservative military. When Phyllis Schlafly appeared on
the commission's American Cultural Values Panel in a rockets-red-
glare red dress and testified directly to the television cameras that
99.8 percent of American women believed "mothering is more important than flying a plane or driving a tank,"[25] short-haired men
sporting American flag lapel pins had murmured, "God bless you,
ma'am," as she left the hotel.

But pregnancy and single mothers had not compromised the
military mission in the Gulf. Though single mothers had drawn cultural sympathy and pregnancy had been elevated to a threat to na-

tional security by women's opponents, the services had learned to cope with women's higher nondeployability rate. "It's all how you approach it from a management viewpoint," says Lieutenant Colonel Mike Lynch, the Air Force representative to the commission. "If you figure you're going to have 5 to 10 percent of your troops nondeployable, and you have to send 100 percent of a unit, then you overman that unit 110 percent." The Navy, too, had adjusted to pregnancy as a reality of women's service. "When you take any group of women between seventeen and twenty-three, you're going to have about a 10 percent pregnancy rate," says Commissioner James Hogg, a retired admiral. "We have a much higher disciplinary problem with the men, unauthorized absenteeism, absence in the brig for more serious offenses. Pregnancy is a wash."

The conservative commissioners had grabbed at straws to build a case against women in combat. Because women had gotten high ratings for their performance in the Gulf war, the conservative bloc had dismissed it as a test on the grounds that little combat had taken place. Vietnam had been substituted as a model, though the majority of the 5,000 women who had served voluntarily in Vietnam were nurses and no servicewomen in the 60s had been weapons-trained. Armed only with her purse, retired General Pat Foote, a Public Affairs officer in 1967, had been dispatched to a field artillery battalion dug in as a decoy to draw the North Vietnamese across the Cambodian border.

The Gulf war was only combat heavy when applied to men. The Tailhook Association had pumped up Marine and Navy fighter pilots by declaring the Gulf war as the country's "first victory in a full-scale war in half a century."[26] The twenty-three Marine women who had earned the Combat Action Ribbon for firing at or being fired at by Iraqi troops[27] and the two Army women who came home to POW medals and Purple Hearts had evidently not gone to the same war. "There are myths and propaganda to contend with as more than 22% of the women deployed to the Persian Gulf 'feel' or believe that they were in combat," read one commission report, "but the Secretary of Defense assures the Congress that no laws excluding women from combat were broken."[28]

The opposing arguments on the commission were irreconcilable, just as they were within the military. Proponents of diversity and equal opportunity looked at women's track record in the air and on the sea and found no rational reason to restrict them. Forty-four thousand women had served on sixty-six of the Navy's support ships over the last fourteen years with no ill effect on the Navy.[29] Women aviators had an enviable track record in high-performance jets. Navy test pilot Lieutenant Lori Melling Tanner testified to the thirty-four different types of aircraft she had flown, including a Soviet MIG-21. Air Force test pilot Jackie Parker testified to the 3,000 hours she had logged flying a wide variety of aircraft, including the Goodyear blimp.[30]

Women's opponents looked at that same performance and saw the cultural negatives. Women on Navy combat ships would lead to "inevitable romantic involvements" and "false" charges of sexual harassment and pregnancy, warned Elaine Donnelly, echoing male concerns aboard an aircraft carrier. Women in the air would become liabilities on the ground.[31]

Female prisoners of war had dominated the combat debate from the moment Hays Parks, chief of the Army's International Law Branch, testified on June 8, 1992, that each of the Army women taken prisoner of war in the Gulf had been "treated more favorably than their U.S. and Coalition male counterparts," though each had been the "victim of indecent assaults."[32]

Five former prisoners of war had given testimony later the same day, including three men held in Vietnam, a World War II Navy nurse interned by the Japanese and Desert Storm POW Major Rhonda Cornum. The commissioners had not asked the male POWs to elaborate on the torture they had endured which had left one unable to lift his arm above the height of his shoulder. Elaine Donnelly zeroed in on Cornum, however, demanding to know the nature of her "indecent assault." Cornum's reply, that she had been "violated manually, vaginally and rectally" the year before in Iraq, had provided an emotional argument against women in combat and generated public interest in the hearings for the first time.[33]

"Sexual Assaults of Female POW's Withheld from Panel," read the story headline in *USA Today*.[34] "Women in War: Ex-Captive Tells of Ordeal" read the front-page story in the *New York Times*.[35] While male POWs had traditionally been viewed as heroes, Cornum had become a victim.

The cultural divide over female POWs was the most graphic to come out of the presidential commission. The female pilots monitoring the commission had been furious at Donnelly for invading Cornum's privacy. "Mrs. Donnelly's disgraceful conduct was an attempt to exploit Major Cornum's courage to further her well-known political agenda opposing women in combat," WMA president Rosemary Mariner wrote to the *Washington Times*.[36] Commissioner Mimi Finch was angry that Donnelly had pressed Cornum for details about her treatment as a POW, but not the male POWS. "Why didn't they call in Jeffrey Zaun and ask him what it was like or what made him talk?" said Finch. "It just seemed very sexist that Cornum would be asked that question and nobody else would."

Cornum had been the least disturbed. "Getting raped or abused or whatever is one more bad thing that can happen to you as a prisoner of war. There's about four hundred bad things I can think of and it's not the worst of them," Cornum had testified, calling her incident an "occupational hazard."[37] The other female POW, Army truck driver Melissa Rathbun-Nealy, dismissed her designation as a "victim of indecent assault." A letter sent on her behalf to the presidential commission reiterated that she "at all times steadfastly maintained that she was not the victim of sexual abuse and continues to so maintain this position."[38]

But another "difference" had been identified between servicemen and servicewomen, another perceived threat to unit cohesion. "There is no question in my mind that I would certainly lean toward giving the enemy something if I knew they were raising hell with a fellow female prisoner," former Vietnam POW and Air Force Colonel Norman McDaniel testified.[39]

The POW issue became a matter of white male "values" in their protectionist arguments against women in combat. "I am not prepared to see America's mothers and daughters paraded down the streets of Baghdad and subjected to abuse, when it's not necessary," testified Rhonda Cornum's battalion commander, Lieutenant Colonel William Bryan.[40] "Now those are my values as an American citizen."

"Values" would motivate General Maxwell Thurman's commission vote against the female pilots. "No people want women to get victimized," Thurman would tell me. "Even if the pilots want to get victimized, we don't want to get them victimized. You follow me? It's not our American value system." The word "values" was never attached to the American concept of equal opportunity or individual choice or the meritocracy in which the military took such pride, but was being denied women.

The POW issue was never about women, but about men. In the commission's final report to the president, every argument against women in combat would revolve around the pain women's capture would cause, not to the women themselves but to their male colleagues. "The mistreatment of women taken as POWs could have a negative impact on male captives," read one rationale against women in ground combat.[41] "The presence of women might cause additional morale problems for male prisoners," read an argument against women in combat aircraft.[42]

The philosophical battle over women in combat was so incendiary that the conservative bloc staged a walkout in the midst of the commission's final votes in November. "The Fadeout Five,"[43] as the *Navy Times* called them, demanded, and would get, their own section in the final report titled "Alternative Views: The Case Against Women in Combat," written before a single vote on combat had been taken. In a parody of DEOMI training, one white male commissioner would cite the Scriptures, the Bible, God and his identity as a "Christian" in his combat case against women.[44]

The presidential commission voted resoundingly against women in ground combat,[45] and even called on Congress to enact a *new* combat exclusion law shielding the Army and Marine Corps from women and a hypothetical draft. (During the Vietnam War, 99.7 percent of draftees had gone to the Army or Marine Corps; during the Korea War, 100 percent, presumably as ground combat troops.)[46] For extra insurance against women, the commission voted to retain the DOD's "Risk Rule"[47] that supposedly distanced women in support roles from combat and against the nonissue of requiring women to register for the draft.[48]

By one vote, the commission voted to lift the combat exclusion law against women on Navy combat vessels, save for submarines and amphibious ships.[49] By the same margin, they voted to reinstate the combat exclusion law against women pilots. The deciding vote against the pilots was based on menstruation.

"I'd like to know, is it true or false that flight schedules are adjusted for menstrual cycles?" asked Commissioner Charles Moskos, who would author the controversial "Don't Ask, Don't Tell" policy for gays in the military.[50]

A chorus of noes came from the pilots in the back of the room.

No, confirmed Commissioner Meredith Neizer.[51]

Commissioner Finch, an Army helicopter pilot, explained that aviators, male or female, had the discretion to adjust their peacetime flight schedules if they hadn't slept well, had hangovers or felt under the weather so as not "to sacrifice the aircraft or themselves." "I do not believe menstruation in any way, shape or form is an issue here," she said.[52]

But pilots' menstrual cycles continued to be a prime concern to the white male commissioners. Commissioner Darryl Henderson, an expert on male cohesion, suggested that during "the highest rate of flow," one study showed that women had an increased susceptibility to decompression sickness and hypoxia.[53]

Commissioner Hogg questioned "menstrual considerations" as well, but reported he had heard it might be a problem for a forty-five-year-old woman pilot, but not for younger women.[54]

The pilots sitting in the back of the room were incredulous at the turn the debate had taken. After nine months of military testimony about their qualifications as aviators, the hundreds of hours they had spent in the air in the Gulf refueling fighter planes and ferrying combat troops, the lives lost like Marie Rossi's, it had all come down to making men feel bad if women were taken prisoners of war and their menstrual periods.

The Clinton administration threw out the presidential commission recommendations on combat in April 1993. Adopting the DEOMI approach to diversity and replacing the defining category of gender with individual qualifications, Secretary of Defense Les Aspin removed the Risk Rule as "no longer appropriate,"[55] and ordered the services to open combat cockpits to women and the eager, post-Tailhook Navy to seek congressional repeal of the 1948 law against women on combat ships. In 1994 the Navy opened combat ships to women and the Army, under pressure from its black male secretary, Togo D. West Jr., muscled the white male club of the Army into opening over 32,000 new jobs to women. Only Army and Marine units engaged in direct combat with an enemy—infantry, armor and much of field artillery—remained closed to women.

The political edict was hailed as a victory by women's supporters. The New York Times editorial "Women Warriors" decried the servicemen and "more than a few Americans," who "carried on as if knighthood were still in flower."[56] The Air Force Times "Women Warriors" editorial decried the resistance of "manly men" and heralded women's entry into the service's "most sacred precincts."[57] But the military culture remained the same.

■

Navy Lieutenant Kara Hultgreen was the first woman combat pilot to die. She was lining up her F-14A to land on the USS *Abraham Lincoln* on October 25, 1994, when she lost an engine and crashed into the Pacific. Her shipmates held a memorial service for her the next day. But while Lieutenant Pam Lyons Carel, an F-18 pilot and college classmate of Hultgreen's, read from the Scriptures and the few other female combat aviators aboard eulogized Hultgreen in words and song, anonymous phone calls and unsigned faxes were already appearing at newspapers and talk radio stations in San Diego. Though Hultgreen was the tenth F-14A pilot to be killed in a training accident since 1992, the anonymous messages charged the Navy with "political correctness" by lowering standards to qualify the first women combat carrier pilots, hurrying women through carrier training and concealing Hultgreen's "inadequate flight skills."

Hultgreen's mother, a lawyer in San Antonio, rose to her daughter's defense and released the flight records the Navy had given her. Hultgreen had ranked third among the seven pilots in her class, all of whom had qualified as carrier pilots. Her overall grade of 3.10 out of a possible 4 was above the average of 2.99. The Navy confirmed the records, stating that Hultgreen was an "average to above average" F-14 pilot.[58] The Navy accident report released four months later, along with videotapes of the accident, attributed the cause of the crash more to engine malfunction than pilot error.[59] Eight of nine Navy F-14 pilots reenacting Hultgreen's final ten-second landing sequence in a flight simulator had also crashed, said Vice Admiral Robert "Rocky" Spane, Pacific commander of the Naval Air Force.[60]

Male complaints grew only more bitter. The deaths of male pilots drew one-paragraph obits in their local papers, but Hultgreen's death had generated national headlines. The Navy had spent at least $100,000 to raise Hultgreen's plane from the Pacific floor, but nothing to salvage the downed planes of male pilots. Unlike male fighter pilots, Hultgreen had been buried at Arlington National Cemetery and top Navy officials had attended the ceremony, including the vice chief of naval operations and the secretary of the Navy.[61] "If I die in a crash should my wife reserve two more seats?" ended a letter to the *Navy Times* from an F/A-18 pilot signed "Name withheld."[62]

The slander campaign escalated when a second, "privileged" Navy report released internally in March 1995 laid Hultgreen's accident as much to pilot error as to engine malfunction. While the Navy's male pilots were dropping out of the skies at an alarming rate

—another pilot off the USS *Lincoln* and four combat jets had been lost since Hultgreen's accident, including two $60 million F-14s that had collided in midair during a photography shoot[63]—the supposedly "privileged" information in Hultgreen's MIR, or "Mishap Investigation Report," was provided by "unofficial sources"[64] to news media, including the *Navy Times,* which ran it on the Internet.

The campaign to discredit women pilots escalated with the theft and release of the flight records of Lieutenant Carey Dunair Lohrenz, Hultgreen's sister F-14 pilot aboard the USS *Lincoln.* By selectively choosing the errors the women had made in flight training and ignoring their accomplishments, the women's enemies built a case against them. Both women pilots had subpar flight-training records and would have been disqualified if they hadn't received special treatment, claimed Elaine Donnelly's Center for Military Readiness, which circulated a report titled "Double Standards in Naval Aviation."[65]

Relations were already strained on the USS *Lincoln.* The men were complaining that women's long hair was a danger on the flight deck, though the women kept their braids or ponytails inside their flight suits. The men were also complaining that the female pilots got preferential berthing; the women had been assigned quarters two decks below the flight deck while the men were berthed right under it. "It's caused a lot of resentment," says Lieutenant Loree Draude, the only female pilot in her VS-29 squadron of Dragonfires on the *Lincoln.*

The young men posted a picture of a female officer over a urinal,[66] and alternately bragged in the ready room about lying to Tailhook investigators or talked bitterly about the promotions still being held up by the Senate four years after Tailhook. In response, the token female pilots adopted the gender camouflage used by female cadets at West Point. "They'll start talking down women and I'm just sitting there going, 'Fine, I'm not going to say anything,' " says Lieutenant Carel, the only female F-18 pilot in her squadron.

The tension intensified after Donnelly's report appeared in the press. Though Lohrenz was referred to as "Pilot B," she was easily identifiable by virtue of being the only surviving female F-14 pilot in the Navy.[67] The pilots on shore faxed the news stories about Lohrenz's apparent failings to the *Lincoln,* where one of her senior officers read them out loud.[68] Copies of Donnelly's report circulated among the training squadrons ashore and were always left where Lohrenz could see them.

Whether or not the evaluations were valid was impossible to determine. Both Hultgreen and Lohrenz had been assigned to fighter-training squadrons at Miramar, a Navy aviation station in San Diego. West Coast squadrons had sponsored twenty of the twenty-two infamous "hospitality suites" at the 1991 Tailhook convention, Miramar squadrons accounting for six of them.

The women had been trained by TopGun instructor pilots, the elite squadron which had stonewalled Tailhook investigators by denying any knowledge of the pornographic movies, strippers, indecent exposure or assaults going on outside the TopGun suite at the Tailhook convention.[69] Three TopGun instructor pilots had testified against women at the presidential commission and brought along a protest letter for Elaine Donnelly signed by twenty-one of the twenty-three instructor pilots back at Miramar Naval Air Station in California.

Lohrenz described her fighter pilot training there as "the year from hell."[70] The first-year male pilots, or "nuggets," had been assigned to the most experienced backseaters and counseled and encouraged by the officers who graded every carrier landing while she had met only sullen silence. Every mistake Lohrenz and the other women pilots made on the *Lincoln* were exaggerated, while the same mistakes made by male pilots were ignored. "If I'd done what one of the guys did, I'd have been in front of a board," says Lieutenant Carel. "There were a lot of double standards."

The Donnelly report provided ammunition for a new wing commander aboard the *Lincoln*. In April 1995, evaluation hearings were ordered of four of the seven female pilots. Two combat pilots, including Lieutenant Lohrenz, were dropped from naval aviation. Another female pilot was put on a six-month probation; her next mistake would be her last. A noncombat aviator resigned after being warned that she would be evaluated if she didn't turn in her wings.[71] The one male pilot evaluated had crashed his F-14A into the sea. He was returned to flight status only to die nine months later in a hot-dogging accident in Nashville, Tennessee.[72]

Air Force Major Jackie Parker would give up her flight status as well. Invited in May 1993 to become the first female F-16 combat pilot in an Air National Guard squadron in upstate New York known as "The Boys from Syracuse," Parker left the 174th Fighter Wing in June 1995. The male leadership had taken no action against the junior officers who had blocked her training, joked about her meeting a violent death, accused her of having an affair with the operations group commander and passed her over for deployment to Turkey.[73]

Pregnancy conspiracies continued in the Navy. The first six-month deployment of women aboard the aircraft carrier *Dwight D. Eisenhower* in 1994 would not be noted for its successful mission to the Mediterranean, the Arabian Gulf and the Adriatic Sea but for the number of women, 39, out of the total of 415, who became pregnant.[74] The academies would lurch from one scandal to another, their male traditions embedded in their white male cultures. In 1995, West Point would win an award in "crisis communication" from the Public Relations Society of America for defusing the potential embarrassment inherent in fifteen female cadets being groped the year before in a gauntlet of two hundred football players. The academy's reported good news was the new confidence among both male and female cadets to report the misbehavior of their peers. The unreported bad news was that all three male cadets turned in by the white cadet brotherhood were black.[75]

The AVF offers unparalleled career opportunities for women. They earn the same pay and benefits as men, advance at the same if not faster rates, and often live the life promised by recruitment ads. "I could do one of those posters selling the Air Force," says Lieutenant Colonel "Happy" Maguire, who spent a year in Thailand and six years in England and Germany.

The male resistance many women encounter often serves to enforce their determination to stay the course. "The men can try and knock me down, but they haven't managed to stop me yet," says a seventeen-year Army veteran. "That in itself keeps me going."

Stepping up the numerical presence of women in the services would mute the consequences of tokenism, though achieving the unlikely gender ratio of 35:65 set by Rosabeth Moss Kanter for women to achieve "minority" group status and the power to influence the male "majority" or the more unlikely gender ratio of 40:60[76] to achieve true balance, seems unrealistic. So does altering the age-old hierarchy of military rank which continues to provide a vehicle for the sexual pressuring of junior women. And nothing has been discovered yet to defuse the dynamic of men in groups and the collective necessity to subordinate women.

Many of the young men who seek masculine military identities can't risk having women do what they do, no matter how well the women do it. The dynamic is hardly new. Writing in 1949, anthropologist Margaret Mead noted that in a great number of human societies, men's sureness of their sex role is tied up with their right, or ability, to practice some activity that woman are not allowed to practice. "Their maleness, in fact, has to be underwritten by preventing women from entering some field or performing some feat," wrote Mead.[77]

Women cleared for combat positions are on a collision course with the male need for masculine reassurance, especially in combat aviation. "There was a guy in my Test Pilot School I got along with real well, but he said, 'Look, I can handle anything, but I can't handle being worse than you,' " Major Jackie Parker had testified to the presidential commission. Senior enlisted men in Special Operations had used that same argument before the presidential commission to protect their men's "fighting spirit." "That warrior mentality will crumble if women are placed in combat positions," a first sergeant had testified. "There needs to be that belief that 'I can do this because nobody else can.' "[78]

The resistance to women will not go away because it can't. Despite the efforts of the diversity instructors at DEOMI and the colonels at West Point, the dynamic of the white male culture that draws men to it depends on exclusivity. "We never were trusted as part of the organization," says retired Marine General Gail Reals, who spent thirty-six years in the Marine Corps. "We were kind of handy for someone making a speech who would showcase their woman general. They tolerated us but they didn't accept us."

Instead of drawing the genders together, the dynamics at work in the military culture often force them apart. Women are to be studied, to be tested, to be found wanting. Judged against the majority male model, women have to be the Wrong Stuff.

Major Marie Rossi was eulogized in 1991 as the "first female combat commander to fly into battle." Lieutenant Kara Hultgreen was eulogized in 1995 as a "warrior" by her sister pilots in the WMA. "Thank you for joining the fight to open combat to women. And thank you for dying for our country," read the WMA tribute to the F-14 fighter pilot.[79] The four years that separated their deaths marked the end of women's professional wars within the military. The cultural wars will never end.

Notes and Sources

THE MAJORITY of interviews with military and civilian sources for *Ground Zero* were conducted in the two years between the end of the Gulf war in 1991 and the assignment of women to combat positions beginning in 1993. During that time period, I went to three DACOWITS conferences, two WMA (Women Military Aviators) conventions, a conference at the Women's Research and Education Institute, a meeting of the Navy's Women Officers Professional Association (WOPA) and the Senate Armed Services subcommittee hearing on women in combat. I attended the gala salute to Military Women Prisoners of War in 1992, the unveiling of the Vietnam Women's Memorial, and several sessions of the Presidential Commission on the Assignment of Women in the Armed Forces. I visited the United States Military Academy at West Point, the now defunct Naval Recruit Training Center in Orlando, Florida, the Defense Equal Opportunity Management Institute (DEOMI) near Cocoa Beach, Florida, and the U.S. Army Military History Institute at Carlisle Barracks in Pennsylvania. In 1994, I met with the air crews in a Naval aviation fleet logistics support squadron in Norfolk, Virginia, and interviewed the first mixed gender crew aboard the USS *Dwight D. Eisenhower*.

The list of sources is not complete. Many military sources asked to remain anonymous. Those who consented to be interviewed on the record are identified in the text by the rank they held at the time of the interview.

Marcelyn Adkins

Amy Alger

Barbara Alt

James L. Anderson

Marjorie Bachman

Peggy Bahnsen

Kathy Ballard

Laurie Barone

Kathleen Batton

Adele Beck

Patricia Beckman

Carolyn Becraft

Barbara Bell

Linda Bisson

Mary Blissard

Alice Booher

Hattie Brantley
Linda Bray
Heidi Brown
Cabell Bruce
Kathleen Bruyere
Julie Buric
Donna Burk
Nancy Duff Campbell
Pam Lyons Carel
Elizabeth Carey
John Anderson Cayton
Daniela Di Ciccio-Harbaugh
Eileen Collins
Mickey Collins
Peter Copeland
Kim Corcoran
Rhonda Cornum
Becky Costantino
Paula Coughlin
Kimberly Line Courtois
Patrick Cummings
Ann Cunningham
Diana Davis
Judy DeBock
Tanya Domi
Elaine Donnelly
Loree Draude
Thomas Draude
Carolyn Dreyer
Tod Ensign
Marsha Filtrante
Mimi Finch
Ann Marie Fleming
Evelyn "Pat" Foote
Fred Francis
David Frederickson
Mike von Fremd
Betty Friedan
Danielle Fuller
Dr. Carole Garrison
Patricia Gavin
Deborah Gill
Alan "Mr. Big" Gorthy
Dr. Stephen Grove
Kelly Hamilton
Randy Hamilton
H. Steven Hammond

Evelyn "Blackie" Harding
Douglas Hart
Bernice Haydu
Karen Heck
Darrald Hert
Vennie Hilton
James Hogg
Victoria Hudson
Joyce Mady Hutton
Evalina Jerido
Ronald Joe
Gloria Johnson
Thomas Jones
Ken Kay
Jeanne Kelser
Terris Kennedy
Valerie Knowles
Bernadette Kucharczuk
Mike Lynch
Happy Maguire
Rosemary Mariner
Beth Martin
Steve Maurmann
Mike McDannell
Anne McGee
Jonathan McGraw
Sally Blaine Millett
Newton Minow
Lisa Moreno
Charles Moskos
Meredith Neizer
Mary Nelson
Brenda Newton
Giles Norrington
Jane O'Dea
Carol Ogg
Eileen O'Hickey
Jennifer St. Onge
W. S. "Bud" Orr
Gail Palmisano
Jacquelyn Parker
Russell Parkinson
Dr. Linda Grant De Pauw
Ted Paynther
Sue Peterson
Linda Phillips
Isabelle Katz Pinzler

Barbara Pope	Woods Thomas
Leo Rathbun	Maxwell Thurman
Gail Reals	Grace Tiscareno
Carol Rivers	Linda Tobin
Karen Roe	Patrick Toffler
Jennifer Rohrer	Madeline Ullom
Paul Rossi	Teresa VandenDolder
Sheryl Rozman	Peggy Walcher
Pierce Rushton Jr.	Carolyn Walter
Dr. Margaret Scheffelin	John Wattendorf
Robert Seigle	Delia Weeder
Sue Phillips Soto	John Weiss
Robert "Rocky" Spane	Stephanie Wells
Doreen Spelts	Babette White
Cecil Stack	Martha Whitehead
Thomas Stafford	Ora Jane Williams
Nora Kinzer Stewart	Pete Williams
Thomas Stoddard	Louise Wilmot
Claude Galbreath Swafford	Cookie Wilson
Jodi Tekell	Clement Wood
Scott Tekell	

PROLOGUE

1. The "fraternization" policy held that because senior personnel could influence if not virtually control a subordinate's assignments, promotions, even the degree of danger into which he or she could be sent, any perceived favoritism toward an individual was a cohesion and morale buster among the other troops.

2. Martin Binkin and Shirley Bach, *Women and the Military* (Washington, DC: Brookings Institution, 1977), p. 66.

3. "Background Study Use of Women in the Military," Office of the Assistant Secretary of Defense for Manpower, Reserve Affairs, and Logistics, Second Edition, September 1978, p. 23.

4. Ibid., p. 22.

5. Ibid., p. 2.

1. THE SILK AND CHIFFON GENERALS

1. 1978 Defense Department definition of combat, cited in Maj. Gen. Jeanne Holm, USAF (Ret.), *Women in the Military: An Unfinished Revolution*, rev. ed. (Novato, CA: Presidio, 1992), p. 338.

2. Martha L. Golar et al., "The Combat Exclusion Laws: An Idea Whose Time Has Gone," Association of the Bar of the City of New York Committee on Military Affairs and Justice, April 1, 1991.

3. "The Netherlands' Female Fighter Pilot," *WMA News*, Summer/Fall 1994, p. 10. (*WMA News* is a quarterly publication of Women Military Aviators, Inc.)

4. Quoted in Kate Muir, *Arms and the Woman: Female Soldiers at War* (London: Sinclair-Stevenson, 1992), p. 45.

5. Ibid., p. 36.

6. Marilyn A. Gordon and Mary Jo Ludvigson, "A Constitutional Analysis of the Combat Exclusion for Air Force Women." Reprinted in *Minerva: Quarterly Report on Women and the Military*, vol. IX, no. 2 (Summer 1991), pp. 1–34.

7. Betty J. Morden, *The Women's Army Corps, 1945–1978* (Washington, DC: U.S. Army Center of Military History, 1990), p. 33.

8. Gordon and Ludvigson, p. 4.

9. Quoted in Holm, p. 118.

10. Gordon and Ludvigson, p. 9.

11. Ibid., p. 6.

12. Holm, p. 118.

13. Melanie Martindale, Ph.D., "Sexual Harassment in the Military: 1988," Defense Manpower Data Center, Arlington, VA, September 1990.

14. Memo to The Hon. Richard Cheney, secretary of defense, from the DACOWITS Executive Committee and Connie S. Lee, chair, Aug. 23, 1989.

15. Dr. Jacquelyn K. Davis, report to Gen. Anthony Lukeman, Aug. 26, 1987, re: DACOWITS 1987 WESTPAC Visit. (WESTPAC is a military acronym for Western Pacific.)

16. John Burlage, "Salvage Ship's CO Draws Allegations of Harassment," *Washington Post*, Sept. 14, 1987, p. 3.

17. "Much Too Macho," *Time*, Sept. 28, 1987, p. 28.

18. Z-Gram 116, Aug. 7, 1972, titled "Equal Rights and Opportunities for Women in the Navy."

19. Ibid.

20. Jean Ebbert and Marie-Beth Hall, *Crossed Currents: Navy Women from WWI to Tailhook* (Washington, DC/New York: Brassey's [U.S.], 1993), p. 220.

21. *Owens v. Brown*, 455 F. Supp. 291 (D.D.C. July 1978).

22. Quoted in Holm, p. 333.

23. Carolyn Becraft, *Women in the U.S. Armed Services: The War in the Persian Gulf* (Washington, DC: Women's Research and Education Institute, March 1991).

24. Brian Mitchell, *Weak Link: The Feminization of the American Military* (Washington, DC: Regnery Gateway, 1989), p. 176.

2. PANAMA, THE PRESS AND ARMY POLITICS

1. Maj. Gen. Jeanne Holm, USAF (Ret.), *Women in the Military: An Unfinished Revolution*, rev. ed., (Novato, CA: Presidio, 1992), p. 427; *Minerva Bulletin Board*, Spring 1990, p. 3.

2. Charles Moskos, "Army Women," *Atlantic Monthly*, August 1990, p. 72.

3. *Soldiers Magazine,* March 1990, p. 22.

4. Ibid.

5. Peter Copeland, "U.S. Women Key Players in Invasion of Panama," Scripps Howard News Service, Jan. 1, 1990.

6. Kevin Buckley, *Panama: The Whole Story* (New York: Simon & Schuster, 1991), p. 240.

7. Peter Copeland interview in Joan R. Vallance Whitacre, "An Evaluation of the Media Coverage Concerning the Mission to Secure the Dog Kennel During the Panama Invasion on December 20, 1989," M.S. thesis, Virginia Commonwealth University, 1990, p. 92.

8. Capt. Mary B. McCullough, "Company Commander Reports from Panama," *Minerva's Bulletin Board,* Spring 1990, p. 1.

9. Charles Moskos, "Women in Combat: The Same Risks as Men?" *Washington Post* editorial, Feb. 3, 1990.

10. United States Southern Command News Release 90-1-8, Quarry Heights, Panama, Jan. 3, 1990.

11. Ibid.

12. Wilson Ring, "Woman Led U.S. Troops into Battle: Captain's Platoon Took PDF Target," *Washington Post,* Jan. 3, 1990, p. A1.

13. "Public Affairs After Action Report, United States Southern Command, Quarry Heights, Panama, Ronald T. Sconyers, Colonel, USAF, Director, Public Affairs, 31 Jan., 1990," p. iii.

14. Jacqueline Sharkey, *Under Fire: U.S. Military Restrictions on the Media from Grenada to the Persian Gulf* (Washington, DC: Center for Public Integrity, 1991), p. 100.

15. Sconyers report, p. 17.

16. Former Army spokesman Paige Eversole interview with Vallance Whitacre, p. 105.

17. Myths and taboos swirled around women and weaponry. During World War II unarmed members of the WAC had driven armed men around combat environments but weren't even allowed by the Army to be photographed near a weapon. Fifty years later it was still more acceptable for women to be fired on by men than it was for women to fire back.

Historians had drawn parallels between the taboo against women and weaponry and society's traditional fear of arming an underclass. (White males had still been uneasy about arming black males during the Korean War, although a decade had passed since President Harry Truman ordered racial integration in 1948.) (Francine D'Amico, "Women at Arms: The Combat Controversy," *Minerva,* vol. VII, no. 2 [Summer 1990], p. 11.) Anthropologist Margaret Mead had suggested that the military taboo against arming women stemmed from the male fear that women would perform their roles too well. "It may be that women would kill too thoroughly and endanger the negotiations and posturings of armies, through truces and prisoner taking with which nations ... eventually manage uneasy breathing spaces between wars," Mead had opined in 1971 ("Women in National Service," *Teacher's College Record of Columbia University* 73:1 [September 1971], quoted by D'Amico in *Minerva*).

18. "Female GI Wins Plaudits for Combat Role in Invasion," *Newark Star-Ledger,* Jan. 4, 1990, pp. 1, 18.

19. "Fire When Ready, Ma'am," *Time,* Jan. 15, 1990, p. 29.

20. Ibid.

21. Eversole interview with Vallance Whitacre.

22. Holm, p. 435.

23. Ring.

24. "A Fresh Shot at Full Equality," *U.S. News & World Report,* Jan. 15, 1990, p. 12.

25. "Fire When Ready, Ma'am," p. 29.

26. *Detroit News,* Jan. 7, 1990, p. 1.

27. "A Combat Soldier Named Linda," *Washington Post* editorial, Jan. 6, 1990.

28. Col. Bill Mulvey interview with Vallance Whitacre, p. 134.

29. John M. Broder, "Female's War Exploits Overblown, Army Says," *Los Angeles Times,* Jan. 6, 1990, p. 22.

30. Ibid.

31. Ibid.

32. Copeland interview with Vallance Whitacre, p. 70.

33. Ibid.

34. Ibid., p. 126.

35. Michael Gordon, "For First Time, a Woman Leads G.I.'s in Combat," *New York Times,* Jan. 4, 1990; Gordon, "U.S. Tells Calmer Story of Woman's Role in Commanding Attack," *New York Times,* Jan. 9, 1990.

36. Valerie Richardson, "Female Heroics Set Off War of Words in Press," *Washington Times,* Jan. 10, 1990, p. A1.

37. Chris Harvey, "Women-in-Combat Bill Faces Up-Hill Battle as Foes Dig In," *Washington Times,* Jan. 15, 1990 p. A5.

38. Valerie Richardson, "Shall Women Soldiers Fight?" *Washington Times,* Jan. 12, 1990 p. A1.

39. Ibid.

40. *World News Tonight* with Peter Jennings, Jan. 10, 1990.

41. Valerie Richardson, "Bray Will Get Medal, but Not the Badge," *Washington Times,* March 1, 1990, p. A4.

42. Ibid.

43. Elmo Zumwalt Jr. and James Zumwalt, "Meddling with Military Medals," *Washington Times,* June 25, 1990, p. F4.

44. Ibid.

45. Valerie Richardson, "Run on Combat Badge Voids Army's Supply —for Men," *Washington Times,* Jan. 31, 1991, p. A3.

46. "2 Army Women Being Investigated for Disobeying Order in Panama," *New York Times,* Jan. 21, 1990; Bill Gertz, "Army Suspects Women Truckers Ducked Panama Combat," *Washington Times,* Jan. 22, 1990, p. A5.

47. Moskos, "Army Women," p. 72.

48. Brian Mitchell, *American Legion Magazine,* May 1990.

49. Peter Copeland, "America's 'First Woman in Combat' Found Burden Too Heavy," Scripps Howard News Service, June 29–30, 1991.

50. Department of the Army, United States Army Criminal Investigation Command, Fort Benning District, Third Region, "CID Report of Investigation—Final," 0545-90-CID013 (0047-90-CID629-60023-7J4), Jan. 8, 1991, p. 1.

51. Army response about women's roles in Grenada and Panama to the Presidential Commission on the Assignment of Women in the Armed Forces, 1992.

52. Presidential Commission on the Assignment of Women in the Armed Forces, "Report to Commission on Findings, Panel Four," p. 55.

53. CBS/*New York Times* poll, Jan. 13 and 15, 1990, Roper Center, University of Connecticut, Storrs.

54. Sconyers report, p. 51.

55. Dr. Theresa Kraus, "Lessons Learned in Operation Just Cause," information paper prepared for the Army's Center of Military History, Washington, DC, Aug. 15, 1990.

56. Presidential commission report, p. 53.

3. PUBLIC VICTORY, PRIVATE LOSSES

1. *The Whirlwind War* (Washington, DC: U.S. Army Center of Military History, 1993), p. 352.

2. Lt. Gen. Walter E. Boomer, quoted in Molly Moore, *A Woman at War: Storming Kuwait with the U.S. Marines* (New York: Scribner, 1993), p. 99.

3. Martin Binkin, *Who Will Fight the Next War?: The Changing Face of the American Military* (Washington, DC: Brookings Institution, 1993), p. 20.

4. OASD-PA-DD1, Desert Shield/Desert Storm Casualties as of January 1992 cycle. This final Pentagon record lists names by state, type of casualty (hostile, nonhostile), sex, race, casualty date, rank, service, hometown and age of Gulf War casualties.

5. Dr. Linda Grant De Pauw, a professor of American history at George Washington University and publisher of *Minerva*, a quarterly report on women and the military, asked Doreen Spelts, editor of *The Keystone Veteran*, the quarterly newspaper of Pennsylvania Vietnam Veterans of America, to document the female casualties in the Gulf. "Linda called me and said, 'Let's do something about these women before they get lost,' " says Spelts, who used casualty lists from the Pentagon and an old national newspaper index to collect the hometown obituaries of the women. Details of the servicewomen's personal histories and military deaths were published in two issues of *Minerva's Bulletin Board* in the summer and fall of 1992.

6. "Women Casualties of the Gulf Operations," *Minerva's Bulletin Board*, Spring 1991, p. 1.

7. "Women Casualties of the Gulf Operations: An Update," *Minerva's Bulletin Board*, Fall 1991 p. 7.

8. *Buffalo News*, March 15 and 16, 1991.

9. Joshua Epstein of the Brookings Institution on *CBS Evening News*, Feb. 11, 1991.

10. Jacqueline Sharkey, *Under Fire: U.S. Military Restrictions on the Media from Grenada to the Persian Gulf* (Washington, DC: Center for Public Integrity, 1991), p. 28.

11. Ibid., p. 139.

12. *The Whirlwind War*, p. 346; Binkin, p. 85. African-American soldiers would account for 16% of the deaths in the Gulf, the low proportion due primarily to the lack of resistance from Iraqi troops during the ground war.

13. *The Whirlwind War*, p. 351

14. Ibid.

15. *Minerva's Bulletin Board*, Fall 1991, pp. 3–7.

16. R. W. Apple Jr., "Death Stalks Desert Despite Cease-Fire," *New York Times*, March 2, 1991, p. A6.

17. The seemingly benign silver "bomblets" which some servicewomen wore as earrings accounted for so many U.S. deaths—at least 25—that Congress ordered an investigation into the mishandling of the unexploded "ordnance" that Allied carpet-bombing runs and rocket launchers had strewn around the desert. (U.S. General Accounting Office, *Operation Desert Storm: Casualties Caused by Improper Handling of Unexploded U.S. Submunitions*, GAO/NSIAD-93-212, August 1993.)

18. Department of the Army, Board for Correction of Military Records—Board Date: July 28, 1993, Docket Number: AC93–08871.

19. Don Terry et al., "After the War: Grief in Western Pennsylvania," *New York Times*, March 4, 1991, p. A12.

20. *The Whirlwind War*, p. 349.

21. Terry et al.

22. Dorothy Schneider and Carl J. Schneider, *Sound Off! American Military Women Speak Out* (New York: Paragon House, 1992), p. xx.

23. Executive Order 10631, The White House, Dwight D. Eisenhower, Aug. 17, 1955; and Executive Order 12633, The White House, Ronald Reagan, March 28, 1988.

24. Executive Order 10631.

25. Testimony before the Presidential Commission on the Assignment of Women in the Armed Forces, June 8, 1992.

26. Wayne E. Dillingham, "The Possibility of American Military Women Becoming POWs: Justification for Combat Exclusion Rules?" *Federal Bar News & Journal*, May 1990, p. 228.

27. Testimony before the presidential commission, June 8, 1992.

28. Elizabeth Vaughan, "Community Under Stress," Vaughan, a sociologist, and her children were prisoners of war in Santo Tomás for almost four years. Her findings were cited by Robert Dussault, deputy director of the SERE Agency in testimony before the Presidential Commission on the Assignment of Women in the Armed Forces, June 8, 1992, p. 233.

29. Presidential commission, June 8, 1992.

30. Ibid.

31. *NBC Nightly News*, Feb. 1, 1991.

32. Dillingham, p. 228.

33. Department of the Army, "Report of Casualty D-0702," Feb. 11, 1991.

34. Response to a Freedom of Information Act request from the U.S. Total Army Personnel Command, Alexandria, VA, July 26, 1993.

35. Letter to Mr. and Mrs. Leo Rathbun from the POW/MIA Division of the U.S. Total Army Personnel Command, Alexandria, VA, Feb. 14, 1991, from Lt. Col. J. G. Cole, chief, POW/MIA Affairs.

36. "Panel One Report to the Presidential Commission," p. 92.

37. Monika Schwinn, "Break Your Teeth on Me," *Der Spiegel*, March 26, 1973, pp. 46–57, from the library archives at Fort Belvoir, VA.

38. Joyce Price, "NOW Cites Woman POW," *Washington Times*, Feb. 4, 1991.

39. Ibid.

40. Rhonda Cornum as told to Peter Copeland, *She Went to War: The Rhonda Cornum Story* (Novato, CA: Presidio, 1992), p. 9.

41. Ibid., p. 13.

42. Ibid., p. 54.

43. Ibid., p. 174.

44. Ibid., p. 113.

45. Ibid., p. 115.

46. Ibid., p. 162.

47. Binkin, p. 52.

48. Cynthia Enloe, "The Politics of Constructing the American Woman Soldier as a Professionalized 'First Class Citizen': Some Lessons from the Gulf." Reprinted in *Minerva*, Spring 1992, p. 28.

4. THE PREGNANCY WARS

1. "U.S. Soldiers Make Babies, Not War," *New York* magazine, "Intelligencer," March 4, 1991, p. 9.

2. *Newsweek*, Aug. 5, 1991, p. 23.

3. Interview by Col. Donald R. Hargrove and Lt. Col. Milton L. Little, March 7, 1977, Senior Officers Debriefing Program, U.S. Army Military History Institute, Carlisle Barracks, PA, p. 45.

4. Toni Carabillo, Judith Meuli and June Bundy Csida, *Feminist Chronicles, 1953–1993* (Los Angeles: Women's Graphics, 1993), p. 61.

5. *Struck v. Secretary of Defense*, 72 U.S. 178 (1972), Jeffrey Rosen, "The Book of Ruth," *New Republic*, Aug. 2, 1993, p. 31.

6. Maj. Gen. Jeanne Holm, USAF (Ret.), *Women in the Military: An Unfinished Revolution*, rev. ed. (Novato, CA: Presidio, 1992), p. 299.

7. *Crawford v. Cushman*, cited in Judith Hicks Stiehm, *Arms and the Enlisted Woman* (Philadelphia: Temple University Press, 1989), p. 117.

8. Holm, p. 302.

9. Ibid., p. 300.

10. Jean Ebbert and Marie-Beth Hall, *Crossed Currents: Navy Women from WWI to Tailhook* (Washington, DC/New York: Brassey's [U.S.], 1993), p. 165.

11. Bettie J. Morden, *The Women's Army Corps, 1945–1978* (Washington, DC: U.S. Army Center of Military History, 1990), p. 308.

12. Ibid.

13. Stiehm, p. 117.

14. Kate Muir, *Arms and the Woman: Female Soldiers at War* (London: Sinclair-Stevenson, 1992), p. 128.

15. Martin Binkin and Shirley J. Bach, *Women and the Military* (Washington, DC: Brookings Institution, 1977), p. 63.

16. "Women in the Army Study," December 1976, cited in *Use of Women in the Military* (Washington, DC: Office of the Assistant Secretary of Defense for Manpower, Reserve Affairs and Logistics, May 1977), p. 35.

17. Ibid., p. 27.

18. Ibid., p. 1.

19. Ibid., p. c-15.

20. Interview with Maj. Gen. Jeanne Holm by Col. Donald R. Hargrove and Lt. Col. Milton L. Little, Senior Officers Debriefing Program, U.S. Army Military History Institute, Carlisle Barracks, Carlisle, PA, p. 47.

21. "Evaluation of Women in the Army," March 1978, cited in Morden, p. 310.

22. Linda Stern, "Launch a Career with Basic Training," *Working Woman,* February 1980, p. 52.

23. U.S. Army Audit Agency, "Enlisted Women in the Army," Report HQ 82-212, April 30, 1982, p. 2.

24. Ibid., p. 26.

25. Ibid., p. 29.

26. Thomas C. Wyatt, John F. C. Kenney Jr. and A. M. Robert Dean, "Qualitative Analysis of Subjective Evaluation of Woman Content in Units (MAX-WAC) FTD," Technical Report No. 111, Sept. 22, 1977. Prepared for the U.S. Army Research Institute for the Behavioral and Social Sciences, Alexandria, VA.

27. Charles C. Moskos, "Female GIs in the Field," *Society,* vol. 22 (September/October 1985), pp. 28–33.

28. 1990 Navy Women's Study Group, "An Update Report on the Progress of Women in the Navy," p. ES-1.

29. P. J. Thomas and J. E. Edwards, *Incidence of Pregnancy and Single Parenthood Among Enlisted Personnel in the Navy* (San Diego, CA: Navy Personnel Research and Development Center [NPRDC-TR-90-1], 1989).

30. Patricia J. Thomas and Marie D. Thomas, *Impact of Pregnant Women and Single Parents Upon Navy Personnel Systems* (San Diego, CA: Navy Personnel Research and Development Center, Women and Multicultural Research Office [Report TN-92–8], February 1992).

31. Thomas and Edwards.

32. Disqualifying profiles, if proved to be "self-inflicted," can result in punitive penalties anywhere from a reprimand to court-martial.

33. The Navy had limited the number of women the service could absorb precisely because of the rotation of men between sea and shore duty. Until 1994, when the Navy opened combat ships to women, it operated

under a precise gender formula established in 1979 which utilized women without penalizing men. "The limit was 49,917 women based on sea-shore rotation," recalls retired Rear Admiral James Hogg, who served as director of military personnel training from 1979 to 1982. As U.S. troops deployed to the Gulf in 1990, the Navy gender ratio remained roughly the same: 50,000 women to 500,000 men.

34. Thomas and Edwards.

35. Navy response to presidential commission question 10: "What is the rationale for the '20th week' policy regarding assignment on ships for women?" generated from the May 4–6, 1992, meeting.

36. Marie D. Thomas, Patricia J. Thomas and Virginia McClintock, *Pregnant Enlisted Women in Navy Work Centers* (San Diego, CA: Navy Personnel Research and Development Center [NPRDC-TN-91-5], March 1991).

37. Thomas and Edwards.

38. Alecia Swasy, "Navy Babies," *Wall Street Journal,* Oct. 3, 1991, p. 1.

39. Thomas and Edwards.

40. Ibid.

41. 1990 Navy Women's Study Group, p. II-76.

42. 1991 DACOWITS overseas trip report.

43. Thomas et al., *Pregnant Enlisted Women in Navy Work Centers.*

44. Kenneth A. Marx, "Issues Relating to the Unique Medical Needs of Women in the Armed Forces," Research Division, Defense Equal Opportunity Management Institute, Patrick Air Force Base, FL, 1990, p. 13.

45. Thomas and Edwards.

46. Dorothy Schneider and Carl J. Schneider, *Sound Off! American Military Women Speak Out* (New York: Paragon House, 1992), p. 199.

47. Connie L. Reeves, "Pregnancy and the Army Pilot," *WMA News,* Spring 1995, p. 15.

48. Connie L. Reeves, "Dual-Service and Single Parents: What About the Kids?" *Minerva,* vol. XIII, nos. 3 & 4 (Fall/Winter 1995), p. 42.

49. Capt. David A. Self, "Reproductive Physiology Concerns Relating to the Exposure of Females to High Gravitation Fields," Laboratory for Aerospace Cardiovascular Research, Armstrong Laboratory, Brooks Air Force Base, TX.

50. *United Automobile Workers v. Johnson Controls, Inc.* (1991).

51. Cited in Elaine Donnelly, "Politics and the Pentagon: The Role of Women in the Military," 1991, p. 66.

52. David Hackworth, "War and the Second Sex," *Newsweek,* Aug. 5, 1991, p. 29.

53. Ibid.

54. Brian Mitchell, "War's Aftermath: The Issue of Women in the Military," address at conference on women in the military co-sponsored by the Center for Defense Journalism and the Rockford Institute, Washington, DC, April 1991.

55. Testimony of Maj. Steve Maurmann, USAF, to the Presidential Commission on the Assignment of Women in the Armed Forces, Sept. 11, 1992, p. 27.

56. Testimony of Lt. Col. Mike Lynch, USAF, to the presidential commission, Sept. 11, 1992, p. 56.

57. Martin Binkin, *Who Will Fight the Next War?: The Changing Face of the American Military* (Washington, DC: Brookings Institution, 1993), p. 17.

58. Lynch testimony, p. 57.

59. Ibid., p. 59.

60. Testimony of Lt. Col. Eugene Brindle, USMC, to the presidential commission, Sept. 11, 1992, p. 68.

61. Ibid., p. 69.

62. Ibid., p. 79.

63. Testimony of Capt. Martha Whitehead, USN, to the presidential commission, Sept. 11, 1992, p. 32.

64. Ibid., p. 31.

65. Ibid., p. 33.

66. Ibid., p. 34.

67. Army nondeployability briefing to the presidential commission, Aug. 8, 1992, p. 21.

68. Testimony of Col. Terry Hulin, USA, to the presidential commission, Aug. 8, 1992, p. 23.

69. Maurmann testimony, p. 30.

70. Hulin testimony, p. 24.

71. Service answers to questions from the presidential commission, July 13–15, 1992, meetings.

72. Rowan Scarborough, "Women Fall Short on Battle Readiness: Pregnancy Cited as Major Factor," *Washington Times*, July 28, 1992, p. 1.

73. Ibid.

74. Ibid.

75. U.S. General Accounting Office, *Operation Desert Storm: War Highlights Need to Address Problem of Nondeployable Personnel*, GAO/NSIAD-92-208, August 1992, p. 3. Report to the chairman, Subcommittee on Readiness, U.S. House Committee on Armed Services.

76. Ibid., p. 3.

77. U.S. General Accounting Office, *Women in the Military—Deployment in the Persian Gulf War*, GAO/NSIAD-93-93, July 1993. This report to the secretary of defense covers the opinion of service personnel about women's roles and performance in the Gulf, ability to endure deployment conditions, effect on unit cohesion and effect on a unit's ability to deploy. Chapter Five is titled "Unavailability for Deployment."

78. 1993 GAO report, p. 2.

79. Fully 100% of Navy and Army personnel cited pregnancy as the number one cause for both, while the other services weren't so sure. Among the Marines, whose service had sent just over 1,000 women to the Gulf, the percentages dropped to 85% and 89%, respectively. In the Air Force, where deployed personnel had been handpicked, the perception of nondeployment caused by pregnancy was a low 43%.

80. 1993 GAO report, p. 50.

81. Ibid., p. 51.

82. Ibid., p. 3.
83. "Panel One Report to the Presidential Commission."
84. 1993 GAO report, p. 46.
85. Thomas et al., *Pregnant Enlisted Women in Navy Work Centers*, p. 4.
86. 1990 Navy Women's Study Group, p. II-79.
87. 1982 Army Audit, p. 29.

5. THE POLITICS OF DIFFERENCES

1. James Thornton, "When Minnesota Moms Go to War," *Minnesota Monthly*, March 1991.
2. Dick Cheney's 3-A classification was a draft deferral for a "registrant with a child or children; or registrant deferred by reason of extreme hardship to dependents." Cited in letter from California Congresswoman Barbara Boxer to Defense Secretary Cheney, Feb. 13, 1991.
3. U. S. House Committee on Armed Services, Military Personnel and Compensation Subcommittee, *Parenting Issues of Operation Desert Storm: Hearing*, 102nd Congress, Feb. 19, 1991, p. 42.
4. *Population Representation in the Military Services Fiscal Year 1990*, Office of the Assistant Secretary of Defense, Force Management and Personnel, July 1991, p. D-23; cited in Connie L. Reeves, "Dual-Service and Single Parents: What About the Kids?" *Minerva*, vol. XIII, nos. 3 & 4 (Fall/Winter 1995), p. 29.
5. Ellen C. Collier, *Women in the Armed Forces*, CRS Issue Brief, Foreign Affairs and National Defense Division, Congressional Research Service, Sept. 21, 1992 (Order Code IB92008), p. 8.
6. "A Mother's Duty," *People*, Sept. 10, 1991, pp. 42–49.
7. Ibid., p. 46.
8. Ibid.,.p. 47.
9. Ibid., p. 45.
10. Thornton, p. 66.
11. *People*, p. 45.
12. *The Whirlwind War* (Washington, DC: U.S. Army Center of Military History, 1993), p. 372.
13. Ibid., p. 368.
14. *Parenting Issues of Operation Desert Storm*, p. 64. Statement of Hon. G. Kim Wincup, assistant secretary of the Army for manpower and reserve affairs.
15. *Larry King Live*, Feb. 2, 1991.
16. In contrast, only 28% thought it was unacceptable to send young fathers. Associated Press Gulf poll, Feb. 20, 1991.
17. Senator John Heinz, ". . . Accommodations Must Be Made," *Washington Post*, Feb. 19, 1991. Reproduced in *Parenting Issues of Operation Desert Storm*, p. 9.

Held to military scrutiny at congressional hearings on Feb. 19, 1991, the proposed legislation raised more problems than it solved. Barbara Boxer's bill, for example, gave voluntary exemptions from combat zones to parents with children up to 19 years old, a conundrum in that active-duty service members were often themselves only 17 and 18 years old and might still have parents on active duty. "Are you going to get both of them out?" asked Mississippi Congressman G. V. "Sonny" Montgomery.

Indiana Congresswoman Jill Long's bill prohibiting the assignment of parents to areas without child care facilities or housing also failed military scrutiny. Not only would the services be legally constrained from sending a single-parent volunteer on "unaccompanied tours" to such hardship bases as Korea or the Sinai, but, as Beverly Byron pointed out, "no member solely responsible for a dependent could ever be assigned on board ship, since the Navy has no dependent care facilities on its vessels."

One by one, the military realities of the All-Volunteer Force were weighed against the restrictive legislation. South Carolina Congressman Arthur Ravenel Jr. expressed concern that unit morale and cohesion would be strained if a unit were suddenly deployed to a combat zone and a single father could say, " 'Oh no, I've got an option here in the law, and I can request not to be deployed.' I would resent it very much if I had to go fight but he didn't because he has a child back home, possibly living with a grandmother. It's a real problem," said Ravenel.

Combat readiness was the issue raised by Virginia Congressman Herbert Bateman, the subcommittee's ranking minority member. "Operation Desert Shield didn't start off immediately as being an area of imminent danger," Bateman said. "Have you given some consideration to what this will do to a military commander if he has a detachment somewhere that is not subject to imminent danger but, all of a sudden, imminent danger does arise and half of his force says, 'Uh, uh, I'd like to opt out, now, thank you'?"

But it was Christopher Jehn who nailed the legislation for what it was. Despite Boxer's claim that her proposed bill would affect more men than women, and her protestations that preventing "war orphans" was "not a woman's issue," but a "family's and children's issue," neither her message nor her numbers added up to Jehn.

"I want to make sure everyone understands this is a woman's issue," said Jehn in a curious role reversal which placed the pale Pentagon technocrat on the side of equality for women and Boxer, the liberal, feminist legislator from California, seemingly against. "While male parents outnumber females, that is because males outnumber females eight to one in the total force. Women are much more likely to be single parents than are men. This legislation threatens to turn back the clock to the time when marriage or motherhood was cause for discharge or discrimination in assignment."

18. *Parenting Issues of Operation Desert Storm,* p. 97.

19. Truman's executive order begins: "It is believed that a woman who is pregnant or a mother should not be a member of the armed forces." Cited in Maj. Gen. Jeanne Holm, USAF (Ret.), *Women in the Military: An Unfinished Revolution,* rev. ed. (Novato, CA: Presidio, 1992), p. 291.

20. Ibid., p. 296.

21. Ibid.

22. *Parenting Issues of Operation Desert Storm*, p. 9; also in Heinz, "Accommodations Must Be Made."

23. "Panel Three Report to the Presidential Commission on the Assignment of Women in the Armed Forces," November 1992, p. 46.

24. *Women in the Armed Forces*, CRS Issue Brief, p. 9.

25. "Population Representation in the Military Services, Fiscal Year 1990," Office of the Assistant Secretary of Defense, Force Management and Personnel, July 1991.

26. Reeves, p. 32.

27. "Incidence of Pregnancy and Single Parenthood Among Enlisted Personnel in the Navy," Navy Personnel Research and Development Center, San Diego, October 1989.

28. *Parenting Issues of Operation Desert Storm*, p. 104. Testimony of Caroline Becraft.

29. "Panel Three Report to the Presidential Commission," 1992, p. 46.

30. Patricia J. Thomas and Marie D. Thomas, *Impact of Pregnant Women and Single Parents Upon Navy Personnel Systems* (San Diego, CA: Navy Personnel Research and Development Center, Women and Multicultural Research Office [Report TN-92-87], February 1992).

31. Ibid.

32. Grant Willis, "Drawdown Eases Child-Care Woes," *Navy Times*, May 17, 1993, p. 17.

33. Thomas and Thomas.

34. Reeves, p. 43.

35. U.S. General Accounting Office, *Women in the Military: Attrition and Retention*, GAO/NSIAD-90-87BR, July 1990; "Panel Four Report to the Presidential Commission on the Assignment of Women in the Armed Forces," 1992.

36. Thomas and Thomas.

37. *The Whirlwind War*, p. 365.

38. *Parenting Issues of Operation Desert Storm*, p. 120. Testimony of Dr. Robert J. Ursano, professor and chairman, Department of Psychiatry, Uniformed Services of the Health Sciences.

39. Ibid.

40. The Persian Gulf Conflict and Supplemental Authorization and Personnel Benefits Act of 1991, Public Law 102-25, Interim Response.

41. Thornton.

42. Shirley Sagawa and Nancy Duff Campbell, "Recommendations to the Presidential Commission on the Assignment of Women in the Armed Forces Regarding Parents in Military Service," National Women's Law Center, Washington, DC, Nov. 14, 1992.

43. U.S. General Accounting Office, *Reserves and Readiness: Appraising the Total Force Policy, 1991*, cited in the *Congressional Quarterly*, Sept. 25, 1992, p. 839.

44. U.S. General Accounting Office, *Women in the Military—Deployment in the Persian Gulf War*, GAO/NSIAD-93-93, July 1993, p. 52.

45. *The Whirlwind War,* p. 364.

46. "A Study of the Effectiveness of Family Assistance Programs in the Air Force During Operation Desert Shield/Storm," Executive Summary, Contract Number F49642-88-D0003.

47. Ibid.

48. Ellin L. Bloch, Ph.D., Anne C. Zimmerman, C.P.A., et al. "The Mental Health Needs of Operations Desert Shield and Desert Storm Veterans and Their Dependents," June 1991, p. 12.

49. "Panel Three Report to the Presidential Commission on the Assignment of Women in the Armed Forces," 1992, pp. 60, 61.

50. "A Study of the Effectiveness of Family Assistance Programs."

51. Martin Binkin, *Who Will Fight the Next War?: The Changing Face of the American Military* (Washington, DC: Brookings Institution, 1993), p. 50.

52. "Panel Three Report to the Presidential Commission," p. 46.

53. Binkin, p. 51.

54. Presidential Commission on the Assignment of Women in the Armed Forces, *Report to the President,* "Recommendation I: Pregnancy and Deployability Policies," Nov. 15, 1992, p. 19.

55. Ibid., "Recommendation H: Parental and Family Policies," p. 15.

56. U.S. House Committee on Armed Services, *Gender Discrimination in the Military: Hearings before the Military Personnel and Compensation Subcommittee and the Defense Policy Panel,* 102nd Congress, July 29 and 30, 1992, p. 88.

57. Reeves, p. 43.

6. THE MILITARY CULTURE OF HARASSMENT

1. Nelson DeMille, *The General's Daughter* (New York: Warner, 1992), p. 94.

2. Ibid., p. 4.

3. S. L. A. Marshall, *Men Against Fire* (New York: Morrow, 1947), pp. 55–56, cited in *Minerva,* vol. VIII, no. 3 (Fall 1990), p. 6; also Kenneth Karst in "The Pursuit of Manhood and the Desegregation of the Armed Forces," *UCLA Law Review* 38 (1991), p. 534.

4. Col. Frank A. Partlow Jr., "Womanpower for a Superpower: The National Security Implications of Women in the United States Army," *World Affairs,* vol. 146, no. 4 (Spring 1984), p. 303.

5. Capt. Carol Barkalow with Andrea Raab, *In the Men's House* (New York: Poseidon, 1990), p. 28.

6. *New York Times,* Feb. 14, 1996, p. D20.

7. Tom Wolfe, *The Right Stuff* (New York: Farrar, Straus, Giroux, 1979), p. 29.

8. Nancy Chapkis, "Sexuality and Militarism," in Eve Isaksson, ed., *Women and the Military System* (New York: St. Martin's, 1988), p. 110.

9. Remarks by a military guide during a tour of the "Women's Corridor" in the Pentagon.

10. *West Point 1991–1992 Catalog, One Hundred Ninetieth Year,* p. 135.

11. Femininity is described as "negative identity" by Erik Erikson in *Toys and Reasons: Stages in the Ritualization of Experience* (New York: Norton, 1977) and used by Karst in "The Pursuit of Manhood and the Desegregation of the Armed Forces," p. 504.

12. George Gilder, *Men and Marriage* (Gretna, LA: Pelican, 1986), p. 183.

13. Susan Faludi, *Backlash: The Undeclared War Against American Women* (New York: Crown, 1991), p. 290.

14. Gilder, p. 183.

15. *Marines: Recruit Training for Women,* p. 6.

16. Ibid., p. 9.

17. Ibid.

18. " 'Rape' Slogan Outrages Marine Corps Commandant," *Minerva's Bulletin Board,* vol. II, no. 4 (Winter 1989), p. 5.

19. Molly Moore, *A Woman at War: Storming Kuwait with the U.S. Marines* (New York: Scribner, 1993), p. 213.

20. Dr. David Marlowe, testimony before the Presidential Commission on the Assignment of Women in the Armed Forces, May 5, 1992.

21. U.S. General Accounting Office, *DOD Service Academies: More Actions Needed to Eliminate Sexual Harassment,* GAO/NSIAD-94-6, January 1994, p. 10.

22. Melanie Martindale, Ph.D., "Sexual Harassment in the Military: 1988," 1988–89 DOD Surveys of Sex Roles, Defense Manpower Data Center, Arlington, VA, September 1990, p. iii.

23. GAO report, p. 10.

24. Martindale, p. xiii.

25. Shirley Sagawa and Nancy Duff Campbell, "Sexual Harassment of Women in the Military," Women in the Military Issue Paper, National Women's Law Center, Washington, DC, Oct. 30, 1992.

26. 1990 Navy Women's Study Group, "An Update Report on the Progress of Women in the Navy," pp. 111–24.

27. Martin Binkin and Shirley J. Bach, *Women and the Military* (Washington, DC: Brookings Institution, 1977), p. 87. Binkin and Bach cite menstruation research which warned that half the crimes committed by women prisoners occurred during the week before their periods (premenstrual syndrome) and that women living in close quarters tended to synchronize their menstrual cycles, leading to possible "physical and psychological effect" on units with high proportions of women.

28. Ibid., p. 89.

29. Peter Lyman, "The Fraternal Bond as a Joking Relationship: A Case Study," in Michael S. Kimmel and Michael A. Messner, eds., *Men's Lives* (New York: Macmillan, 1989), p. 167. *Men's Lives* is an anthology of social science studies and articles about men and masculinity compiled for academic courses in women's studies in the 80s.

30. Ibid., p. 170.

31. Gary Alan Fine, "The Dirty Play of Little Boys," in *Men's Lives,* p. 177. The boys established their superior group identity as white heterosexual males by disparaging outsiders like blacks.

32. Lyman, p. 174.

33. John Stoltenberg, "Pornography and Freedom," in *Men's Lives*, p. 485.

34. Jill Neimark, "Out of Bounds: The Truth About Athletes and Rape," *Mademoiselle*, May 1991, p. 196.

35. Susan Brownmiller, *Against Our Will: Men, Women and Rape* (New York: Simon & Schuster, 1975), p. 107.

36. Ibid., p. 103.

37. Ibid., p. 110.

38. Neimark, p. 198.

39. Brownmiller, p. 105.

40. Marlise Simons, "For First Time, Court Defines Rape as War Crime," *New York Times*, June 28, 1996.

41. Carol Burke, "Dames at Sea," *New Republic*, Aug. 17 & 24, 1992, p. 20.

42. Barkalow, p. 48.

43. Burke, p. 18.

44. Sheila Coronel and Ninotchka Rosca, "For the Boys," *Ms.*, November/December 1993, p. 13.

45. U.S. House Committee on Armed Services, *Women in the Military: Hearings before the Military Personnel Subcommittee*, 96th Congress, November 15, 1979. The House subcommittee held four hearings in November 1979 and one in February 1980 on the expanded utilization of women in the floundering All-Volunteer Force. In 1979 not one service met its recruiting goal, including, for the first time, the Air Force. Without the infusion of 42,000 women into the services in 1979 alone, the All-Volunteer Force would have failed. "Women made the All-Volunteer Force work," says retired Admiral Louise Wilmot. "It's one of the things we're all very proud of. They cannot now say, 'We don't want these women, or women are not equal partners because they can't do (a), (b), (c) and (d). We didn't make the rules. We've lived by them.' "

46. Richardson testimony at 1979 hearings, p. 193.

47. Testimony of Diana Danis at hearings before the Committee on Veterans Affairs, U.S. Senate, 102nd Congress, June 30, 1992, p. 140.

48. Barbara Franco testimony at Senate hearing, p. 241.

49. *Women in the Military*, Nov. 13, 1979, p. 23.

50. Ibid., Nov. 14, 1979, p. 70.

51. Ibid., Nov. 15, 1979, p. 119.

52. Ibid., p. 156.

53. Helen Rogan, *Mixed Company: Women in the Modern Army* (New York: Putnam, 1981), p. 243.

54. *Woman in the Military*, testimony of Pvt. Sarah Tolaro, Feb. 11, 1980, p. 300.

55. Ibid., testimony of Lori Lodinsky, pp. 304–305.

56. Ibid., testimony of Specialist Jimi Hernandez, p. 300.

57. Ibid., testimony of Lodinsky, p. 302.

58. Ibid., testimony of Pvt. Tolaro, p. 304.

59. Ibid., testimony of Jacqueline Lose, p. 302.

60. Ibid., Congressman Antonio Won Pat, p. 302.

61. Ibid., Congressman Sonny Montgomery, p. 303.

62. Ibid., Congresswoman Marjorie Holt, p. 307.

63. Ibid., testimony of Gen. Mary Clarke, p. 337.

64. Ibid., testimony of Congresswoman Patricia Schroeder, p. 339.

65. Ibid., testimony of Congressman Montgomery, p. 343.

66. Ibid., testimony of Brig. Gen. Margaret Brewer, USMC, p. 341.

67. Ibid., testimony of Airman Marilyn Fields, p. 346.

68. U.S. Army Audit Agency, "Enlisted Women in the Army," Report HQ 82-212, April 30, 1982, p. 37.

69. Martindale, p. 34.

70. The military's special exception to legal avenues of redress from its members has been reinforced time and again by the courts. In 1953, in *Orloff v. Willoughby,* 345 U.S. 83 (1953), Supreme Court Justice Robert Jackson deemed the military "a specialized community governed by a separate discipline from that of the civilian." The judicial testing of Title VII thirty years later would not penetrate that "specialized community." In 1983 the Supreme Court, in *Chappell et al.* v. *Wallace et al.,* 462 U.S. 296 (1983), would let stand a lower court ruling that the protections of Title VII did not extend to a group of black sailors trying to sue the Navy for racial discrimination in duty assignments. Military justice was a stand-alone. "The special status of the military has required, the Constitution has contemplated, Congress has created, and this Court has long recognized two systems of justice, to some extent parallel: one for civilians and one for military personnel," Chief Justice Warren Burger wrote in *Chappell* v. *Wallace.* Cited by Judith Hicks Stiehm in *Arms and the Enlisted Woman* (Philadelphia: Temple University Press, 1989), p. 109, and by Karst in "The Pursuit of Manhood and the Desegregation of the Armed Forces," p. 565, note 247.

71. *Women in the Military,* statement of Col. Thomas E. Fitzpatrick, post commander, Fort Meade, MD, Feb. 11, 1980, p. 318.

72. *DOD Service Academies: More Actions Needed to Eliminate Sexual Harassment,* p. 18. The GAO lists a total of ten articles under the UCMJ to which harassment can be attached, including bribery and graft (Article 134) for servicemen offering rewards for sexual favors and Dereliction of Duty (Article 92) for those engaging in sexual harassment to the detriment of job performance.

73. Jean Ebbert and Marie-Beth Hall, *Crossed Currents: Navy Women from WWI to Tailhook* (Washington, DC/New York: Brassey's [U.S.], 1993), p. 187.

74. Tamar Lewin, "A Case Study of Sexual Harassment and the Law," *New York Times,* Oct. 11, 1991, p. 24.

75. U.S. General Accounting Office, *DOD's Policy on Homosexuality,* GAO/NSIAD-92-98, June 1992, p. 10.

76. Randy Shilts, *Conduct Unbecoming: Gays and Lesbians in the U.S. Military* (New York: St. Martin's, 1993), p. 5.

77. Celia Morris, *Bearing Witness: Sexual Harassment and Beyond—Everywoman's Story* (Boston: Little, Brown, 1994), p. 189.

78. J. Harry, "Homosexual Men and Women Who Served Their Country," *Journal of Homosexuality* 19 (1–2), 1984, p. 117, cited in Theodore R. Sarbin, Ph.D., and Kenneth E. Karois, M.D., Ph.D., "Nonconforming Sexual Orientations and Military Suitability," Deputy Personnel Security Research and Education Center (PERSEREC), Monterey, CA, 1989, p. 23.

79. *Face to Face,* Connie Chung, CBS TV, Nov. 8, 1991.

80. B. D. Clark, "The 'Lesbian' Label to Hold Back Women," *Virginian-Pilot and Ledger-Star,* Sunday, Oct. 21, 1990.

81. Jane Gross, "Hiding in Uniform—Homosexuals in the Military," *New York Times,* April 10, 1990, p. A1.

82. Michelle M. Benecke and Kirstin S. Dodge, "Military Women in Nontraditional Job Fields: Casualties of the Armed Forces' War on Homosexuals," *Harvard Women's Law Journal,* vol. 13 (1990), p. 221.

83. Jim Lynch, "Witch Hunt at Parris Island," *The Progressive,* March 1989, p. 26.

84. Ibid., p. 23.

85. Jane Gross, "Navy Is Urged to Root Out Lesbians Despite Ability," *New York Times,* Sept. 2, 1990.

86. Benecke and Dodge, p. 223.

87. Shilts, p. 632.

88. Gross, "Hiding in Uniform," p. A1.

89. Shilts, p. 640.

90. Ibid., p. 637.

91. Cynthia Enloe, *Does Khaki Become You? The Militarisation of Women's Lives* (Boston: South End, 1983), p. 143.

92. Lynch, p. 24.

93. Shilts, p. 595.

94. Philip Shenon, "New Study Faults Pentagon's Gay Policy," *New York Times,* Feb. 26, 1997, p. A10.

95. "Rape in the Military," ABC News *20/20,* Nov. 15, 1996. The Navy men who gang-raped the mechanic reported on went free. The Navy dropped the charges against two of the men without a hearing and dismissed the charges against the third after a one-day hearing because of "insufficient evidence."

7. THE UNDERGROUND WORLD AT THE ACADEMIES

1. Gwen Dreyer would graduate with high honors in 1993 and be named Outstanding Woman Engineer of the Year. She would spend two years at Apple Computer after graduation, then join Hewlett-Packard.

2. Gelareh Asayesh, "Harassed Female Midshipman Quits," *Baltimore Sun,* May 14, 1990, p. 1; see also "Taunted Woman Quits Academy," *New York Times,* May 14, 1990.

3. Scott Harper, "Ex-Mid Says Academy Sexism Lingers," *Annapolis Capital,* May 15, 1990, p. 1.

4. Ibid.

5. "Resignation of Woman Midshipman Triggers Investigations of USNA," *Minerva's Bulletin Board,* Summer 1990, p. 10. The members of NOW carried such signs as "Expel Sexist Middies," "Handcuff the Lying Admiral" and "Gentlemen, Officers, and Thugs."

6. Molly Moore, "Navy, Congress Open Probes of Harassment at Annapolis," *Washington Post,* May 18, 1990, p. A1.

7. "American Notes": "A Probe That Snowballed," *Time,* June 11, 1990, p. 27.

8. Martin Binkin and Shirley J. Bach, *Women and the Military* (Washington, DC: Brookings Institution, 1977), p. 52.

9. United States Naval Academy Board of Visitors (Barbara A. Mikulski, U.S. Senator; Helen D. Bentley, member of Congress; FitzGerald Bemiss; James M. Cannon; Arthur B. Culvahouse Jr., chairperson), *"Report of the Committee on Women's Issues,"* Oct. 9, 1990, p. 13.

10. Women Midshipmen Study Group-90 (hereafter WMSG-90), "The Assimilation of Women in the Brigade of Midshipmen, United States Naval Academy, Annapolis, Maryland," report to the superintendent, July 1990, p. 13.

11. Ibid., p. 3.

12. Ibid., p. 11.

13. The members of DACOWITS were briefed on the findings of the 1990 Women Midshipmen Study Group in April 1991 by the chair of the standing committee, Capt. Dave Davis.

14. Maj. Gen. Jeanne Holm, USAF (Ret.), *Women in the Military: An Unfinished Revolution,* rev. ed. (Novato, CA: Presidio, 1992), p. 94.

15. Jean Ebbert and Marie-Beth Hall, *Crossed Currents: Navy Women from WWI to Tailhook* (Washington, DC/New York: Brassey's [U.S.], 1993), p. 235.

16. Holm, p. 427.

17. WMSG-90, p. 9.

18. Ibid., p. 10.

19. Ibid., p. 25.

20. Ibid., p. 23.

21. Ibid., pp. 23, 24.

22. Ibid., p. 23.

23. Ibid., p. 23. James Gordon Bennett, "Shock Waves at the U.S. Naval Academy," *Glamour,* June 1992, p. 254.

24. Carol Burke, "Dames at Sea," *New Republic,* Aug. 17 & 24, 1992, pp. 16–20.

25. Ibid.

26. *Report of the Committee on Women's Issues,* p. 10.

27. Ibid., p. 9.

28. U.S. General Accounting Office, *DOD Service Academies: More Actions Needed to Eliminate Sexual Harassment,* GAO/NSIAD-94-6, January 1994, p. 20. The survey covers the academic year 1990–91, the year after the Dreyer handcuffing, and includes 10 forms of harassment used in other survey models; derogatory comments; comments that standards have been lowered; comments that women don't belong; offensive posters, T-shirts, etc.;

mocking gestures; derogatory letters or messages; exclusion from social activities; target of unwanted horseplay or hijinks; unwanted pressure for dates by more senior students and unwanted sexual advances. Women at West Point reported significantly more incidents of harassment than did their counterparts at the other academies in nine of the ten categories. The incidence of unwanted pressure for dates by senior students, a violation of the services' "fraternization" policies, was shared equally by 4% of all female cadets and midshipmen.

29. Quoted in Judith Hicks Stiehm, *Bring Me Men & Women; Mandated Change at the U.S. Air Force Academy* (San Francisco: University of California Press, 1981), p. 25.

30. Toni Carabillo, Judith Meuli and June Bundy Csida, *Feminist Chronicles, 1953–1993* (Los Angeles: Women's Graphics, 1993), p. 70.

31. Brian Mitchell, *Weak Link: The Feminization of the American Military* (Washington, DC: Regnery Gateway, 1989), p. 38.

32. Dr. Richard U'Ren, *Ivory Fortress* (Indianapolis/New York: Bobbs-Merrill, 1974), pp. 130–31. Dr. U'Ren, the chief of psychiatry at West Point from 1970 to 1972, quotes a first classman at the time who told a West Point doctor: "The Secretary of the Army found out about the plan and put a stop to it immediately. He realized it would have shot a hole in the argument that women shouldn't be admitted to West Point because they couldn't qualify for combat arms. If cadets were going into noncombat arms branches, why shouldn't women, too?"

33. Quoted in Stiehm, p. 25.

34. Holm, p. 309.

35. Binkin and Bach, p. 49, note 30.

36. Stiehm, p. 33.

37. Mitchell, p. 41.

38. Ibid.

39. Capt. Donna Peterson, *Dress Grey: A Woman at West Point* (Austin, TX: Eakin, 1990), p. 128.

40. Quoted in Stiehm, p. 20; the hearings are covered as well in Holm, Mitchell and Binkin and Bach.

41. 1994 GAO report, p. 21.

42. U.S. General Accounting Office, *DOD Service Academies: Improved Cost and Performance Monitoring Needed,* GAO/NSIAD-91-79, July 1991, p. 30.

43. According to the 1994 GAO report, 49% of female cadets at West Point were being told at least twice a month that they "didn't belong" at the academy, p. 21.

44. Public Law 94-106, Oct. 7, 1975.

45. U.S. General Accounting Office, *DOD Service Academies—More Changes Needed to Eliminate Hazing,* GAO/NSIAD-93-36, November 1992, pp. 76, 77. The GAO report found every primitive rite of male passage identified by Lionel Tiger and Robin Fox in their book *The Imperial Animal* (New York: Holt, Rinehart and Winston, 1971), pp. 158–59: "The initiates are separated from the women and kept in seclusion. They are hazed and humiliated by their elders. They undergo ordeals of endurance and tests of many skills.

. . . They are compelled to learn masses of arcane wisdom, as well as the proper conduct of ritual and the proper cherishing of myths and traditions of the group. . . . Finally, they are sometimes ritually slain and brought back to life as 'men.' "

Though the rigid fourth class system at the academies that traditionally had given license to upperclassmen to use physical force and psychological cruelty to instill manly values in freshmen (plebes) had been tempered, other rituals remained.

Still alive and well was the plebes' recital on demand of "arcane wisdom" which required plebes at the Naval Academy to memorize such trivia as the daily menus, sports scores, the number of bricks in the sidewalk and the number of days until the Army game. At West Point, "fourth class knowledge" extended beyond the memorization of menus to include the names and numbers of every football player on the Army team, the sports news, the number of "butt" days to every significant West Point event from the number of "butt days until Army beats the hell out of Navy" to the butt days "until graduation leave," as well as the daily headlines and front-page stories in the *New York Times*. The Air Force Academy followed suit with its own arcana, justifying the rote memorization to the GAO as a necessary discipline for future aircrews who would have to memorize the exact procedures to follow in an emergency (GAO, p. 31).

"The proper cherishing of myths and traditions" governed every minute of a plebe's day. Plebes at West Point and Annapolis were not allowed to talk to each other outside their rooms, and at the Air Force Academy were allowed only 7 responses to upperclassmen's questions from the obvious "Yes, Sir/Ma'am, No, Sir/Ma'am" to the more urgent "Sir, I will find out." Meals were measured in inches. While upperclassmen yelled demands for "fourth class knowledge," the plebes at the Air Force Academy had to drink without touching the top third of a glass, which must be filled to ½ inch from the top (GAO, p. 31). At the Naval Academy, plebes had to sit at attention on the edges of their chairs, stare straight ahead and eat their meals with "three chews and a swallow" (GAO, p. 16).

The "hazing and humiliation by their elders" was a 24-hour reality to plebes and to upperclassmen deemed unworthy of fraternal membership by their male peers. Though the academy dynamic was little different than the hazing imperative among young males in civilian fraternities, the stress was multiplied a thousandfold for the academy plebes, who spent every moment of every day and every night at the mercy of their only slightly older academy colleagues. Such harsh treatment was necessary, the justification went, to prepare cadets and midshipmen for the possibility of future internments as POWs (GAO, p. 69).

Over half the cadets and midshipmen in all four classes at the academies surveyed by the GAO between 1990 and 1992 reported being insulted or ridiculed as plebes, screamed at by upperclassmen and having to use study hours to memorize the next day's trivia which, if they failed, would result only in more hazing. At the Naval Academy, over half the midshipmen also reported having to assume the exaggerated "stand at attention" posture called bracing which required the plebes to throw back their shoulder blades until they touched, thrust their chests up, arms down, and press in their buttocks and chins—and to remain braced until released.

The cadets at the high-tech Air Force Academy turned out to be the most harassed of all. Over 40% of current and former plebes reported having been subjected at least twice a month to 10 of the 21 areas of "fourth class treatment" identified by the GAO, including enduring extended periods of bracing, having study hours preempted by plebe duties, being forced to do multiple sets of exercises, performing "personal services or errands" and assuming "unnatural positions."

The rites of passage were more brutal in other militarized cultures. The stories of Citadel upperclassmen forcing one freshman "knob" to hang by his fingers over a sword aimed at his testicles, of another being half drowned into unconsciousness and of another being beaten with a rifle butt by a gang of cadets made the pages of *Sports Illustrated* in 1991. The rites of passage in the civilian Corps of Cadets at Texas A&M included such sophomoric rituals as heaving a pumpkin filled with pig feces into the band members' dorm and such illegal hazing rituals as subjecting first-year cadets, called fish, to paddlings with axe handles, forced marches and late-night physical endurance "training" exercises which, in 1985, had left one male cadet dead on the floor of a barracks shower stall at 3 a.m. So fundamental were the rites of passage to men like President Bill Clinton's Secretary of Housing and Urban Development and former cadet Henry Cisneros that he continued to revere the cadets in the all-male corps in the 60s who'd pinioned him spread-eagled on the ground in his underwear, while other cadets poured water on his genitals from an upper-story window. "These were my buddies, the best friends I ever had," Cisneros would tell *Texas Monthly* fondly about the corps tradition called quadding (Mimi Swartzon, "Love and Hate at Texas A&M," *Texas Monthly,* February 1992, p. 100).

46. "Report on the Integration and Performance of Women at West Point for the Defense Advisory Committee on Women in the Services (DA-COWITS)," February 1992, pp. 54, 55. Supreme Court Justice Ruth Bader Ginsburg cited this report in the Court's majority opinion finding the exclusion of women from the Virginia Military Institute (VMI) to be unconstitutional, June 26, 1996, at Footnote 13, supporting the statement "Women's successful entry into the federal military academies . . ." and "Women cadets have graduated at the top of their class at every federal military academy."

47. WMSG-90, p. 15.

48. In 1991 the Naval Academy mission statement was: "To develop midshipmen morally, mentally, and physically and to imbue them with the highest ideals of duty, honor, and loyalty in order to provide graduates who are dedicated to a career of naval service and have potential for future development in mind and character to assume the highest responsibilities of command, citizenship, and government."

49. Since 1987 the West Point mission statement has been: "To educate and train the Corps of Cadets so that each graduate shall have the attributes

essential to professional growth throughout a career as an officer of the Regular Army and to inspire each to a lifetime of service to the nation."

50. WMSG-90, p. 7.

51. "The Superintendent's Annual Historical Review," 1981, United States Military Academy, West Point, NY, p. 42.

52. "Report on Fact-Finding Trip to United States Military Academy, West Point, NY," Presidential Commission on the Assignment of Women in the Armed Forces, Oct. 19, 1992.

53. West Point report to DACOWITS, p. 41.

54. U.S. General Accounting Office, *Military Academy: Gender and Racial Disparities*, GAO/NSIAD-94-95, March 1994, p. 26.

55. Priest et al., "Difference Between Characteristics of Men and Women New Cadets Class of 1980," Report No. 1B5.14-77-010.

56. West Point report to DACOWITS, p. 24.

57. Ibid., p. 12.

58. Transcript of hearings: statement of Phyllis Schlafly, U.S. Congress. Congressional Record—Senate, Armed Services Committee, Subcommittee on Manpower and Personnel, June 18, 1991, p. 938.

59. Grant Willis, "DACOWITS: Academies Missing Point on Sexual Harassment," *Air Force Times*, Dec. 16, 1991, p. 13. DACOWITS echoed the same response Israeli Prime Minister Golda Meir had given 20 years before to the suggestion that a nighttime curfew on women would solve an epidemic of assaults. "Men are attacking women, not the other way around," Meir had said. "If there is going to be a curfew, let the men be locked up, not the women" *(New York Times*, Sept. 28, 1995, op-ed).

60. Col. Patrick Toffler, West Point's director of the Office of Institutional Research, testified as a "witness of fact" in the nonjury trial on the admission of women to the Virginia Military Institute (VMI) in Lexington, Virginia, on April 8, 1991. The lawyers for VMI used his testimony on the post-integration changes at West Point to buttress their case against women being admitted to VMI. These statistics can be found on page 535 of the court transcripts of the trial, which resulted in a first-round victory for VMI. "VMI truly marches to the beat of a different drummer, and I will permit it to continue to do so," ruled U.S. District Court Judge Jackson L. Kiser on June 17 of that year. The decision was later overturned by the Supreme Court.

61. West Point report to DACOWITS, p. 64. In the classes of 1988, 1989 and 1990, respectively, 43%, 50% and 40% of the graduating male cadets felt integration had been successful. That indicates that 57%, 50% and 60% did not.

62. West Point report to DACOWITS, p. 49.

63. A 1988 Air Force Academy study had determined that its female cadets had a significantly higher level of bulimia (12%) than was typically found among women at civilian colleges. This finding would play out in the skeletal images of a 90-pound cadet at the Air Force Academy in 1995 after she became a target for harassment. Fat was considered such a fundamental human failing at West Point it was cause for dismissal. The criteria for

"breach of service agreement" spelled out on page 133 of the 1992 West Point catalogue specifically deemed the cadets failing "to make satisfactory progress" in the academy's Cadet Weight Management Program as liable for dismissal, as were violators of the Honor Code and the cadets who went AWOL.

64. West Point report to DACOWITS, p. 29.

65. *Minerva's Bulletin Board,* Summer 1992, p. 8.

66. West Point report to DACOWITS, p. 23.

67. Ibid., p. 49.

68. Ibid., p. 50.

69. 1994 GAO report on sexual harassment, p. 21.

70. Ibid., p. 22.

71. Ibid., p. 37.

72. Ibid., p. 22.

73. Ibid.

74. U.S. General Accounting Office, *DOD Service Academies: Update on Extent of Sexual Harassment,* GAO/NSIAD-95-58, March 1995.

75. The number of female cadets experiencing recurring sexual harassment rose from 50% in 1990–91 to 70% in 1993–94 at the Naval Academy, and from 59% to 76% at the Air Force Academy. At West Point, the rise was 76% to 80%. Men were included in the GAO's 1995 update; 3% to 4% cited recurring sexual harassment across the GAO's 10 categories (p. 8). The '95 update also found that between 36% and 42% of academy women had experienced unwelcome "contact of a sexual nature" at least one or two times a year, and 39% to 42% had experienced "physical, gender-related conduct" that either interfered with their performance or created an "intimidating, hostile, or offensive environment"; 13% of cadets at West Point experienced such behavior "a couple of times a month or more" (pp. 27, 28); 11% to 22% experienced the acceptance or rejection of sexual advances being tied into their academy careers. The highest percentage was at West Point (pp. 29, 30).

76. "The Annual Report of the Superintendent, 1980," United States Military Academy, West Point, NY, p. 84.

77. Ibid., p. 85.

78. Rosabeth Moss Kanter, *Men and Women of the Corporation* (New York: Basic Books, 1977). Kanter's thesis covers women in a civilian, white-collar male culture. The effects of "tokenism" in the young male academy culture were the same, but greatly exaggerated.

79. Ibid., p. 222.

80. WMSG-90, p. 58, fig. 16.

81. Request for Information: Women in the Military Academies, Submitted by: United States Air Force Academy, March 20, 1992, Table 4i.

82. West Point report to DACOWITS, p. 45.

83. 1994 GAO report on sexual harassment, p. 24.

84. *Military Academy: Gender and Racial Disparities,* pp. 27, 29. Women were found to have lower grades in military performance in four of the five classes between 1988 and 1992.

85. Ibid., p. 29.

86. Answer to question: To what extent do you feel accepted by your classmates in your role as a cadet? prepared by U.S. Military Academy Office of Institutional Research, January 1992; Source: Human Relations Survey, Class of 1991. Of the women, 58% reported feeling "more accepted than not," a higher percentage than Asians, blacks and Hispanics. The same survey found that fewer than half of male cadets in the class of '91 (42.7%) agreed or agreed strongly that the integration of women had been a success, in contrast to 59.6% of women.

87. 1994 GAO report on harassment, p. 20.

8. GROUND ZERO

1. U.S. Congress. Congressional Record—House of Representatives, Committee on Armed Services, Subcommittee on Manpower and Personnel, transcript of hearings: "Utilization of Women in the Military Services," June 18, 1991; statement of Elaine Donnelly, founder and executive director of the Coalition for Military Readiness. Donnelly's coalition included the American Conservative Union, American Defense Lobby, American Defense Foundation, Americans for the High Frontier, Center for the Military and Society, Concerned Women for America, Conservative Caucus, CNP Action, Inc., Coalition for America, Eagle Forum, Family Research Council, Freedom Alliance and High Frontier, Inc.

2. Section 8549, Title 10, U.S. Code.

3. Section 6015, Title 10, U.S. Code.

4. Carolyn Becraft, *Women in the U.S. Armed Services: The War in the Persian Gulf* (Washington, DC: Women's Research and Education Institute, March 1991).

5. U.S. House Committee on Armed Services, *Women in the Military: Hearing before the Military Personnel and Compensation Subcommittee,* 101st Congress, March 20, 1990, p. 53.

6. Ibid., p. 87.

7. The House vote was on May 22, 1991. See Jon Nordheimer, "Women's Role in Combat: The War Resumes," *New York Times,* May 26, 1991, p. 1.

8. Defense Department press release, May 23, 1991.

9. Anne Noggle, *For God, Country and the Thrill of It: Women Airforce Service Pilots in World War II* (College Station, TX: Texas A&M University Press, 1990), p. 11.

10. Sally Van Wagenen Keil, *Those Wonderful Women in Their Flying Machines: The Unknown Heroines of World War II* (New York: Four Directions, 1990), pp. 273, 228.

11. Ibid., p. 347.

12. Noggle, p. 14.

13. Lillian Kozloski and Maura Mackowski, "The Wrong Stuff," *Final Frontier: The Magazine of Space Exploration,* May/June 1990, p. 21.

14. Ibid.

15. Jean Ebbert and Marie-Beth Hall, *Crossed Currents: Navy Women from WWI to Tailhook* (Washington, DC/New York: Brassey's [U.S.], 1993), pp. 252, 255.

16. Lt. Col. Terence J. Lyons, "Women in the Military Cockpit," Brooks Air Force Base, TX, June 1991, p. 2.

17. Barton Gellman, "Women Fliers in Race with Changing Times," *Washington Post*, July 29, 1991, p. A1; also Maj. Gen. Jeanne Holm, USAF (Ret.), *Women in the Military: An Unfinished Revolution*, rev. ed. (Novato, CA: Presido, 1992), p. 493.

18. Marilyn Achiron and Bob Stewart, "Cleared for Takeoff: Second Lieutenant Jeannie Flynn Becomes America's First Female Combat Pilot," *People*, May 17, 1993, p. 46.

19. June 18, 1991, hearing; statement of Elaine Donnelly, p. 886.

20. President Jimmy Carter reactivated registration for the draft and proposed including women in early 1980 following the seizing of U.S. hostages in Iran and the Soviet invasion of Afghanistan in 1979. Congress defeated the president's request to include women after a "Don't Draft Women" campaign spearheaded by Phyllis Schlafly and the Eagle Forum. The male-only registration was challenged in court as sex discrimination by two young men and ended up, on appeal, before the Supreme Court in 1981. In *Goldberg* v. *Rostker*, the Supreme Court upheld the constitutionality of a male-only draft on the basis that the draft existed to raise combat troops and women, by law, were excluded from combat.

21. Statement of Phyllis Schlafly, June 18, 1991, hearing, pp. 940–41. "The Problem of Making Women Liable to Conscription" was one of Schlafly's "problems." Others included "The Pregnancy Problem," "The Motherhood Problem," "The Affirmative Action Quota Problem" and "The Problem of the Feminist Attack on Our Culture."

22. Statement of Elaine Donnelly, June 18, 1991, hearing, p. 884.

23. Ibid., p. 885.

24. Testimony of Gen. Carl Vuono, June 18, 1991, hearing, p. 842.

25. Testimony of Gen. Alfred M. Gray Jr., June 18, 1991, hearing, p. 832.

26. Testimony of Adm. Frank B. Kelso II, June 18, 1991, hearing, p. 833.

27. Testimony of Gen. Merrill A. McPeak, June 18, 1991, hearing, p. 838.

28. Testimony of Gen. Vuono, p. 846.

29. Holm, p. 485.

30. Statement of Lt. Brenda Marie Holdener, a Navy helicopter pilot assigned to Helicopter Combat Support Squadron 6, Naval Air Station, Norfolk, VA, June 18, 1991, hearing, p. 850.

31. Statement of Maj. Christine Prewitt, Air Force senior pilot, flight scheduler, Andrews Air Force Base, MD, June 18, 1991, hearing, p. 851.

32. Statement of Sgt. Jean A. Amico, Headquarters Company, Head-

quarters Battalion, 1st Marine Division, Camp Pendleton, CA, June 18, 1991, hearing, p. 847.

33. Statement of Staff Sgt. Susan Leifeste, motor sergeant, 82nd Airborne, Fort Bragg, NC, June 18, 1991, hearing, p. 847.

34. Testimony, June 18, 1991, hearing, p. 855.

35. U.S. House Committee on Armed Services, Subcommittee No. 3 (Organization and Mobilization), *Subcommittee Hearing on S. 141, to Establish the Women's Army Corps in the Regular Army, to Authorize the Enlistment and Appointment of Women in the Regular Navy and Marine Corps and the Naval and Marine Corps Reserve, and for Other Purposes,* Feb. 18, 1948. Cited in Jean Zimmerman, *Tailspin: Women at War in the Wake of Tailhook* (New York: Doubleday, 1995), p. 162.

36. National Organization for Women News Release, "Statement of NOW Executive Vice President Patricia Ireland Supporting Repeal of Combat Exclusion Laws for Women," June 18, 1991. Other women's groups actively supporting repeal were the American Association of University Women, American Nurses' Association, Center for Women Policy Studies, National Women's Law Center, NOW Legal Defense and Education Fund, and Wider Opportunities for Women.

37. Schlafly statement to the Senate, June 18, 1991, hearing, p. 935.

38. Memo to: Members, United States Senate and Members, United States House Armed Services Committee from Elaine Donnelly, Coalition for Military Readiness, July 15, 1991, Re: Excerpts from June 18th Senate Hearing: Women in Combat, p. i.

39. June 18, 1991, hearing, pp. 844, 845.

40. Lyons, p. 15.

41. *WMA News,* vol. 111, no. 4 (December 1991), p. 9.

42. Rick Maze, "Roth, Kennedy Want Amendment to Let Women Fly Combat Craft," *Navy Times,* Aug. 15, 1991.

43. Gellman, p. A1.

9. THE UNWINNABLE WAR

1. DEOMI Program of Instruction, Class 91-2, May 1991.

2. "Women in Combat," Research Division, Defense Equal Opportunity Management Institute, Patrick Air Force Base, FL, 1990, pp. 2–4. The report's cover reads "Local Reproduction is Authorized and Encouraged."

3. Kenneth A. Marx, "Issues Relating to the Unique Medical Needs of Women in the Armed Forces," Research Division, Defense Equal Opportunity Management Institute, 1990, pp. 6, 1.

4. Testimony of the Rev. John Stewart, a nondenominational Protestant minister, to the Presidential Commission on the Assignment of Women in the Armed Forces, Aug. 6, 1992, Los Angeles.

5. Presidential Commission on the Assignment of Women in the Armed Forces, *Report to the President,* Nov. 15, 1992, p. 50.

6. Testimony of Sgt. Carlos DeJesus, USA, to the presidential commission, July 14, 1992, Chicago.

7. Presidential commission report, p. 25.

8. Testimony of Dr. David Marlowe to the presidential commission, May 5, 1992, Washington, DC.

9. U.S. House Committee on Armed Services, *Gender Discrimination in the Military: Hearings before the Military Personnel and Compensation Subcommittee and the Defense Policy Panel,* 102nd Congress, July 29 and 30, 1992, p. 48.

10. Interview by Serena Cosgrove and Robyn Braverman.

11. "Dissent from the Recommendation on the Exclusion of Women from Combat Aircraft," presidential commission report, p. 85.

12. "Stress During the Early Phase of Operation Desert Shield: Observations of the WRAIR Stress Evaluation Team," paper presented at the Eighth Users' Stress Workshop, U.S. Army Health Care Studies and Clinical Investigation Activity, San Antonio, TX, Sept. 24–27, 1991.

13. Testimony of Capt. David Freaney to the presidential commission, Aug. 28, 1992, p. 157.

14. "Panel Two Report to the Commission on Findings," p. 29.

15. Ibid., p. 55.

16. Ibid., p. 31.

17. Ibid., p. 7, based on a snapshot of male and female Army ROTC cadets during Advanced Summer Camp.

18. Soraya Nelson, "Training Program Toughens Women to Handle Army's Men-only Jobs," *Army Times,* Feb. 12, 1996, p. 3.

19. Kate Muir, *Arms and the Woman* (London: Sinclair-Stevenson, 1992), p. 80.

20. Ibid., p. 77.

21. Ibid., p. 81.

22. Testimony of Staff Sgt. Michael T. Wagner to the presidential commission, Aug. 7, 1992, p. 221.

23. "Attitudes Regarding the Assignment of Women in the Armed Forces: The Military Perspective," Roper Organization, unpublished, September 1992, p. 123.

24. Ibid., p. 127.

25. Testimony of Phyllis Schlafly to the presidential commission, June 9, 1992, Washington, DC.

26. Tailhook Association submittal to the Defense Department inspector general contained in U.S. Department of Defense Inspector General, *Tailhook '91, Part 2: Events at the 35th Annual Tailhook Symposium,* February 1993, p. B-5.

27. Presidential commission report, p. 94.

28. "Panel One Report to Commission on Findings," p. 63.

29. Presidential commission report, p. 31.

30. Testimony of Lt. Lori Melling Tanner, USN, test pilot, Patuxent River Naval Air Station, MD, and Capt. Jacquelyn Parker, USAF, test pilot, Wright-Patterson Air Force Base, OH, Aug. 29, 1992, Dallas.

31. Elaine Donnelly, Commissioner Statements in the presidential commission report, p. 102.

32. Testimony of Hays Parks, chief of the International Law Branch of the International and Operational Law Division Office of the Judge Advocate General, USA, to the presidential commission, June 8, 1992, Washington, DC.

33. Testimony of Rhonda Cornum to the presidential commission, June 8, 1992.

34. Laurence Jolidonin, "Sexual Assaults of Female POW's Withheld from Panel," *USA Today,* June 11, 1992.

35. Elaine Sciolino, "Women in War: Ex-Captive Tells of Ordeal," *New York Times,* June 29, 1992, p. A1.

36. Letter from Cmdr. Rosemary Mariner to the *Washington Times,* June 28, 1992.

37. Testimony of Rhonda Cornum to the presidential commission, June 8, 1992.

38. Letter to the presidential commission, June 11, 1992.

39. Air Force Col. Norman McDaniel was one of the prisoners of war giving testimony to the presidential commission on June 8, 1992. The others were the Hon. Everett Alvarez Jr., Col. Fred Cherry, USAF (Ret.) and Lt. Mary Rose Harrington Nelson, USN (Ret.).

40. Testimony of Lt. Col. William Bryan, USA, attack helicopter battalion commander, U.S. Army Aviation Center, to the presidential commission, Aug. 7, 1992, Los Angeles.

41. "Issue K: Ground Combat," presidential commission report, p. 25.

42. "Issue L: Combat Aircraft," presidential commission report, p. 28.

43. George Wilson, "Opinion/Commentary," *Navy Times,* Nov. 30, 1991.

44. Commissioner Ronald D. Ray, Commissioner Statements in the presidential commission report, p. 116.

45. "Issue K: Ground Combat," pp. 24–27.

46. "Panel Four Report to Commission on Findings," p. 22.

47. "Issue O: Risk Rule," presidential commission report, p. 36.

48. "Issue Q: Conscription," presidential commission report, pp. 40, 41.

49. "Issue M: Combatant Vessels," presidential commission report, p. 31.

50. Commissioners' discussion and vote on women in combat cockpits, Nov. 3, 1992.

51. Ibid.

52. Ibid.

53. Ibid.

54. Ibid.

55. Memorandum from Secretary of Defense Les Aspin to the Secretaries of the Army, Navy and Air Force, the chairman of the Joint Chiefs of Staff, and the Assistant Secretaries of Defense for Personnel and Readiness and Reserve Affairs, Jan. 13, 1994.

56. "Women Warriors," *New York Times* editorial, April 30, 1993.

57. "Women Warriors," *Air Force Times,* May 10, 1993.

58. "Navy Records Highly Rated Woman Pilot Who Crashed," *New York Times*, Nov. 21, 1994, p. A16.

59. Investigation into the VF-213 F-14A Aircraft Accident on 25th October 1994 that Resulted in the Death of Lt. Kara S. Hultgreen, USN, and Injury to Lt. Matthew P. Klemish, USN, Feb. 14, 1995, from Cmdr. Preston C. Pinson to Commander, Carrier Air Wing Eleven, p. 6.

60. "The Vindication of Navy Pilot Lt. Kara Hultgreen," *Nightline*, Feb. 28, 1995.

61. Patrick Pexton, "Women Rise, Tension Reigns," *Navy Times*, Jan. 2, 1995, p. 22.

62. Anonymous letter to the *Navy Times*, Jan. 23, 1995.

63. Patrick Pexton, "What's Wrong with Navy Air?" *Navy Times*, Feb. 13, 1995, p. 20.

64. Becky Garrison, "Internal Report Confirms Hultgreen's Error," *Navy Times*, April 3, 1995, p. 6.

65. "Double Standards in Naval Aviation," Center for Military Readiness, Michigan, cited in Susan Barnes, "Sibling Rivalry in the Navy: Tom Cruise Meets His Little Sister," *Minerva's Bulletin Board*, Winter 1995, p. 11, and Linda Chavez, "Did Navy Policy Cost Pilot Her Life?" *USA Today*, "Counterpoints," May 10, 1995. Barnes, a lawyer for the WANDAS Fund and WANDAS Watch, a pro bono organization for servicewomen in Denver, is representing Lt. Lohrenz. She is suing Elaine Donnelly's Center for Military Readiness, the *Washington Times* and the parent company of the *San Diego Union-Tribune* for libel and invasion of privacy.

66. Barnes, p. 11.

67. Ibid.; James W. Crawley, "Navy Grounds F-14 Pilot for Evaluation of Flying Skills," *San Diego Union-Tribune*, June 30, 1995, p. B-1.

68. Barnes, p. 11.

69. "Tailhook '91, Part 2," p. E-58.

70. Barnes, p. 10.

71. Ibid., p. 11.

72. Becky Garrison, "The Grounding of Morale at Air Wing 11," *Navy Times*, March 18, 1996, p. 6.

73. Vargo Muradian, "Embattled NY Fliers Face New Era," *Air Force Times*, Jan. 15, 1996, p. 21.

74. Becky Garrison, "Deployed and Pregnant," *Navy Times*, April 3, 1995, p. 6.

75. D'Ann Campbell, "Servicewomen and the Academies: The Football Cordon and Pep Rally as a Case Study of the Status of Female Cadets at the United States Military Academy," *Minerva*, Spring 1995, p. 8.

76. Rosabeth Moss Kanter, *Men and Women of the Corporation* (New York: Basic Books, 1997), p. 208.

77. Margaret Mead, *Male & Female: A Study of the Sexes in a Changing World* (New York: Morrow, 1949, 1967), p. 160.

78. Trip Report to the Presidential Commission from Maj. C. B. Johnson, USMC, Oct. 26, 1992.

79. *WMA News*, Winter 1995, p. 1.

Index

Abarbanel, Gail, 160
ABC News, 62–63, 80, 182, 241
Abortion, 109, 114–15, 150
Air Force Academy, bulimia at, 213, 214; dropouts from, 207–8; GAO reports about, 187, 191, 205; harassment at, 184, 187, 191, 203, 204, 205; opening to women of, 184, 191–93, 194, 203
Air Force, U.S., 24, 249; and combat exclusion laws, 23, 25–26, 27, 32, 33, 57, 221–24, 226–27, 228, 229–30, 235, 237, 239, 248, 252; diminishing career/job opportunities for pilots in, 27, 28, 33, 221; discharge for motherhood from, 137–38; discharge for pregnancy from, 105, 106–7; gender quotas for pilots in, 226–27; harassment in, 27, 153, 168, 237; lesbian-baiting in, 177; male pilots in, 153, 156, 235, 239; nondeployability for the Gulf, 120–21, 125; parenthood in, and parental deployment problems to Gulf, 143; physical strength in, 248; and pregnancy for pilots in, 116–17, 235; resignations/ discharges from, 227; strain on families in, 147–49. *See also* Air Force Academy; *specific person*
Air Force, U.S.: and combat exclusion laws, 23, 26, 27, 28, 32, 33, 36, 221–224, 226, 227, 228, 229–30, 235, 239, 252; and harassment, 153, 156, 229–230; and pregnancy, 116–17, 235; training of, 24, 156

Air National Guard, 258–59
All-Volunteer Force, 15–16, 138–39; dependency on women for, 16, 18, 107–8, 141–42, 150; resignations/ discharges from, 107–8. *See also specific branch of service*
Alt, Barbara, 141, 166–67
American Civil Liberties Union (ACLU), 31, 106, 237
American Conservative Union, 40
American Legion, 225
American Nurses' Association, 237
Anderson, James L., 197, 201, 248
Armed Services Committee (U.S. House), 25, 64, 78, 164, 172, 191–92, 193–94, 220–24, 233
Armed Services Committee (U.S. Senate), 64, 149, 181, 186, 187, 224–225, 229, 231–34, 239–40
Army Aviation Hall of Fame, 17
Army, U.S., 15, 16, 133, 246; basic training in, 36; bias against single mothers in, 140, 141; cadence calls in, 162, 163; career/job opportunities in, 27, 33, 255; and combat exclusion laws, 26, 27, 33, 45, 57, 102, 230, 231, 232, 238, 248–49, 254, 255; first hearings on harassment, 69–172; harassment culture in, 162, 163; lesbian-baiting in, 177, 178, 180; parenthood in, 133–34, 142–43, 145–146, 147, 148; physical strength in, 248–49; pilots in, 17, 36, 115–16, 226, 238; and pregnancy, 105, 108, 109, 110–11, 115–16, 120, 122–23, 125,